PENGUIN BUSINESS
THE NEW RULES OF BUSINESS

Rajesh Srivastava is an alumnus of IIT Kanpur and IIM Bangalore. He has over three decades of corporate and academic experience. At United Spirits (now Diageo India), he played a significant role in creating some of India's most recognized, beloved and enduring alcohol brands that include McDowell's Signature, Royal Challenge, Bagpiper and Blue Riband Duet. He later became the president of J.K. Helene Curtis Ltd, where he re-energized the company and the deodorant category by relaunching Park Avenue deodorant as a perfume. Today, 'perfume' has become a generic benefit for the deodorant category.

Since 2008, he has directed his focus towards teaching and conducting corporate workshops. As an educator, he has taught at IIM Indore and SP Jain School of Global Management. As a corporate trainer, he has worked with prestigious companies like Siemens India, Mercedes-Benz Research Centre and Reliance Industries, among others.

Throughout his career, his writings have appeared in various publications, including *Outlook*, the *Telegraph*, *Mid-Day*, *Business Standard* and *Mint*.

He lives in Mumbai with his wife, Shaily, and their son, Kautuk.

PRAISE FOR *THE NEW RULES OF BUSINESS*

'I liked reading Rajesh's work a lot. First, it was an easy read, full of anecdotes, so, a perfect flight companion. It was consistent in its narrative and drilled down on a few points very thoroughly. How every part of an organization should focus on making the consumer the centre of every decision is shown again and again through different examples. His personal experience in leadership positions makes him adept at answering the questions facing the readers and that is probably why I found this book very practical. It made me take a few notes as well, which I can use as guiding principles for the future' —**Neeraj Kakkar, co-founder, Paper Boat**

'At a time when change and disruption is the new order, Rajesh's insightful book is a brisk read and a "corporate guide" to navigating these times—putting the consumer, as always at the centre with a desire to win. Filled with relevant examples from both global and Indian brands, *The New Rules of Business* is a must-read for all practitioners of marketing and business'—**Neeraj G. Roy, founder and CEO, Hungama Digital Media Entertainment**

'Rajesh's book on sixteen new rules of business is an interesting and insightful read. Being an accomplished brand creator and manager, Rajesh draws extensively from his personal success stories. His narrative is authentic and rich, and draws from the Western world and marketplace. Roughly two thirds of the rules focus on marketing dimensions like customer, brand, channel, communication, while the remaining focus on employees, workplace, leadership and business strategy. This lucidly written and concise book will find great acceptance among management students and practitioners'—**N. Ravichandran, professor (retired), IIM Ahmedabad, and former director, IIM Indore**

'Highly interesting and extremely relevant. "Big and complex" ideas have been explained using stories drawn from the world of business and from the lives of people we admire. The storytelling format makes the book extremely readable. It provides a wonderful summary of what new-age business leaders should know to stay relevant. I found this book extremely useful'—**Ashish Bhasin, CEO APAC and chairman, Dentsu Aegis Network (India)**

'Rajesh Srivastava's marketing brain is a rare combination of clarity of vision, remarkable insight, superfast ability to spot trends and a passion for innovation. His sixteen new rules for business, with scores of examples of winning strategies of companies from across the planet, will be invaluable to students, managers and teachers trying to make sense of an increasingly volatile, uncertain, complex and ambiguous world'—**Sandipan Deb, former editor,** *Financial Express*

'We live in a new world, a world that is ever-changing. This change is about geopolitics, brands and marketing equally as all else. In such a world, where nothing is really static, and nothing can ever be predicted to be the same, how does one grapple with business and its many challenges? Rajesh Srivastava attempts to answer this with stories well-captured and well-told, in a language that is completely friendly and even fun in this delightful book. Do classrooms prepare managers? Or do markets? Or life-experiences? Or contemporary books? Or living in the real world, as opposed to the unreal one of our own making that most of us find ourselves trapped within at times? I do believe that books written with an honest intent to accept that we live not in a "ready-made world" of business, but one that is "WIP" (Work in Progress) help. This is one such book. I, therefore, enjoyed reading it. I am sure you will as well. Long live change. Long live disruption. Without it, business would be so, so boring'—**Harish Bijoor, brand-strategy specialist, and founder, Harish Bijoor Consults Inc.**

'It was very enlightening reading Rajesh's book, which has some home truths that are not given weight in our day-to-day working. He has the uncanny knack of bringing out very powerful messages and insights in a simple, relevant and relatable way'—**Ashok Capoor, former president and managing director, United Spirits (now Diageo India)**

'An excellent book with so many examples to illustrate and drive home "the newly minted rules" (as Rajesh calls it) to run businesses successfully in today's ultra-VUCA world. The examples are drawn from disparate industries and different geographies, to show that these principles work widely'—**Raju Venkataraman, leadership coach, corporate trainer, and former CFO and head of strategy, Walt Disney SEA**

'Rajesh has taught marketing at SP Jain School of Global Management and always got outstanding feedback from the students. His secret: bringing contemporary content into the classroom and illustrating it using examples drawn from businesses. He has used the same strategy for this book. He has studied new-age, well-run companies across the globe and shared what makes them valuable, consolidating everything in sixteen simple rules. This book will arm you with insights, tools, techniques and a direction to tackle business challenges. Highly recommended'—**Nitish Jain, president, SP Jain School of Global Management, Dubai, Mumbai, Singapore and Sydney**

'In his book *The New Rules of Business,* Rajesh Srivastava manages to pack his many decades of experience and wisdom into a handy volume of lessons and rules for success. The book traverses a wide terrain, from nudging customers to serving customers better, to building a "supercool" brand, to getting employees to perform better, to building a great workplace and more. Each of the sixteen rules comes with many examples drawn from both the Indian and international arena, often juxtaposed with Rajesh's own rich experiences and anecdotes. All in all, this makes the book a compelling read'—**Ambi Parameswaran, independent brand strategist, and author of *Nawabs, Nudes, Noodles* and *Sponge: Leadership Lessons I Learnt from My Clients***

'Rajesh Srivastava has the amazing ability to explain new business concepts simply and backed by real-world stories. That's what defined the popular column and YouTube video series he started in Founding Fuel, also titled "New Rules of Business". I'm delighted to see it evolve into a lucidly written book that provides the ideas, toolkit and case studies to navigate the new world of business. It should become a must-read for every young business professional'—**Indrajit Gupta, co-founder and director, Founding Fuel**

'*The New Rules of Business* by Rajesh Srivastava introduces the reader to sixteen curated "new rules" for doing business. Each new rule is explained through examples drawn from Rajesh's own career and from well-run companies in India and across the world. It is written in a storytelling format and is an easy read. It is a must-read for budding entrepreneurs and management graduates. The book will leave you feeling motivated, energized and brimming with new ideas'—**Raj Nayak, founder and managing director, House of Cheer, and former COO, Viacom18**

'Drawing upon his own journey and a wide variety of global examples, Rajesh Srivastava deftly illustrates the hows and whys of creating a great consumer experience. The lessons are accessible and relevant across sectors and geographies'—**Deepa Prahalad, co-author of *Predictable Magic***

'The book is very well written, in a simple, fluent and easy-to-read style. The many interesting examples reinforce the rules articulated and are cogent to the narrative. It's also amazing that the root guiding principles for a sustainable business remain the same over time, even as the business landscape changes so rapidly'—**Anil Nair, former managing director and CEO, Avaya Global Connect, Aegis Consulting, Securitas India and AGC Networks**

'"Thoughtful", "conversational" and "wise" are not adjectives often used to describe a business book. But they go perfectly with *The New Rules of Business*. Rajesh has used a light touch in describing the depths of change that have overtaken both consumer markets as well as the businesses that serve them'—**Sreekant Khandekar, co-founder and director, afaqs!**

'In this dynamic, rapidly changing world, where the rate of obsolescence has escalated, this book equips you to be one of the drivers of change. In a simple, engaging manner, Rajesh helps you understand the intricacies of today's marketplace and outlines the appropriate strategies to effectively tackle them. In today's complex business environment, where the modification of consumers' hierarchy of needs and their media consumption habits is continuous, this book provides a template for overcoming the challenges. The real-life examples further illustrate and bring to the fore the ground realities which the reader will easily empathize with, and learn ways and means of addressing them with ingenuity. Unlike typical management books, its narrative, storytelling style are very well crafted, and it will undoubtedly benefit the professional development of any practising manager. A definite must-read for all management students and practitioners'—**Kamal Oberoi, chairman, QUO India, former chairman and managing director, M&C Saatchi (India), and former president, J. Walter Thompson (India)**

'In this disrupting world, retention and enticement of the customers remain the biggest challenge. Customers were never as sensitive, knowledgeable and smart as they are now. Rajesh Srivastava's book provides new rules of business, bringing the best in class, national and international practices in marketing, and builds a case for creating an internal ecosystem to help remain and thrive in business. Written in a lucid style, the book is a must-read for every business executive and corporate leader'—**Anil K. Khandelwal, former chairman, Bank of Baroda**

'Rajesh has poured his lifetime of experience into this book. It's an easy read and full of business stories that provide valuable insights. It will also introduce a business aspirant to ideas of several thought leaders and gurus. This book is a good gateway to connect young talent with the wisdom of great experienced leaders. My best wishes to Rajesh and the readers of this book to continue on the journey of transformation that begins from within'—**Prashant Jain, managing director, GE Power India**

'This book by an industry veteran, Rajesh Srivastava, is a game changer. It gets you practical knowledge for entrepreneurs and start-up founders with case studies and examples, which makes it a quick and easy read. Practical knowledge always has its merit over theoretical knowledge of an issue and Srivastava's book scores here. For any entrepreneur, start-up founder, or a student of business management, this should be a must-read'—**Saurabh Shukla, founder and editor-in-chief, News Mobile**

'Rajesh Srivastava offers new rules to succeed in this "disruptive" world. Each rule is explained through examples drawn from the world of business. This makes it easy to read and internalize. Entrepreneurs and corporates will get insights and directions in building, nurturing and growing a business. Business students will get introduced to contemporary ideas, concepts and frameworks which will help them to think in new and unexpected ways'—**Indu Shahani, president and chair, Indian School of Design and Innovation (ISDI), Indian School of Management and Entrepreneurship (ISME), ISDI WPP School of Communication**

'Keeping customers satisfied and happy enough to return is a continuous challenge, offline and online. And more so in the brutally competitive marketplace that is India. Rajesh Srivastava brings in his decades-long experience as a CEO and marketeer to everyday challenges that almost all brands face and may or may not be able to overcome but nevertheless must learn from'—**Govindraj Ethiraj, financial journalist, and founder, BOOMLive, IndiaSpend**

THE
NEW
RULES
OF
BUSINESS

GET AHEAD
OR
GET LEFT
BEHIND

RAJESH SRIVASTAVA

PENGUIN
BUSINESS

An imprint of Penguin Random House

PENGUIN BUSINESS

USA | Canada | UK | Ireland | Australia
New Zealand | India | South Africa | China | Singapore

Penguin Business is part of the Penguin Random House group of companies
whose addresses can be found at global.penguinrandomhouse.com

Published by Penguin Random House India Pvt. Ltd
4th Floor, Capital Tower 1, MG Road,
Gurugram 122 002, Haryana, India

First published in Portfolio by Penguin Random House India 2019
Published in Penguin Business 2021

ISBN 9780143446927

Typeset in Adobe Caslon Pro Manipal Technologies Limited, Manipal

Printed at Manipal Technologies Limited, India

www.penguin.co.in

I dedicate this book to—

My late father, who believed that I had the talent to be a writer. I am happy to have lived up to his expectations.

My mother, who believes that I can achieve anything I put my heart into. I am happy I have proved her right yet again.

My wife, Shaily, who happily reviewed multiple drafts and played the role of a professional dissenter to perfection.

My son, Kautuk, a published author, who made me a better writer by insisting I write every word, instead of someone ghost-writing it for me.

My students, many of whom took sweet revenge when they got the manuscript to review. They circled in red almost everything in this book. But their critical inputs proved to be invaluable.

My friends and well-wishers who invested their valuable time to review and make valuable suggestions. It has made the book practical and interesting.

In times of change, learners inherit the earth, while the learned find themselves beautifully equipped to deal with a world that no longer exists.

—Eric Hoffer

Contents

Why Was This Book Written?

The mind, once stretched by a new idea, never returns to its original dimension.

—Ralph Waldo Emerson

Night had fallen and darkness was all-pervasive except around a dimly-lit lamp post. Here, an old lady, half-bent, seemed to be searching for something.

A young passerby thought it was his duty to help the old lady in distress.

'Madam, what have you lost?' he asked politely.

'My house keys,' she informed him.

'Where did you lose them?' he asked, so he could confine his search to that area.

'In my garden,' she replied.

'Where is your garden?' He probed.

'Over there,' she said, pointing to a spot away from the lamp post, which was covered in complete darkness.

Bewildered by the answer, he probed further, 'If you lost the keys in the garden, then why are you searching for them under the lamppost?'

'Because the light is here,' replied the lady nonchalantly.

The young man shook his head in disbelief.

You must have heard some version of this old parable and I'm sure you share the young man's sentiments. However, unknown to us, we might be doing the same.

In our careers, we are constantly faced with business challenges. Most of us, like the old lady, search for the answers in the areas 'lit' by our current level of knowledge. The solution may very well lie outside of it.

This book is an attempt to help you look for business solutions in the right places or at the least widen the light of your knowledge with which to search for them.

This is necessary because the rules of business have well and truly changed.

I can sense a question arising in your mind: 'I am a veteran. I have overcome many business challenges. What new tools, techniques, and frameworks can this book teach me?'

Let me get Professor Albert Einstein to answer this. In 1942, he was teaching a course in Physics, at Oxford University, to senior-class students. As a course requirement, he conducted an examination.

While walking in the campus, he was accompanied by his assistant, who posed a question to him. 'Prof. Einstein, this exam you just gave to the senior students is exactly the same exam you gave to the same class a year ago?' he asked.

'Yes, Yes, I did,' nodded Prof. Einstein. 'The questions remain the same, but the answers have changed.'[1]

Similar is the case in business. By and large the business challenges have largely remained the same but the solutions for satisfactorily resolving them have changed.

---

[1] Paul Rulkens, 'Why the Majority is Always Wrong', YouTube video, 11.25, posted by Tedx Talks on 21 October 2014, https://www.youtube.com/watch?v=VNGFep6rncY

This book will introduce you to new thoughts, ideas, tools, techniques, and frameworks which will help you come up with impactful answers to business challenges.

How can you get the most out of this book?

To get most out of this book:

- **Empty your cup:** A student believed that he was a learned man. But to be doubly sure, he decided to visit his master who had earned a reputation of being the most learned person.

  'Master, I think I know most things. But still, I believe you know more than me. I want you to teach me those things which I do not know,' requested the student.

  'Of course,' said the master. 'Let me get you a cup of tea first.'

  Shortly, he emerged from the kitchen carrying a tray laden with a teacup, saucer and a kettle. He kept the tray on the table and started pouring tea from the kettle into the cup. Soon, the cup was full but the master continued to pour. Now the tea was overflowing into the saucer.

  The student was surprised. 'Master, can't you see the tea is overflowing?' he exclaimed.

  'Yes, I can see the tea is overflowing,' said the master. 'The same is true for you. Your mind is like a cup that is full to the brim. If I impart more learnings, it will overflow. If you sincerely wish to learn, empty your cup first.'

This is a classic tale in Zen Buddhism. You, too, should empty your 'cup' before reading this book. This will help you get rid of old ideas because as French political philosopher, Montesquieu warned us, 'Old ideas weaken new ideas.' Once old ideas are unlearned, the mind can be filled with new thoughts, ideas, tools, techniques and more.

- **Internalize each rule**: Rakesh Jhunjhunwala is arguably India's most successful investor in the stock market. People flock to him for investment tips to make money. 'I give them tips. But you cannot make money from borrowed knowledge,' he says.[2]

  The same may apply to you. You cannot profit by merely reading this book (read: by acquiring borrowed knowledge). To benefit, you must internalize these rules. Therefore, while reading you should frequently pause and reflect on what you have read. Then pose yourself a question: Can I apply this rule to my company? If yes, then how can it be applied? Introspection coupled with a desire to apply these rules will help you internalize and profit from them.

- **Involve your team**: Helen Keller had said: 'Alone you can do so little; together we can do so much.' Alone you may find it daunting to implement these rules;

---

[2] Kripa Raman and Rakesh Jhunjhunwala, 'I give tips but you can't make profit from borrowed knowledge', *Mumbai Mirror*, 27 October 2013, https://mumbaimirror.indiatimes.com/others/sunday-read/rakesh-jhunjhunwala-i-give-tips-but-you-cant-profit-from-borrowed-knowledge/articleshow/24772526.cms

together with your team, you may find the going easier. If you find ideas in this book valuable, communicate and clarify them to your team. Getting them on board will make for a smoother implementation of these new rules.

- **Act:** Merely ruminating over an idea will not deliver results. Indecisions lead to delays. In this matter, it is best to follow the advice of Johann Wolfgang von Goethe: 'What you can do, or dream you can, begin it; boldness has genius, power, and magic in it.' Not only must you act soon and decisively, you must also act often.

A word of caution—do not apply these rules blindly. Intelligently adapt them to suit your business requirements.

Postscript: Then and Now!

I started my career all the way back in 1985. A lot has changed since then:

- I used to get the news from the newspaper. Now, I get it from a screen.
- I used to go to taxis stands or hail a taxi. Now Uber comes where I want it.
- I used to go to a cinema hall at the time of the show. Now, I see a film at home; that too, whenever I want.
- I had to visit a restaurant earlier if I wanted to grab a bite. Now, I can get food delivered at home.
- I used to visit a bank branch for all the bank work. Now, I do basic banking from my home at my convenience.

- I used to go to the store and carry my shopping bags back home. Now I can shop online at my convenience, and get everything delivered at my doorstep.
- Snail mails took days to reach once upon a time. Now, emails reach in seconds.

Newspapers, taxies, cinema halls, restaurants, banks, Shopping centres, postal services and many more industries have been disrupted by new age companies. They are quietly dismantling the old rules and installing new rules of business. Result: customer's expectations are changing. They are getting used to the delightful experience delivered by Amazon, Flipkart, Uber, Ola, Oyo Rooms, Netflix, et al. They expect the same from you. If you fail to provide it, then they are likely to shift their loyalty to those who do. You run a real risk of becoming irrelevant and gradually extinct. It is in your interest to adopt these New Rules of Business. It will ensure that you secure your company's future.

A glance at the rules—for example, Rule 1: 'Love Your customers, Serve Your Customer' or Rule 5: 'Treat Your Employees as You Treat Your Best Customers'—may make them seem like 'old' rules. After all, were we not told to treat the customer like God and our employees well? What is new in that?

True, but what is of interest for us is the change in their importance and implementation. Earlier companies either ranked these rules lower on their list of priorities or merely paid lip service to them. Times have changed. The best run companies are placing these and other 'new' rules at the center of decision-making. So, should you.

I wrote this book to introduce you to these new rules of business.

It is said that the journey of a thousand miles begins with a single step. Take the step and embark on this journey. You will future-proof your business.

Rajesh Srivastava
7 September 2019, Mumbai.

CUSTOMER

RULE 1

Love Your Customer,
Serve Your Customer

There is only one boss. The customer. And he can fire everybody in the company from the chairman on down, simply by spending his money somewhere else.

—Sam Walton

Neeraj Kakkar, founder of Paper Boat—a ready-to-drink beverage made from traditional recipes—was on a flight. When he spotted a lady holding a Paper Boat pack in her hand, he was elated. But what he witnessed next horrified him. She was struggling to open the cap. Finally, in desperation, she used her mouth to force it open. Neeraj was appalled about a customer being forced to exert herself this way. He resolved to solve it at the root itself so that, in future, customers do not have to undergo this frustrating experience.

This led to the creation of a cap that is so user-friendly that it can be opened with two fingers. There is a simple lesson in this. Kakkar exhibited compassion towards his customers. He not only felt one customer's pain but acted upon it[1].

Many companies go one step further. They strive to keep customers' interests ahead of their own. Amazon, for one, represents this style of decision-making. The company started off as an online bookseller. It encouraged its readers to write reviews and also give ratings for the book. Naturally, some of the reviews were negative. This prompted a customer to shoot off a letter to Jeff Bezos: 'You don't understand your business. You make money when you sell things. Why do you allow these negative customer reviews?'

'And when I read that letter, I thought, we don't make money when we sell things. We make money when we help customers make purchase decisions,' said Bezos.[2]

Jeff Bezos kept the customers' interests ahead of Amazon's.

A few companies have raised the bar even higher. They strive to safeguard customers' well-being and welfare even before their own. Let me share an example of this from my own career, when I was working as president of J.K. Helene Curtis.

One day my secretary walked into my room, looking alarmed. 'There is a caller from Ahmedabad who is threatening to lodge a police complaint against us,' she said.

'What happened?' I asked her.

---

[1] 'Neeraj Kakkar & Shripad Nadkarni, Paper Boat, The New Rules Of Business 2.0 Episode 2', Youtube video, 36.30, posted by Founding Fuel, 22 September 2016, https://www.youtube.com/watch?v=jvSmbLJGriU&t=1391s

[2] Adi Ignatius, 'Jeff Bezos on leading for the long-term at Amazon', *Harvard Business Review,* https://hbr.org/2013/01/jeff-bezos-on-leading-for-the

'Sir, he refuses to give me the reason. He insists on speaking to a senior person.'

'Put him on,' I told her.

I took the call. The caller asked me, in an aggressive tone, about my designation.

'I am the president of the company,' I informed him.

'I don't care who you are,' he said and continued his tirade. 'I am going to the police station to file a complaint against your company!'

'Why?' I asked him.

'My family and I could have been killed!' he roared.

Puzzled, I asked him to explain.

'I bought your company's room freshener and placed it on the car's dashboard. When I reached home, I parked the car and was walking to my house when I heard a loud thud. I turned and saw it had come from my car. When I went closer I noticed that the room freshener had burst,' he explained

I immediately realized what had happened. If an aerosol can is exposed to direct sunlight, it can explode. In the car, the can was exposed to direct sunlight. So it burst.

'Was anybody hurt?' I asked him.

'Nobody was hurt but they could have been,' he said.

I was relieved. 'Has any damage been caused to your car?' I asked

'Yes,' he said, his voice rising, 'the windscreen is damaged.'

'Don't worry,' I said. 'Our sales representative will get it repaired.'

As soon as he heard this, he asked in a calmer tone, 'When will your sales rep come?'

'Soon,' I said. 'But may I share something with you?'

'Yes,' he said. He was more receptive to me now that his problem had been addressed.

'You should not expose an aerosol can, including a room freshener, to direct sunlight. It is likely to burst. Every aerosol can carries this warning,' I informed him.

'I am sorry,' he said contritely. 'I did not read the instructions.'

Although the fault lay with the customer in this case, I took the decision to bear the expense of repairing the windscreen.

All three stories point to a fundamental rule of business. The customer's well-being and welfare are the top priority of a company, overriding even its own welfare.

The Rule in Operation

Let us analyse how lessons from these stories are operationalized.

Steve Jobs was a charismatic business leader. He disrupted music, personal computing, animation and retailing industries. Have you ever wondered how he took decisions? I hear many of you say that his thinking and decision-making process were surreal and beyond our capacity to grasp.

I too thought this way till I understood his philosophy. He believed that everything starts with a great product. 'My passion has been to build an enduring company where people were motivated to make great products.' he said.[3]

---

[3] Jennifer Magnolfi, 'Why Apple's New HQ is Nothing Like the Rest of Silicon Valley', *Harvard Business Review*, 26 June 2017, https://hbr. org/2017/06/why-apples-new-hq-is-nothing-like-the-rest-of-silicon-valley

Based on this insight, I surmised that Steve Jobs took decisions by posing one question to himself and his team:

- Will it make Apple a great product for customers? If yes, green-light it. If not, junk it.

The cumulative impact of many big and small decisions focused on making Apple a better product was that Apple customers were handed an amazing experience that enriched their lives. In 2018, Apple was crowned the world's most valuable company.[4]

Let us now evaluate Jeff Bezos' decision-making process. After all, under his watch Amazon has disrupted retail industry.

Jeff Bezos too would be intuitively posing 'one question' to himself and his team while making decisions:

- Will it reduce friction in the shopping process and improve the shopping experience?[5] If yes, green-light it. If no, veto it.

You may be wondering whether such a simple question can deliver results on the ground. Let me share with you a partial list of initiatives Amazon has introduced which have reduced friction in the shopping process:

---

[4] Lucinda Shen, 'Here Are the Fortune 500's 10 Most Valuable Companies by Lucinda Shen', *Fortune*, 21 May 2018, https://fortune.com/2018/05/21/fortune-500-most-valuable-companies-2018/

[5] Geoff Colvin and Ryan Derousseau, 'Jeff Bezos's War With Friction', *Fortune*, February 2, 2017, https://fortune.com/2017/02/02/jeff-bezoss-war-with-friction/

- **1-Click** ordering is an easy and fast way to order that saves time.
- **The Amazon Dash** button lets customers reorder household items by the simple process of pressing a button.
- **Amazon Echo** allows customers to place an order on Amazon using voice command.
- **Frustration-free packaging** makes it easier for customers to open parcels.
- **Amazon Go** does not have checkouts, thereby facilitates faster shopping.

Let us finally evaluate how Zappos, a shoe and clothing online retailer, acquired by Amazon in 2009, takes decisions. It, too, has framed one question which the team refers to while making decisions:

- Will it make our customers happy? If yes, go ahead; if no, trash it.

'The company's service representatives know they can do whatever it takes to meet that goal—without having to get approval from their superiors. So they will refund defective products and replace them for free, send flowers to a customer who says, "Mom is sick," and spend as much time on the phone as necessary to resolve a problem.'[6] Zappos finds a place among Fortune's list of 100 best companies to work for![7]

---

[6] George Stalk, Jr. and Sam Stewart, 'Avoiding Disruption Requires Rapid Decision Making', *Harvard Business Review*, 23 April 2009, https://hbr.org/2019/04/avoiding-disruption-requires-rapid-decision-making.

[7] 'Zappos Makes FORTUNE 100 Best Companies to Work for List!' Zappos, 16 January 2014, https://www.zappos.com/about/stories/zappos-makes-fortune-100-best-companies-to-work-for-list

Steve Jobs, Jeff Bezos and Zappos intuitively leaned on one question—which I call '1 Central Question' (1CQ)—to make decisions.

When decisions are taken by referring to one lodestar (read: 1CQ), then there is consistency in decision-making and this has the power to put your company on the path of success.

Does 1CQ Deliver Results?

For that let me share a parable of the Fox and the Hedgehog. The fox knows many ways of trapping the hedgehog—chasing it, pouncing upon it, ambushing it or mounting a guerrilla attack. Every time it faces defeat and withdraws with its spout prickled by spines. This is because the hedgehog has mastered one art to perfection: of defending itself.

The moral of this parable was succinctly summed up by Greek poet Archilochus: 'The fox knows many things, but the hedgehog knows one big thing.'

Does the moral have any relevance to modern business?

Jim Collins, in his book *Good to Great*[8] points out that organizations are more likely to succeed if they identify the one thing that they can do best—their 'Hedgehog Concept'.

By framing 1CQ you will identify your, 'Hedgehog Concept' which will help you not only in defending but growing your business.

How Can You Frame Your 'One Central Question' (1CQ)?

Always keep the customer at the centre of decision-making and frame the question in such a way that whenever it is

---

[8] Jim Collins, 'Good to Great' (Harper Business, 2001)

answered, it will further the interests of customers, not the company. The irony is that when the companies continuously take decisions in customers' interests, customers reciprocate by displaying a cultish loyalty towards the business.

A word of caution: if you frame a question that appears to be favouring customers on the surface but surreptitiously serves the company's narrow self-interest, then this strategy may backfire.

For that, let us get Mark Zuckerberg into our discussion. He seems to have intuitively formulated 1CQ which seems to be focused on serving customers but ends up serving company's interest.

- Will it get more users on the Facebook platform? If yes, implement the decision. If no, shoot it down.

The game plan is simple: get the maximum number of users on the platform, which acts as bait to attract advertisers. In 2018, 98 per cent of FB's revenue came from advertising. This in turn boosted its valuation.[9]

Zuckerberg's 1CQ is in favour of Facebook (henceforth, FB) to help it maximize its revenue, which in turn would boost its valuation. It does not seem to favour customers. Blindly answering the 1CQ has landed FB in hot water and attracted bad press.

---

[9] Tony Silber, 'Facebook Ad-Spend Growth from National Marketers is Slowing, Intelligence Firm's Data Shows', *Forbes*, 31 December 2018, https://www.forbes.com/sites/tonysilber/2018/12/31/facebook-ad-spend-from-national-marketers-is-slowing-intelligence-firms-data-shows/#13647a661591; Note for Facebook Revenue: Fortune 500, https://fortune.com/fortune500/facebook/

Building Relationships with Customers

In addition to framing a 1CQ, to love and serve customers would require you to build a deep relationship with your customers. Let me share with you strategies required for building and deepening relationships with customers:

- **Be compassionate towards customers:** In 2003, Ratan Tata, then Chairman of Tata Sons, noticed a family of four on a scooter: the father was driving it, a child stood in front holding on to the handlebar, while the mother rode pillion with another child on her lap. This sight evoked compassion in Ratan Tata and he posed a question to himself: could one conceive of a safe, affordable and all-weather form of transportation for such a family? This led to the development of Nano, the world's first affordable car. For various reasons, it was withdrawn, but it earned global acclaim for being an innovative solution.[10]

- **Keep customers in mind while taking a decision:** Do you feel that it is difficult to implement this strategy? Draw inspiration from Amazon. At their meetings, a seat is left empty for the customer who is an absent presence.[11] It is a silent reminder that decisions need to be made in the favour of the customer.

---

[10] Saurabh Sharma, 'How a scooter on a rainy day turned into Ratan Tata's dream project Nano,' *Business Today*, 14 April, 2017, https://www.businesstoday.in/current/economy-politics/how-a-scooter-on-a-rainy-day-turned-into-ratan-tatas-dream-project-nano/story/239035.html

[11] John Koetsier, 'Why every Amazon meeting has at least 1 empty chair,' *Inc.* April 4, 2018, https://www.inc.com/john-koetsier/why-every-amazon-meeting-has-at-least-one-empty-chair.html; George Anders,

- **Act with alacrity on customer feedback:** Dissatisfied customers can email Jeff Bezos directly and he'll forward the message to the right person—with one dreaded addition: '?'

Brad Stone writes in *The Everything Store: Jeff Bezos and the Age of Amazon*:[12]

When Amazon employees get a Bezos question mark e-mail, they react as though they've discovered a ticking bomb. They've typically got a few hours to solve whatever issue the CEO has flagged and prepare a thorough explanation for how it occurred, a response that will be reviewed by a succession of managers before the answer is presented to Bezos himself. Such escalations, as these e-mails are known, are Bezos's way of ensuring that the customer's voice is constantly heard inside the company.

- **Repose trust in customers:** I have always trusted my customers. Let me give you an example. As head of a company, I had a rule that all customer complaints should come to me. In the early 2000s, the internet had not evolved; most customer complaints were received through telephone or letters sent by post. I made it a point to acknowledge every complaint.

'Inside Amazon's Idea Machine: How Bezos Decodes Customers', *Forbes*, 4 April 2012, https://www.forbes.com/sites/georgeanders/2012/04/04/inside-amazon/#4d8bc0096199

[12] Brad Stone, 'The Everything Store: Jeff Bezos and the Age of Amazon' (Little, Brown and Company, 2013)

In fact, I wrote a personal letter to every complainant along the following lines:

I wish to apologize for the bad experience you may have had with our product. We are taking steps to ensure that you do not face the same problem in the future. As a gesture of gratitude, I am taking the liberty of sending you a gift hamper containing our company's range of products. I hope they live up to your high expectations . . .

I would get my sales representative working in the complainant's area to deliver my letter along with a gift hamper at the address mentioned in the letter and also collect the offending product so that we could analyse it at our R&D centre.

My team members advised me against pursuing this strategy. They said that by admitting our products are defective, we were offering opportunities for legal cases to be filed against us. I would counter that objection by pointing out that at no point had I admitted that our product was defective; I was merely apologizing for the unsatisfactory experience our product may have offered.

The other objection of my team was that if the word spread that we give a gift hamper to every person who sends a complaint, many people would misuse our generosity. Of course, I admitted, some people may misuse our generosity, but that number is likely to be small. At this point I posed a counter-question to my team: to prevent a small number from misusing our generosity should we penalize genuine customers who make the effort to bring our shortcomings to our notice?

By the way, I did not come across a single case of misuse of our generosity. I have always believed that when we trust people, they become more trustworthy.

- **Be sensitive to your customers' sensibilities:** We should not expect customers to change their habits to suit our requirements. On the contrary, we should make products keeping our customers' sensibilities in mind. Take McDonald's for instance. In most parts of the world, Big Mac stands for a beef patty. But for many in India, beef is taboo. Bowing to customer sensibilities, McDonald's launched McChicken Burger and the Maharaja Mac, which use chicken. In addition, they launched a plethora of vegetarian options such as McAloo Tikki Burger and McSpicy Paneer Burger.

- **Go where customers want you:** Usually, when I shop, I have to physically walk to a store and then carry the merchandise home. But when I shop at Flipkart, I realize it is always close to me. In fact, it is in the palm of my hand. I have to tap a few times on my smartphone and voilà, the merchandise is delivered to my doorstep.

For my eye check-up, I had to travel to my optician's clinic. But Lenskart's optician visits you at home at your convenience; it also offers you a choice of frames for selection. Who is growing? Traditional stores or online retailers? Traditional opticians or Lenskart? The answer is obvious.

- **Ask Customers for suggestions on how best to serve them:** Let me get Marc Benioff, the CEO of Salesforce to weigh in on it. 'In 2008, Howard Schultz returned to Starbucks as CEO, after being out of that role for eight years. The company had lost touch with consumers, and Schultz was determined to fix that. The first thing he did was create an app that asked customers how they thought the coffeehouses could be improved. The company consolidated the top ten responses and put them to a consumer vote. Then it implemented the top five fixes. The process engaged customers in the turnaround and helped restore revenue growth.'[13]

   Take a leaf from Howard Schutz playbook and ask your customers for suggestions of how you can serve them better. They will not disappoint you.

Empowering Your Employees to Take Decisions

I was travelling back to Mumbai from Dubai. Since the security check at Dubai airport mandates that we remove metal items, I put my pen and watch in my cabin bag.

When the flight was to land in Mumbai, I retrieved my pen and Titan Nebula watch from my bag. I noticed that the glass cover of the watch was missing. More disappointment awaited me. Upon putting it on, I felt a biting sensation on my wrist. When I turned the watch over, to my horror, I found the bezel-steel case which sits at the base of a watch,

---

[13] Brian Gallagher, 'United Way's CEO on Shifting a Century-Old Business Model', *Harvard Business Review*, September–October 2018, https://hbr.org/2018/09/united-ways-ceo-on-shifting-a-century-old-business-model

was also missing. To complete my misery, the watch had stopped working.

How could this happen? I recollected that before going to Dubai I got the battery of the watch replaced at an authorized Titan showroom in Belapur, Navi Mumbai. The mechanic had been able to open the watch but was not able to close the steel case. It required specialized instruments. I was requested to come the next day and collect the watch. As I looked at my wrecked watch now, I intuitively felt that the answer lay at the authorized store in Navi Mumbai.

I took the trouble of visiting the store again. The store manager, Vivek, greeted me with a smile. He listened patiently to my issue. During this period, not once did he let his smile slip. He did not dispute my allegations but requested me to hand over the watch so that he could get it examined by his technician. After a quick consultation with the technician, Vivek informed me that they would order the glass and steel case from the company, but it would take fifteen days to arrive. I had no option but to agree to Vivek's suggestion.

When the spare parts arrived, he called to get my approval for the total cost of the repair. But he said that his boss had given his approval to reduce the cost. And then Vivek said that since the problem had occurred under his watch, he would penalize himself: he would bear a significant part of the cost.

I was amazed. A company employee was willing to offer money from his own pocket to assuage a customer's dissatisfaction.

I visited the store to collect my watch. As promised, the watch was in working condition. But I insisted that Vivek contribute nothing to the cost of the repair. I felt that his behaviour itself was sufficient compensation.

This incident offers an important learning. Occasionally, service is bound to fail. The acid test is how quickly it recovers. Nothing infuriates a customer more than being told, 'I will have to check with my boss and then revert.'

Vivek took decisions on the spot to defuse the situation. In short, he 'empowered' himself to take decisions due to which the service recovered quickly. In the process, he converted a dissatisfied customer into a brand advocate.

You may be thinking that employees like Vivek are rare. In fact, you may not be lucky enough to have even one in your organization. More importantly, you may be wondering if this level of commitment towards providing service can be inculcated in every member of the organization. Seems implausible?

If you don't know of them already, let me introduce you to the Mumbai dabbawalas (lunchbox-delivery men), who have won world-wide acclaim in achieving the Six Sigma level of service delivery: 3.5 incorrect deliveries per million deliveries. The dabbawalas have managed such a high rate of success despite the fact that they do not have formal academic qualifications, nor can they converse in English or use technology.

Harvard Business School did a case study on them and global companies study their way of working to gain insight into what enables them to deliver a Six Sigma level of performance.[14]

The dabbawalas' high level of performance can be attributed to the fact that they do not see their job as a courier

---

[14] Stefan Thomke and Mona Sinha, 'The Dabbawala System: On-time Delivery, Every time', Harvard Business School, 2010, https://hbr.org/product/the-dabbawala-system-on-time-delivery-every-time/610059-PDF-ENG

service delivering food to the right address. If they did, dabbas would get lost with monotonous regularity. They look upon the person to whom they have to deliver the dabba (lunchbox) as God; for them, delivering the dabba to that person is akin to serving prasad to their deity, Lord Ganapati. If you were entrusted with the responsibility of delivering offerings meant for the god you worship, what would be your level of commitment? Casual? Or would you do everything in your power to make sure the offerings reach in time?

The dabbawalas also believe that delivering food is akin to delivering medicine to the sick. Consider yourself. If a loved one was in the hospital and you had to deliver the medicine that would help her recover, how would you act? Casually? Or do everything in your power to deliver the medicine, at any cost and as fast as possible?

Mumbai dabbawalas can deliver a Six Sigma level of performance because they have discovered 'purpose' in their job. This purpose motivates them to impose restrictions on themselves: they do not have their own lunch till they deliver the last dabba.

What Should You Do to Love and Serve Your Customer?

- **Spend time framing your 1CQ:** It should be framed keeping the customer at the centre of decision-making. You and your team should refer to it while making big and small decisions.
- **Build strong relationships with customers:**
  o Be compassionate towards them.
  o Keep customers' interests ahead of the company's.

o   Create products that are sensitive to customer sensibilities.

o   Repose trust in customers.

o   Empower your employees to make decisions regarding customer service on the spot.

o   Never forget to tell your customer that you value the business that they bring you.

o   Look upon customer complaint as feedback that reflects a larger malady. Industry folklore suggests that if twenty-five people have a bad experience with your product, only one person will take the trouble of writing to the company about it; but each of those twenty-five customers will speak to approximately twelve people about their bad experience. In this age of social media, they even post about their negative experiences. All these result in bad buzz for the business.

o   Never stop surprising and delighting customers.

o   Help your employees assign a higher purpose to their job.

If all this sounds complicated, remember this golden rule: in every situation do what is good for the customer. Period. Your business will always be in fine fettle.

RULE 2

Deliver a Delightful Customer Experience

Nothing ever becomes real till it is experienced.

—John Keats

There can be several strategies to win a customer's heart, but the foremost would be to deliver a pleasurable experience to them. A customer who has had a pleasurable experience with a brand is likely to develop an emotional bond with it. Once that happens, customers display a cultish devotion towards it.

To identify strategies that can deliver a pleasurable customer experience, we'll have to go back to the birth of the product economy at the dawn of the Industrial Revolution.

Back then, consumers bought 'standardized' items. The product economy viewed this as merely a transaction. No more, no less. In many cases, consumers had to further 'invest' in the product to make it consumption-ready. Take instant coffee for instance. After purchasing the product, a customer had to add water, milk and sugar and heat the concoction before she could enjoy it. After consuming it, she had to invest additional resources in disposing of or cleaning the waste generated: the dirty utensils and other leftovers.

The service economy stepped in to overcome the shortcomings of the product economy. It presented customers with ready-to-consume products. It gave greater convenience to the customer. Brands charged a premium for this convenience and customers were more than happy to pay it. The service economy was an improvement over the product economy and was widely adopted by brands to gain a competitive advantage; industries moved from selling their brand as a product, to selling it as a service, to commanding a price premium.

However, despite its myriad advantages, even the service economy has its drawbacks.

Take the case of a kiosk selling coffee. It serves us coffee in return for money. Once we finish our coffee and move on, we forget about the service (coffee) that we just consumed. It is because the kiosk only provided coffee as a service and nothing more. There is hardly any attempt on the part of the kiosk owner to establish a relationship with the customer.

This is where the experience economy stepped in. It seeks to deliver a service as an experience so remarkable that it evokes positive emotions which linger over an extended period of time, long after the brand has been consumed. This results in the forming of a relationship between the experience provider and the customer. Over time, as the relationship deepens, it starts maturing into an emotional bond and is finally reflected as loyalty.

Delivering a Pleasurable Customer Experience

How do brands deliver a pleasurable customer experience? Human beings experience pleasure through the five senses:

sight, sound, smell, touch and taste. When the five senses are engaged in unison, they heighten the experience and evoke positive emotions which are stored in the brain as memory.

Let's stay with coffee. Starbucks is arguably regarded as a purveyor of fine quality coffee. It achieved this status not by marketing coffee as a product (it would have been deemed an expensive coffee), not by marketing coffee as a service (it would still be perceived as expensive), but by marketing it as an experience. It stimulated all five senses of its customers to deliver a pleasurable experience.

Here is how Starbucks does it:

- **Smell:** Upon entering a Starbucks outlet, the coffee aroma hits the customer, reinforcing its image as a purveyor of one of the world's finest coffees.
- **Sight:** The barista welcomes customers with a smile, making her likeable, confident, knowledgeable and approachable. Would you not like to be guided by her in navigating the menu?
- **Sound:** A barista is trained to greet a regular customer by name. This simple behaviour makes the customer feel welcome. A barista is also trained to remember the previous order of a regular customer. This simple act makes the customer feel important.

  If the customer is new then the barista greets them enthusiastically and strives to engage them in conversation. She does this by posing open ended questions. Conversations build relationships.

  For example, I was once asked at a Starbucks, 'I saw you going through the menu board. What kind of coffee do you like?' This is a much better question than 'Would you like coffee?' which can elicit a monosyllabic response.

As the customers answer the question, the barista engages them to get a better idea of the type of coffee they may desire. Coupled with a smile and a warm tone, it makes the customers feel special.

Once the order is placed, the barista invariably poses the next question: 'your name, please?' The customers write the response on the side of the cup.

While waiting, the customers hear the sound of a coffee machine in the background which reinforces the core value of Starbucks as a specialist in coffee.

When the order is ready, the barista calls out the customer's name. Again, it makes the customers feel special. They walk over to collect the order and go back to their table to savour it.

- **Taste:** Starbucks strives to customize each and every order. Therefore, the barista takes all inputs at the time of the order to ensure it is handcrafted to the customer's liking.

  In the unlikely event the customer is not satisfied with the taste and complains, the order is remade without any questions asked.

  This is part of the 'Just say yes to customers' policy. Starbucks is not in the business of winning an argument with the customer but of delivering a pleasurable customer experience.

  Also, a guest can request the barista for a taste of the coffee before they purchase it. This reduces post-purchase dissonance.

- **Touch:** The feel of the coffee cup, the tray, the upholstery of the seats and the cutlery are all aimed at heightening the experience of touch.

This has worked for me too. I have almost always had an enjoyable experience at Starbucks. The positive emotions evoked by these experiences have been stored in my brain as memories. Whenever I think of getting a coffee, I remember Starbucks and positive emotions flood me. Since I want to have an enjoyable experience again, I make an extra effort to visit Starbucks. This is how Starbucks builds loyalty among its customers.

The Business Impact of Customer Experience

According to a study[1], emotionally-engaged customers are more valuable because they:

- Buy more
- Visit more often
- Care less about price
- Pay attention to your communication
- Follow your advice
- Recommend you to others

A word of caution: while customers who experience a great customer experience exhibit this desirable behaviour, the converse is also true. If they are at the receiving end of bad

---

[1] 'The New Science of Customer Emotions', *Harvard Business Review* video, 8.44, August 8, 2018, https://hbr.org/video/5819564758001/the-new-science-of-customer-emotions

experiences, they will lose no time in taking their business away from you!

Customer Experience in a Service Industry

Customer experience offers so many advantages that many businesses are leaning on it to secure a competitive advantage. Singapore Airlines (SIA) is a great example of quality customer experience.

I had to travel to Singapore quite often for business. I opted to fly SIA. On every flight, I had an enjoyable experience. When I tried to analyse the reasons, I concluded that SIA looks upon the flying time of five-and-a-half hours between Mumbai and Singapore as a stage, and the aircraft, air hostesses, food and drinks, crockery, upholstery and entertainment as props. Using the stage (flying time) and the props, SIA strives to stimulate all my five senses in unison to deliver a pleasurable customer experience.

When I board the aircraft, the airhostesses welcome me with a smile. They ask for my boarding pass and while they escort me to my seat, I am addressed by my name. The seats are super large and the entertainment available on every flight is well curated. I love to catch up on documentaries and the latest blockbusters. During the flight, I am served beverages of my choice. My vote is always for the Singapore Sling! Thereafter, piping hot food is served. The entire five-and-a-half hour flight passes off in a blink. I de-board the aircraft filled with positive emotions.

Whenever I have to fly to Singapore, I think of SIA and positive emotions flood me. I therefore insist on flying SIA, resulting in repeat business for them.

How Can Technology Companies Deliver Customer Experience?

The strategy of engaging the five senses in unison to deliver an enjoyable experience is good for businesses where customers come in face-to-face contact with them.

How can technology companies, such as Ola, deliver a customer experience when customers do not come in contact with the employees?

According to me, engineers working in ride-hailing companies identify every touch point between the customer and the app, from the customer keying in the destination and ordering the ride, the ride itself and payment options to the rating of the driver at the end of the ride. They strive to make each touch point in the app user-friendly.

Here is how they deliver a customer experience:

- **Use of existing devices:** The app has to be hardware agnostic. It can run on customers' existing devices. In case of Ola it is a smartphone. This means that riders do not have to invest in acquiring an additional device to access it.
- **Intuitive:** The app is intuitive and does not require riders to acquire new cognitive skills to engage with it.
- **Least number of 'taps' required to get serviced:** To engage with the app users have to 'tap' a few times. In most cases it is not more than three times. The best companies have reduced this to merely one step. For example, Amazon has patented its 1-Click ordering which places an order with just one tap.

- **Limited choices:** If a large number of choices are offered, it leads to decision fatigue and postponement of the decision. Therefore, limited choices are offered to customers for selection. Further, these choices are based on their past habits.

- **Keeping the user updated in real time:** The app is designed to update users on various aspects of the ride: the driver's profile and his rating, time to reach the pickup point, time to the destination and more. This ensures that uncertainty and anxiety are kept at bay. The ride hence becomes even more enjoyable.

- **Designed to make drivers and riders behave better:** This is done by having a rating system for the driver and the rider. The earnings of the driver are directly linked to favourable ratings. Riders, too, are dependent on a good rating: if they misbehave, then the next time they book a ride they will get a lower preference. Therefore, the system is designed to self-correct.

All these features are intelligently embedded in the app to ensure that riders have a pleasurable customer experience.

Technology companies—such as Ola, Uber, Flipkart, Amazon, Oyo Rooms, Airbnb and Google—have a similar strategy, or a variation of it, to deliver a pleasurable experience to their customers and win their loyalty.

Creating Extraordinary Moments

New research warns us that over time we tend to remember the best, worst and last moments of an experience and forget the rest. To overcome this problem, Chip Heath and Dan Heath proposed that we should build short meaningful moments: short experiences that are both memorable and meaningful.[2]

I believe that meaningful moments are made up of three elements. This is a minor variation of the proposal made by the Heath brothers.

- **Elevate:** Engineer an ordinary moment to transform into an extraordinary experience. At Singapore's Changi Airport, at the immigration counter, after stamping my passport, the officer says, 'Welcome to Singapore.' Just ahead there is a bowl filled with sweets. This is how I am always welcomed in Singapore. This is in sharp contrast to the experience I have upon returning home. Do ensure, wherever possible, that these moments come as a surprise to customers.
- **Physiological change:** These 'extraordinary' moments of surprise should have the power to bring about physiological changes in customers. For example, if a moment causes extreme pleasure, then a pleasure hormone, dopamine, is released which causes a physiological change in the body.
- **Shareable:** The extraordinary moment should be shareable.

Let me illustrate these with an example. We were to sign a joint venture pact with a leading global beverage company. Their senior team was visiting us for this purpose. For many

---

2   Chip Heath and Dan Heath, 'The Power of Moments' (Bantam Press, 2017).

members of the team it was their maiden visit to India. We booked them in a five-star hotel in the vicinity of our office. And we requested the hotel staff to welcome our guests in traditional Indian style, by putting a tika on their forehead and garlanding each team member. For many of our foreign guests, it was a novel experience. They were enthralled and clicked selfies with the lady and each other. A few among them shared these pics with folks back home.

Years later, I met some of my guests in their home country. They still remembered the check-in moment! An ordinary event of a check-in was transformed into something extraordinary by engineering the three elements into it.

What Derails Customer Experience?

'God has heard my prayer!' my friend told me excitedly.

'What happened?' I asked.

'Finally, a fairness cream for men has been launched. It promises to make men fairer. I am buying it,' he replied.

Time flew by and it was almost a month later that we met again.

'Did you use the fairness cream?' I asked my friend.

'I did, but to no avail. My complexion has not changed. I feel angry and cheated,' he said with disappointment written all over his face.

My friend was a victim of post-purchase dissonance. It is a feeling of disappointment and misgiving that sets in after customers buy a product, start using it and realize that it has not lived up to its promise. They feel short-changed and, at worst, cheated. This feeling, if left unattended, could lead to a negative emotion becoming associated with the brand. This results in customers not giving it additional business; moreover, they will speak negatively about the company and the brand, damaging its reputation.

Strategies to Prevent Derailing of Customer Experience

Prior to purchase, provide the customer with opportunities to sample the brand or find a way to demonstrate your promise.

Car companies encourage potential customers to test-drive the car before signing the cheque; food companies routinely make people sample the products prior to purchase. If on-the-spot sampling is not possible, they hand out product samples to customers prior to purchase.

Newspapers and magazines offering subscription schemes provide a guarantee to subscribers that if they are not entirely satisfied they can cancel the subscription—anytime. These small steps ensure that post-purchase dissonance is kept to a minimum, if not entirely eliminated.

Let us shift our conversation to product demonstration. Let me share with you a personal experience of product demonstration that made us happily pay a premium for it.

My wife, Shaily, and I were in Dhaka and no visit to Dhaka is complete without purchasing a Dhaka sari (Dhakai). We decided to seek references from our friends about which sari shop to buy one from.

As we entered the recommended sari shop, I realized it was frozen in time. There were mattresses placed on the floor on which we made ourselves comfortable.

When the shopkeeper heard the name of the person who had recommended the store, he was even more welcoming.

He immediately issued instructions to his assistant to serve us water and snacks.

Then, he got down to showing saris to Shaily. The craftmanship and workmanship evident in every sari were extraordinary. The large number of choices he placed before Shaily overwhelmed her. Noticing this, he said, '*Boudi* (the term for elder brother's wife), please select the saris you really like, so that I can remove the rest of them from here.' It was agonizing for Shaily to shortlist some saris, but she finally succeeded. Now she had to make a choice from three saris.

Hesitantly, she asked about the prices. The price range indicated by the shopkeeper made Shaily's face fall: they were all expensive.

Seeing indecision writ large on her face, the shopkeeper called out to his assistant and asked him to shake open the sari Shaily seemed to like the most.

The sari now lay in front of us in a huge pile.

'*Boudi*, can I have your ring?' asked the shopkeeper.

Puzzled at this request, Shaily asked, 'Why?'

'I require it for just a moment and then I will return it to you,' he replied.

Shaily took off her ring and uncertainly handed it to the shopkeeper. What he did next was extraordinary. He slipped one end of the sari through the ring—just enough for the assistant to get hold of it at the other end. Then, the assistant started to walk away from us. Magically, the whole sari passed through the small ring.

Without saying a word the shopkeeper had demonstrated the excellent quality of the fabric used in his saris. Now when we juxtaposed the price against the high quality of the sari, we felt that it was not all that expensive and ended up buying it, without bargaining.

Product demonstration has the power to get customers to willingly buy the product and also pay a premium for it.

This is how the high-end audio specialists Bose compelled us to purchase a music system we had no intention of buying.

Window-shopping in a mall, Shaily and I noticed a Bose store. For a lark, we walked inside with no intention of purchasing anything.

As we entered, a salesperson greeted us with a broad smile and posed an open-ended question: 'What kind of music system are you looking for?' The question was designed to help the salesperson understand our requirements.

He listened intently to what we had to say, interjecting occasionally to better understand our requirements. Then he led us to a section where a music system closest to our requirement was displayed. He switched on the music system and a high-performance sound filled the room.

Shaily tugged at my shirtsleeve to indicate that we should leave. I took the hint and we started moving towards the exit, assuring the salesperson that we would be back later to make the purchase.

As we neared the exit, he posed an innocuous question: 'Sir, do you have five minutes?'

'Of course,' I said, not wanting to disappoint him. After all, he had been helpful and courteous to us!

'Sir, please follow me,' he said.

He took a few steps inside the store and opened a door for us to enter. The door led us into a room that looked like a mini theatre, holding approximately ten seats. He made us sit in the front row, dimmed the lights and switched on the projector. Breath-taking imagery accompanied by sharp, deep and rich music surrounded us. He quietly exited the theatre leaving us to enjoy the audio-visual extravaganza in solitude.

The booming sound made me look in the direction from where it was emanating. I noticed massive rectangular speakers on either side of the screen. I surmised the sound was emanating from them; after all, the size of the speakers had to match the intensity of the sound.

As if on cue, the salesperson came back to the theatre, and before our eyes, walked towards the first speaker and removed it.

What I had thought was a speaker was merely a cover; inside it was the minuscule Bose Cube, this was the actual speaker through which the booming sound was emanating. Similarly, he moved to the second 'speaker' and removed the cover to unveil another cute minuscule speaker.

Shaily and I were dumbfounded. We hadn't expected such resonant sound to come from such tiny speakers. Through this simple demonstration, Bose proved to us, beyond doubt, that it is peerless when it comes to sonic engineering!

The salesperson switched off the audio-visual and asked us, 'Did you enjoy the experience?'

'Yes' was the only thing we could mumble, still reeling from the demonstration!

He guided us out of the theatre to a sitting area and asked, 'May I show you the music system you just experienced in the theatre?'

'Of course!' Shaily and I said in unison. The experience in the theatre had us determined to possess the music system.

Once we had made the decision to buy it, he made us sit down so that he could get the invoicing done. After the payment formalities were completed, the salesperson took down the address of our residence where the music system was to be installed and politely asked us a convenient time for his people to come and install it.

At the appointed time the Bose team came and installed the system. They left after reassuring us that they were just a call away should we face any problems—which they assured us was unlikely to happen!

Along with providing samplings and demos, you may choose to follow a simple but time-tested axiom: under-promise and over-deliver. This will further reduce chances of post-purchase dissonance. The businesses will not be the judge of how well they have delivered on the promise. That will be left to the customers. If they feel that the business has not lived up to the promise, then the latter ought to self-penalize. As Domino's does. It promises to deliver hot pizza at our doorstep in thirty minutes. If it fails to come good on its promise, it chooses to penalize itself by offering the pizza for free.

Customer Experience Strategy for B2B

From B2C (business-to-consumer), let us shift our discussion to B2B (business-to-business) companies. How can B2B companies demonstrate their promise? By introducing potential customers to existing customers and letting them take direct feedback.

In addition to what we have discussed, make sure that you deliver on the attributes discussed below; the lack of these attributes will adversely impact customer experience.

- **Reliability**: You should design a system that delivers reliable and accurate service. Take the Mumbai dabbawalas (lunchbox-delivery men). They are known to deliver Six Sigma level of performance: 3.5 defects per million deliveries. If they can deliver Six Sigma, why not you?
- **Assurance**: Provide assurance to customers that you will stand by your promise or guarantee. Look at Hampton hotels.[3] When guests check in they are greeted by a prominently placed notice that reads: 'If you're not satisfied, we don't expect you to pay. That's our commitment and your guarantee.' Indeed, there are guests who call in the guarantee. The hotel does not contest it but asks them to give the specific reasons why they felt let down in writing. This feedback helps the hotel to eliminate, at the root, the problems which lead to loss of revenue. Over time they progressively become better and better.
- **Responsiveness**: The system should be primed to respond with speed: it should be able to provide a response within an acceptable time frame. This should happen without the customer having to follow up.

Where the service is offered face-to-face, two additional components become important:

- **Demeanour and conduct of people delivering the service**: The people interacting with your customers must be careful about how they conduct themselves. They have to possess a friendly demeanour, exhibit positive body language and display impeccable

---

[3] About Hampton by Hilton,

conduct, so that customers are not in any way intimidated or inconvenienced.

- **Compassion:** Service people should not only 'empathize' with their customers but also 'act' in a manner that delights them. Take Ritz Carlton for instance. The service staff are trained to anticipate each guest's needs' and strive to fulfil them.[4]

Companies That Fail to Deliver on Customer Experience

Most companies realize the benefits that accrue when they deliver an enjoyable customer experience and therefore invest top dollar in creating infrastructure, systems and processes to do so. This is corroborated through research which indicates that 80 per cent of companies believe they deliver 'super experiences'. But this research also points out that only 8 per cent of customers agree that they had super experiences.[5]

The gulf between companies' assessment and customers' experience is staggering. This presents a golden opportunity for you to hit a home run: by not only delivering a superb customer experience but also ensuring that the customers actually experience it. This will be decided by the customers, not you.

---

[4] Carmine Gallo, 'Stop listening and start anticipating your customers' needs', *Forbes*, 28 May 2014, https://www.forbes.com/sites/carminegallo/2014/05/28/stop-listening-and-start-anticipating-your-customers-needs/#6f0bf216b4f2

[5] James Allen, et al., 'Closing the delivery gap', Bain & Company, 2005. http://www2.bain.com/bainweb/pdfs/cms/hotTopics/closingdeliverygap.pdf

Benefits of Providing a Good Customer Experience

You will reap a host of benefits by providing a good customer experience. A partial list includes:

- Commanding a price premium
- Developing stronger brand loyalty, leading to brand advocacy
- Greater retention and repeat-business from customers
- Creation of positive buzz by the customers, leading to lowering of customer acquisition cost
- Enhanced ability to up-sell and cross-sell existing and new services

What Should You Do to Deliver Good Customer Experience?

Let us move the discussion to what you should do to deliver a pleasurable customer experience. These principles, as discussed previously, are applicable to both B2C and B2B businesses.

- When your customer visits your office, attempt to stimulate all the five senses in unison to create a pleasurable experience:
  - o **Sight:** Be appropriately dressed and welcome your customers with a smile.
  - o **Sound:** Greet them by their name. During conversation use positive words.
  - o **Smell:** Spray the meeting room with a natural room freshener.

- o **Touch:** Your furniture, cutlery and other things with which customers come in contact should be of good quality.
- o **Taste:** Taste could be interpreted metaphorically. Take them around your office/factory and give them a taste of your culture, product and people.

- In case of technology companies, where customers do not come in face-to-face contact, design a customer experience so good that it evokes positive emotions in them.
- Focus on converting ordinary moments into extraordinary moments by incorporating these three elements:
  - o Elevate the customer experience.
  - o Bring about psychological changes: pleasurable moments cause dopamine—the pleasure hormone—to release, which results in psychological changes.
  - o Make the customer experience shareable.

- In both B2C and B2B:
  - o Build a system that recognizes customers and is also reliable, responsive and provides assurance.
  - o Create opportunities for your customers to either sample the product or find a way to demonstrate the promise, prior to purchase.
  - o Under-promise and over-deliver.
  - o Keep taking feedback from customers at regular intervals, to ensure that they are indeed experiencing the promise made by you.

o   If the promise is not experienced, then proactively
    self-penalize yourself.

Today's customers shop at Amazon, search on Google and
ride an Ola. They are used to receiving good experiences.
They expect the same good experience every time they deal
with your company. When you deliver on that, loyalty for
your brand and business will grow. The bad news is that when
customers have a bad experience, then as many as 25 per cent
of them will bid goodbye. Companies have no choice but to
deliver enjoyable experiences to customers. Today, customer
experience is regarded as the number one source of competitive
advantage, ahead of product differentiation and prices.

RULE 3

Transform Your Customers into Brand Advocates

The only path to profitable growth may lie in a company's ability to get its loyal customers to become, in effect, its marketing department.

—Frederick F. Reichheld

Let's begin our conversation with a question. What would you want your customers to be: satisfied or loyal to your brand? Some of you may want your customers to be satisfied because they would then invariably be loyal. Others might choose loyal customers because loyalty is a higher-grade benefit compared to satisfaction. If you ask me, I want neither.

'So, what do you want?' I hear you ask.

I yearn for brand advocates: customers who are not just satisfied or loyal to my brand, but who shout from the rooftops to everyone who cares to listen about the great brand they are using.

A brand advocate is a loyal customer who creates buzz about the brand at almost every opportunity: both offline, by spreading the good word and online, by posting reviews, ratings and actual experiences. They possess the following qualities in varying degrees:

- Strong loyalty towards the brand they advocate
- Early adopters of new brands launched by the company
- Price-insensitive
- Source for new ideas and can be counted upon to work along with companies to co-create new offerings
- Unlikely to desert the brand when it faces reputation issues
- Extend support to the brand for a long period, if not for life

Are Customers Influenced by Brand Advocates?

Many people feel that companies only highlight the positive features of a product in advertisements. But actual customers have no axe to grind and are likely to post balanced reviews.

Not surprisingly, paid advertisement lacks credibility and pales in comparison to the power of real consumers' authentic reviews, ratings and actual experiences. Which is why there is a shift away from paid advertisements towards actual customers' ratings, reviews and experiences. Simply put, buyers are predisposed towards being influenced by buzz: how fellow customers review and rate a brand.

Research Findings

Are there hard numbers to support these hypothesis?

Consider the findings from the Nielsen Global Online Consumer Survey 2009 conducted on over 25,000 Internet users across fifty countries[1] :

- 90 per cent of people trust brand recommendations from people they know.
- 70 per cent people trust customer opinions posted online.
- Only 24–62 per cent of people trust advertising.

Since then, this trend has gathered momentum. Nielsen's 2012 report 'Global Trust in Advertising', which surveyed more than 28,000 respondents across fifty-six countries, concluded that 92 per cent of consumers trust 'earned' media—that is, reviews, ratings and recommendations from friends and family posted online—above all other forms of advertising.[2]

No wonder online consumer reviews are the second most trusted form of advertising with 70 per cent of global consumers that surveyed online indicating they trust this platform (an increase of 15 per cent in four years.)

I can sense another question popping up in your mind: do actual customers show a tendency towards posting online?

---

[1] 'Global Advertising Consumers Trust Real Friends And Virtual Strangers The Most', Nielsen, August 7, 2009, https://www.nielsen.com/us/en/insights/article/2009/global-advertising-consumers-trust-real-friends-and-virtual-strangers-the-most/

[2] 'Global trust in online, social and mobile advertising grows', Nielsen, 10 April, 2012, https://www.nielsen.com/us/en/insights/article/2012/consumer-trust-in-online-social-and-mobile-advertising-grows/.

Truth be told, older generations give it a miss, but the young adults armed with smart devices have embraced it and are expressing their opinions on anything and everything with full gusto, watching gleefully as technology amplifies their voices until it reverberates across the globe.

Possibility of Misuse?

If the voice of customers has so much potency, can unscrupulous companies manipulate the system by 'bribing' people to post glowing (in other words, fake) reviews? Indeed, a handful of companies do resort to it. They pay money to 'influencers'—celebrities, bloggers, micro-influencers, domain experts and thought leaders—to post positive reviews about their brands.

However, I would advise against doing this because when customers, influenced by 'paid' reviews, buy the product and feel disappointed, they tend to vent their anger online and offline. This has the potential of damaging your company's reputation. Also, the option is not sustainable because fake reviews ensure, at best, that the customers buy the product once. They will not give that product a second chance. So, it is not a sustainable strategy in the long run.

Strategies for Cultivating Brand Advocates

Since it offers so many benefits, it must be every company's dream to have an army of brand advocates who voluntarily and without financial rewards spread the word about the brand. Indeed, many companies try to cultivate brand advocates, but few succeed.

Let me share strategies pursued by companies to cultivate and nurture brand advocates.

Look at Google for instance. To gain insight into its strategy, permit me to pose a question to you: 'I need to search for information. Where should I go?'

Your likely response would be 'Google'.

Did you notice that you acted as the brand advocate of Google? Like you, there are a sizable number of people around the globe who use and recommend Google as a one-stop destination for searching information. No wonder the term 'Googling' has become a verb.

Let us get back to the original question: what strategy did Google adopt to achieve this miracle?

In its formative years, its founders drew inspiration from Coca-Cola, one of the most recognizable trademarks across the world. The brand was synonymous with 'refreshment'.

The founders desired Google to become synonymous with 'search' across the world. To translate their dream into reality, they hired Sergio Zyman[3], a marketing consultant and former marketing head of Coca-Cola. They tasked him with drawing up a strategy that would get the world excited about their new company and make it synonymous with 'search'.

In due course, Zyman presented the strategy document but the founders rejected it. It turned out that Coca-Cola had achieved world-wide recognition by investing billions of dollars on advertising. This was a strategy that the founders of Google were unwilling to do. They were willing to spend big money, but not on advertising. Instead, they wanted to invest

---

[3] Fred Vogelstein, 'Dogfight: How Apple and Google Went To War and Started a Revolution' (William Collins, 2013), p.59

in making the 'search' product better so that users would get the best possible experience. This would convert them into brand advocates for Google. After all, when real people say that Google is good, the believability would be higher. It would generate more trials, which in turn would create more brand advocates, setting in motion a self-perpetuating virtuous cycle.

Google states on its site:

> Since the beginning, we've focused on providing the best user experience possible. Whether we're designing a new Internet browser or giving a new tweak to the look of the homepage, we take great care to ensure that they will ultimately serve you, rather than our own internal goal or bottom line.[4]

If you feel that Google is a hard act to follow then let's draw inspiration from a humbler tech company: Dropbox. Its founders committed themselves to making storage on the cloud easy and affordable. But when the time came to launch Dropbox, they discovered that they didn't have the financial resources. To surmount this problem they zeroed in on a business model of offering limited storage space for free.[5] The user got this upon signing up with them. He or she could get further space on payment.

The 'free' bait worked, and Dropbox was able to attract users. Since the 'product' was good, users had a satisfying

---

4   Google Site: https://www.google.com/about/philosophy.html?refresh=
     1pli%3D1
5   Dropbox Site: https://www.dropbox.com/basic

experience. They started posting positive reviews online. Dropbox rewarded this desirable behaviour by providing positive reviewers with additional storage space for free.

The strategy of rewarding desirable behaviour encouraged users of Dropbox to post more positive reviews online, leading to the creation of online buzz. This resulted in more people signing up with Dropbox. As more and more people signed up, it set in motion a virtuous self-perpetuating cycle.

Nurturing Brand Advocates

Companies should show genuine care towards brand advocates by:

- Listening to their voices, and more importantly, acting upon them
- Proactively seeking their feedback
- Making sure that they are the first to see new offerings
- Rewarding them occasionally
- Recognizing them often

Do Indian Companies Subscribe to Brand Advocacy?

A large number of Indian companies, including Raymond and PVR Cinemas, have been successful in cultivating brand advocates.

Let me share my experience with the Raymond Group. At the time, I was the president of J.K. Helene Curtis, part of the Raymond Group. As part of a delegation consisted senior executives, I visited Raymond's state-of-the-art manufacturing plant in Chhindwara, a small town in Madhya Pradesh.

As we entered the factory, a board nailed to the wall schematically outlined the process followed to produce fine fabrics. It showed raw material going in as input, undergoing processing and coming out as fine fabrics.

Light-heartedly, I commented to a colleague standing next to me, 'I now know how Raymond makes money. It puts raw material from one side and sells the finished fabrics that comes out from the other side. Who knew it was that simple?'

As soon as I said this, a senior member of the company, who was walking ahead of us, turned around slowly, looked at me and said, 'Srivastava-ji, you are wrong. It's not that simple. Raymond does not make money simply by putting raw material from one side and selling the fabrics which come out from the other side. It puts in quality between the input and the output.'

I was embarrassed beyond words. I wanted the earth to open up and swallow me. That day I got a deeper insight into Raymond's way of working. Raymond's product quality delivers the best possible experience which converts its customers into brand advocates who spread the word about it.

This strategy has many takers, including cinema halls. They too have focused on investing in improving customer experience so that their customers transform into brand advocates.

When I was in college, there were only single-screen cinema halls. Most of them were fitted with basic amenities: barely passable projection systems, canteens which served a limited spread, wooden chairs and mega size fans whirling in the hall to keep the air circulating. Many a times the fans drowned out the dialogues.

Overtime, cinema hall owners invested resources in improving the cinema-viewing experience by installing central air-conditioning and plush push-back seats, carpeting the floor, and offering a wider range of food and drinks. In recent times, cinema halls have given way to multiplexes, which have upped the viewing experience by installing world-class projection and sound systems, making tickets available online, offering reclining seats and introducing the option of getting food and drinks delivered to the seat. All these features, cumulatively, deliver an amazing viewing experience and transform customers into brand advocates.

There is an important lesson in this: Invest resources in improving the product quality to deliver the best possible customer experience. This is likely to transform your customers into brand advocates who will not only create a positive buzz but will also display loyalty. Loyalty drives revenue growth which will have a positive impact on your business.

Benefits of Brand Advocacy

Indeed, revenue growth would be an obvious benefit of brand advocacy. But did you know that it also results in the following benefits?

- **Cost reduction:** Brand advocacy leads to buzz, which results in decreased spending in advertising and sales promotions (A&SP). Buzz may not entirely replace paid advertising, but it can support it.

- **Loyal customer:** Attracting a new customer costs a company five times more than retaining an existing customer.[6] Brand advocates remain loyal for a longer period of time.

- **Referral power:** Brand advocates have indirect referral power. A Nielson survey suggests that 92 per cent of respondents trusted referrals from people they knew. According to an estimate, 84 per cent of B2B decision-makers start the buying process with a referral.[7] Companies with formalized referral programmes experience 86 per cent more revenue growth compared to the rest.[8]

- **Bottom line improvement:** Bain & Company has concluded that in financial services a 5 per cent increase in customer retention rate can increase the company's profitability by 25 per cent.[9] Brand

6 Jia Wertz, 'Don't Spend 5 Times More Attracting New Customers, Nurture The Existing Ones', *Forbes*, 12 September 2018, https://www.forbes.com/sites/jiawertz/2018/09/12/dont-spend-5-times-more-attracting-new-customers-nurture-the-existing-ones/#7028468c5a8e

7 Laurence Minsky and Keith A. Quesenberry, 'How B2B Sales Can Benefit from Social Selling', *Harvard Business Review*, 6 November 2016, https://hbr.org/2016/11/84-of-b2b-sales-start-with-a-referral-not-a-salesperson

8 Shubhomita Bose, '86 Percent of Companies with Referral Program See Growth, Study Says, Small Business Trends', 5 January 2016, https://smallbiztrends.com/2016/01/b2b-referrals.html

9 Fred Reichheid, 'Prescription for cutting cost', Bain & Company, https://sedonapies.com/wp-content/uploads/2017/04/BB_Prescription_cutting_costs.pdf

advocates tend to remain loyal towards business they advocate.

- **De-risks the overall business:** When a company has a loyal and ever-increasing base of brand advocates the indications are that its future is secure. Around 65 per cent of the business comes from existing customers and 80 per cent of future profits are likely to come from 20 per cent of existing customers.[10] Brand advocates are loyal customers.

You will notice that brand advocates help in growing revenue, reducing cost, expanding margins, increasing the bottom line and de-risking business.

Can Brand Advocacy Be Measured?

The Net Promoter Score (NPS) measures brand advocacy. It is an important number that you should keep an eye on because analysis done by Bain & Company shows companies achieving long-term profitable growth have an NPS that is two times higher than an average company.[11]

To calculate NPS, customers are requested to score on a single question: based on your experience, how likely are you to recommend the product to your friends and family on a scale of 0 to 10?

---

[10] Matt Mansfield, 'Customer retention statistics: The ultimate collection for small business', Small Business Trends, 26 December 2018 (last update), https://smallbiztrends.com/2016/01/b2b-referrals.html

[11] Net Promoter System, Bain & Company, http://www.netpromotersystem.com/about/measuring-your-net-promoter-score.aspx

NET PROMOTER SCORE

Based on your experience, how likely are you to recommend to your friends/family on a scale of 0 to 10?

(0) (1) (2) (3) (4) (5) (6) (7) (8) (9) (10)

Not at all likely   Extremely likely

The company collects this feedback from many customers, and based on their response, customers get classified as:

1. **Promoters (9–10):** Happy and loyal customers who buy from the company and recommend it to their friends.
2. **Passive (7–8):** Barely satisfied customers who can be easily coaxed away by competitors.
3. **Detractors (0–6):** Unhappy customers who are prone to defecting. They account for more than 80 per cent of negative buzz.[12] This impacts the company's reputation, demoralizes employees and puts off new customers.

NPS is calculated by subtracting the 'percentage of promoters' from 'percentage of detractors.[13]

---

[12] Jeff Sauro, 'Do Detractors Really Say Bad Things About A Company?' Measuring U, 27 November 2018, https://measuringu.com/detractors/
[13] Net Promoter System, Bain & Company, https://www.bain.com/insights/introducing-the-net-promoter-system-loyalty-insights/.

So, what is a good NPS score to aim for? It should always be positive and you should aim to keep improving it all the time.

I would strongly recommend that NPS should be used along with another metric: the Customer Effort Score (CES).[14] CES measures how easy or difficult it is for customers to get 'help' from the company. If the customer finds it difficult to get help, she may not give repeat business nor remain loyal to the company.

CES is measured by asking customers to rate their response to a single question: 'Overall, how difficult was it to get the help you expected?' on a scale of 1 (extremely easy) to 5 (extremely difficult).

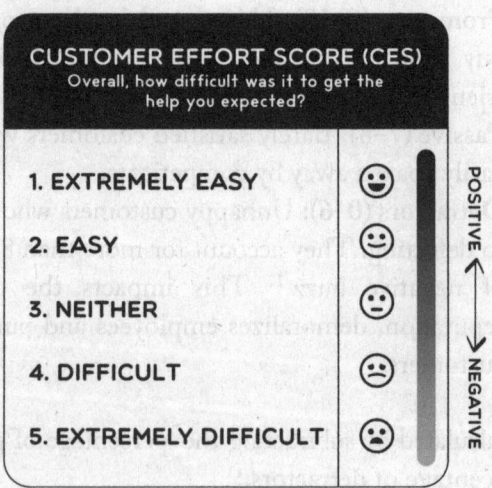

CUSTOMER EFFORT SCORE (CES)
Overall, how difficult was it to get the help you expected?

1. EXTREMELY EASY ☺
2. EASY ☺
3. NEITHER 😐
4. DIFFICULT 🙁
5. EXTREMELY DIFFICULT ☹

POSITIVE ↑ ↓ NEGATIVE

---

[14] Jordon Bryan, 'What's Your Customer Effort Score?' Gartner, July 12, 2018, https://www.gartner.com/smarterwithgartner/unveiling-the-new-and-improved-customer-effort-score/

Let me share my experience which led to my belief that the two metrics should be used concurrently.

A large private bank opened a branch on the ground floor of our building. A few days later the branch manager along with a colleague called upon us at our home. Even before we could say anything, the colleague handed my wife a small pot containing a fortune plant. My wife was happy.

The manager said, 'We have recently opened our branch on the ground floor. It will be convenient for you to bank with us. Our representative will come home and complete the formalities for opening an account. You will enjoy banking with us.'

As promised, a representative of the bank made an appointment and came home to complete the formalities for opening a bank account. The entire experience was extremely pleasant.

If we were asked to rate them on NPS, without hesitation we would score them 9.

A few months later, we had to take a personal loan. Since we had had a good experience with the bank, we decided to approach them. The service they provided was superlative. They gave us a comprehensive list of documents to fill up as well as a list of original documents that had to be submitted. They also sent their team to our home to do due diligence. The entire formalities for sanctioning the loan were completed in a short span of time without in any way inconveniencing us. The money, too, was disbursed promptly.

Some days later an official mail arrived from the bank giving the details of the original documents that had been submitted to them. On close scrutiny we found that one original document was missing on the list. When we pointed this anomaly to the branch, they seemed unmoved and passed the blame on to us. Despite us having a note of acknowledgement from a bank employee stating the receipt of the document.

'You have not submitted it,' a bank representative claimed. Thereafter we had a torrid time dealing with them. Each time we raised a query, it was stonewalled or ignored. The tide had turned. Earlier they were eager to serve us. Now we were chasing them to serve us—but with little success. Finally, after great difficulty, the matter was resolved.

Will we do business with the bank again? Of course not.

Could the bank have been alerted to our growing negative sentiment so that it could take corrective action to win back our loyalty? More importantly, can the bank install a system that can forewarn it about any negative sentiments brewing among its customers?

The answer lies in regularly measuring the Customer Effort Score. CSE indicates customers' intention of continuing to do business with the company. If the bank had asked us to rate it on CES, we would have given it 5, indicating to the bank that as customers we were finding it extremely difficult to get ourselves serviced and, if this continued unchecked, we would cease to do business with them.

To keep your business in robust health, it would be prudent to measure both NPS and CES. If by chance NPS has not captured customers' sentiments, then CES should be able to do so. And your job should be to get good scores on both NPS and CES. You need to maximise brand advocacy and minimize customer effort. This will ensure your customer base displays loyalty towards your business and keeps it in good health.

Let me take a moment to drive home the point of the importance of these two metrics. For that let me introduce you to the concept of a flywheel. It was designed 200 years ago to capture, store and release energy. It helped power the Industrial Revolution.

The function of a flywheel is to rotate and with every rotation, its speed increases. The key task is to keep on increasing the speed of flywheel, which can be achieved by adopting a two-pronged strategy of applying force and reducing friction.

Let me use the metaphor of flywheel for business. The job of a manager is to keep the business running at a fast clip. Therefore, 'force' has to be applied and friction has to be reduced. When NPS is maximized it is akin to force being applied to 'business'; when CES is kept to a minimum, metaphorically speaking the friction is reduced. When NPS and CES work in sync, the flywheel of the business rotates at a brisk speed, resulting in ever growing business.

Employee Advocates

In addition to customers, employees are now turning into advocates of their company.

A *survey* conducted by Edelman indicated that customers trust employees' voices more than that of the CEO, marketing team or the company spokesperson.[15] A study done by Cisco

---

[15] Cameron Brain, 'The employee engagement survey from Edelman', Everyone Social, February 1, 2017, https://everyonesocial.com/blog/employee-engagement-survey/. 2018 Edelman Trust Barometer https://www.edelman.com/sites/g/files/aatuss191/files/2018-10/Edelman_Trust_Barometer_Implications_for_CEOs_2018.pdf

also indicates that employees' posts generate eight times more traction than when the same content is shared through the brand handle.[16]

Employee advocacy involves empowering employees to share the company's content and their experiences of working with the company on their own social channels.

I, too, wanted to formalize an employee advocacy programme in my company which encouraged technology-savvy employees to post about their experiences of working with us. My HR team insisted that we put a policy in place for employees to adhere to while posting online.

I shared a General Motors story with them. Being a hundred-year old company, it had several pages introducing its employees to its complex dress code policy. But with the winds of change, it was decided to reduce it to two words: dress appropriately![17]

Mary Barra, who is leading General Motors and the driving force behind these two words wondered: if employees can't handle 'dress appropriately', then how can they be trusted to handle bigger business decisions?

To convince my team that GM strategy was not an exception, I shared the story of Nordstrom, the chain of luxury department stores. It is renowned for its customer service and

---

[16] Christine Bailey, 'Employee advocacy: Marketing engine of the future?' Cisco (Blogs), September 21, 2015, https://blogs.cisco.com/socialmedia/employee-advocacy-marketing-engine-of-the-future.

[17] Bill Murphy, 'GM Has a 2-Word Dress Code, and It's Actually Brilliant', *Inc.*, June 8, 2018, https://www.inc.com/bill-murphy-jr/this-giant-company-has-a-2-word-dress-code-its-actually-kind-of-brilliant.html

is reputed to have the *shortest employee handbook* to guide their behaviour while providing outstanding customer service.

Here is their entire rulebook:

Nordstrom Rules:

Rule 1: Use best judgment in all situations. There will be no additional rules.[18]

We too requested our employees who wished to put out posts to use their best judgement in all cases. Period. But we did invest in training them on the use of this medium.

What we experienced delighted us: we started receiving better quality CVs. This experience made me wonder: if employees' online voices can benefit us, then why not get other stakeholders—vendors, industry experts and industry bodies—to also share their experiences of dealing with our company? To me, it offered a zero-cost opportunity for building our online reputation.

It's a worthy idea and I would strongly recommend you use it!

What Should You Do to Cultivate Brand Advocates?

- Invest your resources in creating an insanely great product / services that converts customers into brand advocates who then spread the good word.

---

[18] Bill Taylor, 'Trust Your Employees, Not Your Rule Book', *Harvard Business Review*, 20 April 2017, https://hbr.org/2017/04/trust-your-employees-not-your-rulebook

- Craft a strategy to induce trial of your product among your brand advocates.
- Activate your brand advocate by starting Referral Program, opportunities for posting testimonials.
- Refrain from influencing brand advocates by bribing them with money.
- Measure NPS and CES and take business decisions to maximize brand advocacy through NPS and minimize customer efforts through CES.
- Cultivate employee advocates. Trust them to use their best judgement in all cases.
- Seek out advocacy from other stakeholders. For example, vendors.
- Reach out to experts and industry bodies to endorse your business.

RULE 4

Convert Your Customers into 'Employees'

Alone we can do so little; together we can do so much.

—Helen Keller

Let me ask you a question: can companies increase customer satisfaction by cutting costs? The problem, though perplexing, has been resolved. The corporate world has arrived at a solution that is simple, elegant and cost-effective.

The irony is, customers are unknowingly an integral part of the solution.

To increase customer satisfaction, corporates are 'hiring' customers as partial employees. Once customers become partial employees, complaining about bad service is tantamount to complaining about themselves.

Take McDonald's for instance. You stand in queue to place your order, pay for it, collect the food on a tray, walk back to your seat, consume it and deposit the waste in the bin. So, were you only a customer at McDonald's? No, you were also a partial employee. You did things that should ideally have been done by employees hired and paid for by McDonald's.

But did McDonalds pay you for the services you performed for it? Of course not.

Is McDonalds the pioneer in recruiting customers and converting them into partial employees? Read on.

Say's Law of Markets

Way back in 1916, a grocery chain, Piggly Wiggly[1], owned by Clarence Saunders, devised a store format that we now take for granted: self-service. Prior to this, a person always stood behind the counter to serve the buyers. In Saunders' self-service model, customers had to step inside the store and pick up products from the range displayed inside the store. Then they had to cart it to the cash counter where a cashier made the bill and bagged the purchase.

Much to Saunders' delight, sales in this new format were more than in the earlier format. How did this miracle happen? He had unknowingly put into play Say's Law of Markets,[2] which states that 'supply will create its demand'! It simply means that if people get access to 'supply', they will find ways to use it.

Many companies we admire have drawn upon Say's Law and principles of behavioural science to build innovative business models.

IKEA, the world's largest home furniture company, is a prime example. It has been successful in attracting buyers to its store because it has built a sterling reputation of delivering

---

[1] Piggly Wiggly, Wikipedia, https://en.wikipedia.org/wiki/Piggly_Wiggly

[2] Will Kenton, 'Say's Law Of Market', Investopedia, 12 March 2019, https://www.investopedia.com/terms/s/says-law.asp

consistently on its promise of offering a wide range of well-designed home furnishings products at low prices.[3]

It has intelligently interwoven three concepts to give birth to a profitable business model:

- **Say's Law:** Supply creates demand.
- **Do-It-Yourself (DIY):** The phenomenon of carrying out tasks without the support of experts leads to a sense of satisfaction and accomplishment among buyers.
- **Effort Justification:** When we put in our efforts, the outcome seems more valuable to us.[4]

IKEA is a self-service store and the store layout is designed in a circuitous manner; the entrance and exit are on either end of the store and the path between them winds through almost every section. This has been deliberately done to ensure that anyone who enters the store looks at all the products before they can make their way out. Seeing the merchandise (supply), the buyers most often deviate from their shopping list and end up buying things they did not know they needed till they were exposed to it!

Upon reaching home, IKEA's Do-It-Yourself and 'Effort Justification' comes into play. The furniture needs to be assembled before it can be used. Guided by simple and clear instructions, the buyer—now owner—gets down to assembling it. The process of assembling the furniture requires the buyer

---

[3]   Ikea Site: https://www.ikea.com/sg/en/this-is-ikea/about-us/

[4]   Effort Justification, Wikipedia, https://en.wikipedia.org/wiki/Effort_justification

to put in effort (read: sweat) and time. Upon completion of the activity, when the buyer surveys the creation, he or she feels a sense of satisfaction, accomplishment and pride. The assembled furniture appears more valuable and appealing to them: after all, their sweat has gone into making it!

The strategy pursued by IKEA is tantamount to 'outsourcing' the assembly process of the furniture to the customers in exchange for providing a lower price and a feeling of satisfaction, accomplishment and pride.

Every Brand Can Do It

Any company can convert its customers into partial employees, provided the customers see value in taking on the additional responsibilities.

Let me take you to my childhood. During our school summer vacations, my sister and I would buy a pack of Rasna, a popular ready-to-make soft drink concentrate. We would then assemble all the materials required in one place for making and storing our creation: a medium-sized vessel, water, sugar, a large spoon and a glass bottle.

We would plonk ourselves on the floor and get down to the serious business of preparing the drink by following the clearly mentioned steps: we poured the ingredients into the vessel and then started the cumbersome process of stirring it till all the ingredients were completely dissolved. We then carefully poured the mixture into the empty bottle and stored it in our refrigerator.

Whenever we were thirsty, we would make ourselves a drink and relish every sip of it: it tasted so sweet. After all, our 'sweat' had gone into making it! When guests came calling,

the time came to celebrate our father's birthday
stead of buying a ready-made cake this time, my
ought a ready-to-make cake mix. These mixes
cally left a few processes unfinished, to be completed
o baking the cake. My sister poured the mix into a
ner and, as per the instructions, added milk, eggs and
and mixed the batter till all the ingredients had blended
and the consistency was right. She poured the batter into
aking container and put it into the oven to bake. While
e freshened up, the cake was ready! She garnished it to her
eart's content.

With a sense of accomplishment and pride she placed
the 'baked' cake on the dining table and excitedly called out
to us to assemble for the cake-cutting ceremony! How did
my sister feel this time round? Happy, satisfied and, most
importantly, guilt-free, because she had not taken the easy
route and got a ready-made cake, but had put in effort to
bake the cake—although the whole process took barely
twelve minutes!

My sister had, of her own volition, become a partial
employee of the ready-to-make cake mix brand and willingly
bartered effort and sweat to reduce her feeling of guilt and
inner tension.

Companies are now creating products which reduce
feelings of guilt, tension and anxieties and replacing them
with feelings of accomplishment and pride. And the market
is giving these products a thumbs up.

Nowadays, companies from almost every industry,
ranging from airlines to banks to e-commerce companies,
are drawing up strategies for converting their customers into
partial employees.

we served them Rasna with [...] them to take the first sip and p[...] in making it. The guests never fa[...] extraordinary Rasna-making abiliti[...] with pride. We lapped it up and, mu[...] the kitchen to get them a refill.

Even as children, we felt a sense of pr[...] and self-worth in making and serving the[...] had put our 'sweat' and 'effort'—no matter h[...] into making it. For Rasna, my sister and I [...] happily became its partial employees because [...] our labour to experience a sense of pride, self-[...] accomplishment!

Let's fast-forward a few years. My sister had now [...] working and it was our father's birthday. She decided to [...] a cake for him but her hectic schedule prevented her f[...] doing so. Therefore, she decided to buy a ready-made ca[...] from a store. Later that evening, she confided in me that she felt guilty and anxious. She had a nagging feeling that she had not done the right thing by buying a ready-made cake instead of putting in the effort of baking one with her own hands for someone so precious to her.

This feeling of guilt, anxiety and inner tension afflicts many people because they are unable to find time to do things they morally and ethically feel the need to do. Who or what is the culprit? Growing affluence among people results in them being cash-rich but time-poor. How do they manage to come to grips with this reality? By giving away cash to buy time.

Let's return to the cake saga. Over time, my sister rose up the ranks and became busier at work, so much so that she was now cash-rich but always hard-pressed for time.

Companies have discovered yet another way of making customers their 'employees'. This involves offering them convenience, peace of mind, control over their time and relief from frustrating experiences. Let me share with you how airlines have made us their partial employees by catering to these requirements.

In 1985, the year I started my corporate career, flying was a highly sought-after perk and it was available to a select few. To buy an air ticket, I had to invest time, effort and money in travelling to the airline agent's office. He would listen to my requirements, draw up an itinerary, issue the ticket and collect the payment. The ticket would be the size of a mini booklet. The airline paid a commission to the agent for providing these services: an expense that chipped away at their bottom line.

At the airport, the airline secured sufficient space to put up kiosks and had it manned by trained staff for issuing boarding passes. This resulted in further expenses for the airline.

As a flyer I had to arrive early, stand in queue and wait patiently to collect my boarding pass. Invariably, the queue would be long and move at a snail's pace. This experience left me feeling exasperated and helpless.

Fast-forward to 2019. When I have to travel, I log on to a travel site, key in my travel details. And voilà! I get a host of choices. I opt for the airline of my choice, choose the most convenient flight, make an online payment and, seconds later, the e-ticket is in my mail box. A few days prior to the departure, at my convenience, I log into the airline site and check myself in; I also get to choose the seat I like from what is available or I can use a self check-in kiosk at the airport terminal building and then directly proceed for security check and boarding.

In the new system, airlines have 'outsourced' a slew of jobs to me which were previously done by airlines staff. In the process they have made me a partial employee but not paid me a dime.

What strategy have airlines adopted to willingly make us their partial employees? They have deployed a strategy that exploits the 'certainty bias': we feel good when we are certain about outcomes and are in control of situations; uncertainty makes us feel uncomfortable, anxious and inadequate.

Take the process of self check-in, for example. I can do it at my convenience and choose my seat. I do not have to reach the airport early, nor stand in a line which moves at a snail's pace, nor worry about what seat I will get. I am in control of my time.

As a partial employee, I cannot complain about any lapse in the service, because I am in charge of providing it to myself. Result: savings for airlines and increased guest satisfaction. By pursuing this strategy, airlines are discovering that the satisfaction level of guests are going up, while their costs are going down!

From airlines, let us shift our focus to courier companies. They, too, have offloaded a major chunk of their jobs to customers without paying them a penny.

As a partial employee of a courier company, a customer has to carry the parcel to their office, pay the courier charges, and get the receipt. Then, he or she has to track the progress of the parcel herself till it reaches its destination.

Take Tesla, for example. It can be ordered online. In the process, it is side-lining the dealers who booked orders and delivered it.

States Tesla on its site:

> Ordering your Tesla is just like any buying experience on the Internet. Simply choose your options and enter your contact information. Your Tesla will be custom-built in California and delivered to your nearest service centre.[5]

Customers are happily doing 'jobs' which were done by a salesperson at a car dealership.

Customers As Full-time Employees

Companies are not satisfied with merely transforming us into partial employees. Now they are working on converting us into 'full-time employees'.

Amazon, for instance, has introduced Amazon Go, a bricks-and-clicks store that leans on the internet, intelligent technology and smart devices to convert shoppers into its full-time employees. It has no employees or check-out counters. Shoppers switch on the Amazon Go app prior to entering the store, shop for merchandise and just walk out of the store: there is no check-out line, no waiting in the queues! The app automatically totals the value of the purchase and bills it to the shopper's credit card.

The shoppers, unknown to them, have become employees at Go!

Banks too have warmed up to the concept and are pushing the envelope even further. Not only do they aspire to make every customer their full-time employee, they also penalize them if they do not carry out the new responsibilities in a manner that profits the banks!

---

[5] Tesla site: https://www.tesla.com/support/how-ordering-works

Banks have identified banking activities which the customers can carry out so as to result in cost-savings for them. Take the case of issuing bank statements. The bank expects its 'full-time employees' to download it from net banking. But if a customer makes a request for it, the bank usually levies a charge for providing it. Or take cheque-leaves. Banks expect their 'full-time employees' to make payments using internet banking, not by issuing cheques. For emergency situations, a minimum number of cheque-leaves are issued every quarter; if more are ordered, customers are charged.

Customers As Revenue Producers

Companies are attempting to convert customers into their 'employees' and saving on 'cost'. Progressive companies are pushing the envelope. They are motivating customers to design products which can generate revenue for them and/ or suggest strategies to help them meet their business goals.

Take Lego. It is one of the most popular toys in the world. It invites its customers (read: fans) to be a Lego Designer. This is how it works:

Lego Designers can use the existing Lego bricks or Lego Digital designer tools to create new products. Once done, its image has to be submitted along with a description. The company reviews it, and if found suitable, publishes it on its site. The Lego Designer has to get her family, friends, colleagues, acquaintances—in fact, anybody and everybody to vote for their idea. If the ideas receive more than 10,000 votes and the Review Board's nod, then it goes into commercial production. Thereafter, it is available across the world for customers to buy. The Lego Designer gets fame, glory and royalty![6]

Does this concept work only for children's category? Of course not. It holds good for every category, provided a company gains insight into what motivates a customer to become a co-creator and embeds it into the offer. One universal motivation is compensation.

Take iPhone for instance. Can you imagine your iPhone without the apps? To me it would mean defanging it—with the apps, I can do so much more. Who makes these apps? Apple invites the developers, provides them with resources which are designed to help them create it.[7] The developers keep 70 per cent of the revenue while Apple gets to keep the balance.[8] Apple estimates that $100 billion was paid to developers over a decade.[9] The balance is kept by Apple. Apple has made the developers into its 'employees' and makes revenue from their effort.

Heineken, too, has leveraged this insight to motivate people to solve a business challenge it was facing—to make its packaging more sustainable. A financial reward of $10,000 awaited the winner.

The winner proposed a device—Heineken-o-meter—which transformed recycling into a game. People who took

[6] Lego Ideas, Lego website, https://ideas.lego.com/#all

[7] App Store, Apple Website: https://www.apple.com/in/ios/app-store/

[8] Shira Ovide, 'The 30 Percent App Fees Are Too Damn High', *Bloomberg Business Week*, 7 January 2019, https://www.bloomberg.com/news/articles/2019-01-07/the-30-percent-fees-app-developers-have-to-pay-are-too-damn-high

[9] Tim Bradshaw, 'Apple estimates $100bn paid to developers over decade', 4 June 2018, *Financial Times*, https://www.ft.com/content/146ebf2e-681f-11e8-b6eb-4acfcfb08c11

the trouble of returning the bottle stood a chance to win $1000.[10]

You too can engage your customers as co-creators and seek their expertise to grow revenue, achieve business goals or seek their expertise in solving business challenges with minuscule investments.

Factors Promoting This Concept

Laying the runway for this phenomenon are certain irrevocable trends:

- **Lack of time:** People are becoming increasingly time-poor and they detest wasting their time waiting or standing in queues.
- **Desire for peace of mind and convenience:** People wish to have peace of mind and convenience; hence, they prefer to handle some things themselves.
- **Technology:** The deep penetration of the Internet, large-scale adaptation of smart devices, and enthusiasm for technology have given young adults the tools to become willing employees. And they relish the 'control' that this provides.

Designing of Self-Service Platform

A start-up promising weight loss to its customers offered a perk to its employees—breakfast. Not surprisingly it had a

---

[10] Jacques Bughin, 'Three ways companies can make co-creation pay off', McKinsey & Company, December 2014, https://www.mckinsey.com/industries/consumer-packaged-goods/our-insights/three-ways-companies-can-make-co-creation-pay-off

healthy menu. The fruit section offered bananas and oranges. If an employee came late, she would invariable find that the bananas were over and only oranges remained. Most employees walked away without taking an orange.

Why did they exhibit this behaviour? The answer lies in a simple fact—banana is easy to peel and consume. Therefore it is preferred, although orange is tastier.

The Banana Principle is not new. It was advanced a century ago, by Guillaume Ferrero, a philosopher, who postulated that humans operate on the Principles of Least Effort: given several paths, we pick the easiest. [11]

The banana principle applies to business too. Till recently companies spent money on making a better product and trained people to provide after sales serve. But times are changing. New age companies are investing in making good products and designing an easy to use self-service platform. They provide tools to customers and empower them to help themselves.

Lesson for you: Follow the Banana Principle. Invest resources in providing a self-service platform which is obstacle-free, easy-to-navigate, offers frictionless checkout and is secure. People will, on their own volition, choose to work on it.

Measuring a Self-Service Platform

How will you know whether you have succeeded in scoring a bullseye in providing this kind of a platform?

---

[11] Tania Luna and Jordan Cohen, 'To Get People to Change, Make Change Easy', *Harvard Business Review*, 20 December 2007, https://hbr.org/2017/12/to-get-people-to-change-make-change-easy

Do a poll among users of your platform and pose the following open-ended question to them?

- Do you look forward to using the platform? Yes or no?

The majority response will give you an indication about whether your platform is user-friendly or otherwise.

If majority of the responses are 'yes', then that is good for you. But do not rest on your laurels. Conjure up strategies which will make the platform more customer-friendly so that more of your customers get converted into partial employees. If majority of the responses are 'no', immediately start working on strategies to make it customer-friendly.

Another way of determining whether your customers are happy becoming your partial or full-time employees is to do the Four Delta Test. I was introduced to this by Kunal Shah, founder of FreeCharge.[12] This involves seeking answers to two questions.

Take an airline. If it wishes to determine whether its guests are happy becoming its partial employees, it could record their response for two questions:

FOUR DELTA TEST

STATEMENTS	I was in tears	Extremely bad	Very bad	Bad	Neither good nor bad	Just acceptable	Good	Very Good	Extremely Good	Delighted beyond words
My experience while booking Ticket, making Payment & Checking in										
	1	2	3	4	5	6	7	8	9	10
BEFORE I BECAME A PARTIAL EMPLOYEE										
AFTER I BECAME A PARTIAL EMPLOYEE										

12 'Kunal Shah, Founder & Chairman, FreeCharge, New Rules of Business 2.0', YouTube video, 42.50, posted by Founding Fuel, 13 January 2017, https://www.youtube.com/watch?v=iXUbIPIviHs&t=101s

If the improvement is 4 points or more, your customers will willingly and happily continue to be your partial or full-time employees.

How Can You Apply This Concept to Your Business?

You too should invest in developing strategies and resources in converting your customers into 'employees' and seek there assistance to save cost, generate revenue, achieve business goals, and solve business challenges.

Customers will become 'employees', provided they see benefits in taking up additional responsibilities. You should focus your resources on the following things:

- Providing tangible benefits like financial benefits to customers, who become your 'employee'. When you do that, the word will spread. It will motivate more customers to become your 'employees', thereby setting in motion a self-perpetuating and virtuous cycle.
- Offering intangible benefits like a sense of accomplishment, feeling of pride, increase in self-worth or the notion that they are in control of their time. Or reducing anxiety, feeling of guilt and inner tension.
- Providing a platform which is easy to use, navigate, discover and obstacle-free. At regular intervals, administer Four Delta Test and act upon the results.
- Providing intelligently-embed principles of behavioural sciences to influence customers indirectly without overtly coercing them into anything. Remember to not manipulate them to help achieve your goals.

Then, you may sit back and witness how:

- Customer satisfaction scores soar, even as costs and customers complaints plummet.
- Business revenue heads upwards, margins expand and business challenges get slayed.

Is this not enough of a reward for converting your customers into 'employees'?

EMPLOYEE

RULE 5

Treat Your Employees As You Treat Your Best Customers

If you take care of your people, your people will take care of your customers and your business will take care of itself.

—J.W. Marriott

A widely held view is that the customer is God. In the new way of thinking, God seems to have changed its avatar. Today, it is felt that employees should be treated as equal to, if not better than, customers.

The basis for this paradigm shift in outlook is the inference that if employees are happy, they will make customers happy. When customers are happy, they will come back with repeat business and gradually transform into brand advocates.

Result: there is a positive impact on the company's bottom line.

Take this simple test. You are booking a hotel for a well-deserved family vacation. You have two options:

- Hotel A treats its customers like gods. It caters to each and every whim of customers, even if it means mistreating its employees.
- Hotel B respects its employees. It pampers them, and they in turn take good care of the customers.

Which one would you prefer? Chances are you will find staying in Hotel B more pleasurable because pampered employees will in turn pamper you.

Employee First

Does any company follow this seemingly quixotic strategy? Ritz-Carlton, the luxury chain of hotel, does. It proudly proclaims, 'We are ladies and gentlemen serving ladies and gentlemen.' Because the luxe hotel chain treats its employees as 'ladies and gentlemen', they behave likewise and, in turn, treat their guests like ladies and gentlemen, providing them genuine care and comfort.

Ritz-Carlton's guests, consistently exposed to its legendary service, transform over time into brand advocates. They speak well of the brand and the positive buzz generated is free advertising for it.

Other than Ritz-Carlton are there others who believe in this philosophy?

Southwest Airlines chairman emeritus, Herbert 'Herb' Kelleher, says: 'If you treat them (employees) well, then they treat the customers well and that means your customers come back and your shareholders are happy.'[1]

---

[1]   Kevin and Jackie Frieberg, '20 Reasons Why Herb Kelleher Was One Of The Most Beloved Leaders of Our Time', *Forbes*, 4 Jan 2019,

Walking the talk has resulted in Southwest Airlines recording forty-five consecutive years of profit in an industry plagued by bankruptcy.[2]

I too have focused on caring for my employees and witnessed magical results.

I got the mantle of leadership at an FMCG company with the mandate of revving up the company's growth. I realized that I had to conceptualize strategies for improving customer and employee satisfaction, product development, and relationships with channel partners and vendors.

My dilemma was which strategy to act upon first.

I turned to Starbucks chief executive Howard Schultz for inspiration. He believed that employee (or 'partner' in Starbucks' lexicon) satisfaction leads to customer satisfaction.

I too decided to begin by focusing on employees. My first port of call was the sales team because they bring in revenue. While doing an assessment, I observed that many salespeople were:

- Inappropriately dressed during sales calls and carried the order book in a plastic shopping bag
- Diffident, if not apologetic, while engaging with the channel partners
- Lacking in basic knowledge about the product they were entrusted to sell

---

https://www.forbes.com/sites/kevinandjackiefreiberg/2019/01/04/20-reasons-why-herb-kelleher-was-one-of-the-most-beloved-leaders-of-our-time/#1ae08addb311

[2] Jim Schleckser, 'Why Southwest Has Been Profitable 45 Years in a Row', *Inc.*, 28 August 2018, https://www.inc.com/jim-schleckser/why-southwest-has-been-profitable-45-years-in-a-row.html

- Showing poor body language which made them less effective during a sales call

To address these issues, I decided to get to the root cause of the problem. When I delved deeper I discovered:

- We were not paying competitive salaries.
- Our daily allowance was a pittance. It could barely buy a thali lunch in Mumbai.
- We had not issued a sales bag in the recent past.
- We had not held any formal sales training programmes.

I presented the findings to our board and got approvals for making the salary competitive for deserving people, enhancing daily allowance, issuing sales bags and organizing sales training programmes. We implemented all the initiatives, except the salary hike.

I candidly told the team that we should first show performance in the market before taking the salary hike. The sales team agreed with my suggestion. They seemed motivated by the other initiatives that we had already implemented.

They went into the market, with renewed zeal and energy. It took time for results to come, but they did come. Our sales grew at 30 per cent CAGR over three years from 2002 to 2005—at a time when the FMCG industry grew at a single-digit rate.

What delighted me was that despite working longer hours, our sales team was more satisfied. This improvement was reflected in the Employee Satisfaction Score which went up a few notches. Incidentally, so did our Customer Satisfaction

Score. This proved the point that happy employees make for happy customers.

The business lesson is simple: shift your focus from the customers to your employees. Make them feel special by showing care. They, in turn, will look after your business and provide a competitive advantage.

Of course, it goes without saying that treating employees better does not mean mistreating your customers. They are the ones providing you with business. The only change in your business policy should be: treat employees as first among equals.

Dealing with Rude Customers

At times, ugly situations may arise. What if some customers misbehave with your employees? Simple. Show them the door. You will lose their business, but you will gain the goodwill and loyalty of your employees, who will work with redoubled efforts and turn into passionate employee advocates. Moreover, when you make an example of a rude customer by putting them in his or her place, other customers will not risk crossing the line.

Does any company follow such a counter-intuitive strategy?

Zappos, an online retailer that is a part of Amazon, does not hesitate to 'fire' a customer who is rude to its employees.

In an article, Zappos chief executive Tony Hsieh shared 'Seven Ways to Achieve Exceptional Customer Service.' The third point clearly states: 'Fire customers who are insatiable or abuse your employees.'[3]

---

[3] Tony Hsieh, 'How I did it: Zappos's CEO on going to extremes for customers', *Harvard Business Review*, July–August 2010, https://hbr. org/2010/07/how-i-did-it-zapposs-ceo-on-going-to-extremes-for-customers.

This may sound counter-productive in the short term, but don't underestimate the strong emotional bond that grows between the employees and the company. When staffers know the company has their back, they will go the extra mile to ensure that it prospers. These feelings are reflected in higher attendance rates, lower attrition rates, and increased productivity and creativity. All this leads to higher customer satisfaction scores, a source of competitive advantage for a business.

Network of Commitment

Once you have started treating your employees as first among equals, what strategy should you put in place to increase their performance levels? Develop and implement systems and processes which foster a 'network of commitment' among the employees.

In a network of commitment, employees work together as a team to help the company deliver the promise it has made to its customers.

A good example is Domino's Pizza, which promises to deliver 'hot and fresh' pizza in thirty minutes to your doorstep. The company has created systems and processes where employees work in a network of commitment to deliver the company's promise. Every time.

From the time an order is received, everybody in the system knows that a 'hot and fresh' pizza has to be delivered to the customer's residence within thirty minutes. Hence, every member—from the chef to the person packing it to the person making the invoice and the person delivering it—assists others in a symbiotic relationship that delivers on their company's promise. They are so confident the system will deliver that they penalize themselves if the delivery takes more than thirty minutes.

Here also, Domino's has empowered its employees to take appropriate decisions, on the spot, in the unlikely event of delayed delivery.

Bottom line: a company should foster a network of commitment where every employee knows his or her role in the ecosystem and must coordinate their collective action to help the company deliver on the promises it makes to its customers.

Dealing with Disinterested Employees

I can read your thoughts. You are thinking: 'This can happen in a company populated with self-motivated employees who put customers' and the company's interests above their own. But in my company, employees are unproductive, lack motivation, are neither self-driven nor engaged with their work and are not committed to the company. This is the state of my employees, in spite of the fact that they are fairly remunerated. How will this strategy work in my company?'

Indeed disengaged employees display many more behavioural traits that are harmful for the growth of a company. A partial list includes:

- They display more enthusiasm while leaving than coming to office.
- They are clock-watchers.
- They do not work harmoniously.
- They are fault-finders.

- Their work quality is tardy.
- They spread negativity.
- They do just enough to keep their jobs and take the monthly salary check.
- They share their frustration with the customers.

You can take solace from the fact that your company is not alone in facing this problem. A survey done by Gallup between 2011 and 2012 revealed that in India, a mere 9 per cent of employees were engaged, 60 per cent were not engaged, and 31 per cent were actively disengaged.[4] The second group of the employees were previously engaged but due to reasons such as lack of career growth or promotions, unhappiness with their boss or feeling unrecognized, they ceased to be engaged in their jobs. The third group were dissatisfied and unhappy, and showed it through their gestures, words and behaviour. They actively expressed their dissatisfaction and therefore spread negativity in the workplace. In short, they ended up demotivating other employees, making them feel bad about the workplace.

There is a solution to this seemingly intractable problem, that too, at near zero cost.

According to Maslow's hierarchy of needs, human beings have five types of needs. These are organized in ascending order, from the most basic to the most complex. They are in order: physiological (basic need for food, clothing and shelter); safety (need for security of employment, protecting

---

[4] Steve Crabtree, 'Disengaged Employees may Be Impending India's Growth', Gallup, 29 October 2013, https://news.gallup.com/businessjournal/165608/disengaged-employees-may-impeding-india-growth.aspx

them from harm, etc.); love and belonging (need for friendship and community); esteem (desire to feel confident, striving for achievements, and maintaining self-respect); self-actualization (need to be creative, to be a problem solver).

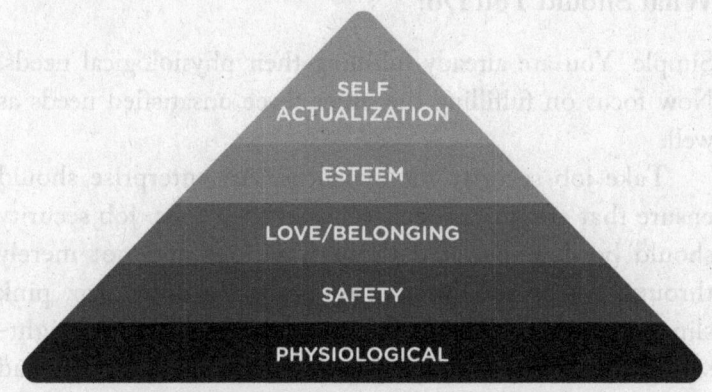

MASLOW'S HIERARCHY OF NEEDS

Could it be that your enterprise merely fulfils your employees' physiological needs by providing them a salary that takes care of their basic requirements of food, clothing and shelter but does precious little to satisfy the next three needs: safety, love and belonging, and esteem? Yet, you expect your employees to perform at the level of self-actualization—where they become more productive and engaged, and cooperate with each other.

Let us go back to the three unfulfilled needs. When they are not adequately fulfilled, employees do not display any overt discomfort, but internally become anxious and stressed. In this state, they cannot be productive or apply themselves wholeheartedly to their work. They become wary of the enterprise. Their energies are diverted from performing their jobs to protecting their narrow self-interest at the expense of the enterprise.

What Should You Do?

Simple. You are already fulfilling their physiological needs. Now focus on fulfilling the other three unsatisfied needs as well.

Take job security for instances. An enterprise should ensure that employees feel secure in their jobs. Job security should be demonstrated through actions and not merely through words and intentions. During a downturn, pink slips should not be distributed under the garb of right-sizing. Be honest and open up about the need for this and how many jobs need to be cut. On other occasions, when your bottom line is under pressure, employees should not be asked to make sacrifices to bolster the bottom line. If an enterprise indulges in such behaviour, the remaining employees feel insecure and anxious. They will cease to be self-motivated, believing what has happened to their colleagues may befall them too.

The next two hierarchies of need—love and belonging, and esteem—can be addressed by focusing on one element: infuse a sense of ownership so that they feel 'this is my company'. How do you do this?

By actively pursuing two initiatives:

- Engaging and empowering employees.
- Instilling in them a sense of purpose and connecting it to their daily work.

So, how have companies succeeded in operationalizing these initiatives?

Engaging and empowering people: It involves adopting a multifaceted approach—

- **Recruit the right people**

You should go the extra mile to recruit employees who will delight customers. Better still, who will sacrifice their life in the service of customers? Sounds unreal? Can employees display such altruistic behaviour in today's time?

Yes, the employees of Taj Mahal Palace hotel, Mumbai, displayed this behaviour when terrorists laid siege to the hotel on 26 November 2008. The hotel staff formed a human chain to evacuate guests to safety; in the process many sacrificed their lives. Karambir Singh Kang, the general manager of the hotel, continued to help guests escape to safety. But his wife and children fell victim to the terrorists' bullets.

What made Taj employees sacrifice their lives for their guests? Rohit Deshpande[5], professor at Harvard Business School, has addressed this question.

It perhaps has something to do with the kinds of people they recruit to become employees at the Taj and then the manner in which they train and reward them,' he says.

Taj does not recruit for grades, but for character, most specifically, respect and empathy. It shows a marked

---

[5]   Rohit Deshpande and Anjali Raina, 'The Ordinary Heroes of the Taj', *Harvard Business Review*, December 2011, https://hbr.org/2011/12/the-ordinary-heroes-of-the-taj

preference for selecting those hailing from small towns and second-tier business schools. This profile of people are keen on making a career with Taj rather than focusing on their salary package.

At the Taj, the team has identified around forty to forty-five guest-employee interactions that an employee can have with a guest in twenty-four hours, where they have an opportunity to display care, respect, kindness and empathy.

If a guest gives a positive review about an employee, then she is recognized. When desired behaviours are routinely recognized and swiftly rewarded, employees become 'conditioned' to display these behaviours at every opportunity. B.F. Skinner, a psychologist from Harvard University, has termed this phenomenon 'operant conditioning'.

When the attack on the Taj occurred, employees displayed the behaviour they were conditioned to display—showing care, concern and empathy towards their guests. It came naturally to them.

Bottom line: you should invest your time in recruiting the right people. Also, identify in advance the behaviours you would like them to display and establish a system that will routinely recognize and swiftly reward them, so that they become conditioned to display it. This would delight customers no end.

A word of caution: while hiring people make sure that they are not joining you for the lure of money.

I can sense a question brewing in your mind: I am not a soothsayer, so how can I guess if she is joining for money or the opportunity the company offers?

We can turn again to Zappos, which has solved this problem by paying new recruits to quit.

Here's how it works. After following the due process of selection, the trainees are given four weeks of intensive training where they are introduced to various facets of Zappos' culture, particularly its obsession with its customers. At the end of the training period, Zappos makes 'The Offer'[6] to the new recruit: salary for four weeks plus $1000 to quit. Many recruits take this offer and leave. Those who refuse are the ones that Zappos wants.

Does it leave you wondering that Zappos is wasting money by making this offer? Remember the old saying: one bad fish spoils the pond. Similar is the case in companies. Bad recruits are infested with rotten habits; unfortunately they are contagious. These spread silently and in due course, adversely impact overall performance in the company. It is wise to eliminate a bad hire at the outset, even if an expense has to be incurred. In the long run, this tends to be more cost-effective.

I seem to have captured your interest. But another question seems to be stirring in your mind. This strategy will work while hiring; but what should be done for people who are already working in the company and are dissatisfied?

Let me share with you Jeff Bezos' strategy for addressing a similar issue.

Amazon got bad press for working conditions at its fulfilment centres. Bezos sought inspiration from Zappos and launched the 'Pay to Quit' programme for its fulfilment centre employees. Every year they get an offer to be paid to

---

[6]   Bill Taylor, 'Why Zappos Pays New Employees to Quit-And You Should Too', *Harvard Business School*, 19 May 2008, https://hbr.org/2008/05/why-zappos-pays-new-employees

quit Amazon. In the first year, it is $2000 and it increases by $1000 every year up to a maximum of $5000.[7]

When people are rewarded to quit but decide to stay back, they are less likely to feel frustrated with their work and the company. Why? They can only blame themselves for their plight.

- **Set up a frictionless workplace**

In many companies, with the passage of time, bureaucracy takes root. Systems and processes take precedence over outcomes; change is resisted and employees' initiatives are given the cold shoulder. Employees' energies are consumed in fighting internal bureaucracy, leaving many exhausted. As a result, the company's goals take a back seat. 'As a leader your job is to remove roadblocks so that they can be successful in what they do,' is Sundar Pichai's advice. Do follow it.[8]

- **Establish a fair and transparent system**

A company's internal system should be robust enough not to be influenced or manipulated by a section of self-seeking employees. Nothing creates more distrust than violating this tenet. In the absence of a fair and transparent system, employees start feeling that the system is stacked against

---

[7]   Martha C. White, 'Amazon Will Pay You $5000 to Quit Your Job', *Time*, 11 April 2014, https://time.com/58305/amazon-will-pay-you-5000-to-quit-your-job/

[8]   Suman Singh, 'Here's what you can learn from Google CEO, Sunder Pichai's success story', CNBCTV18, 22 March 2019, https://www.cnbctv18.com/entrepreneurship/google-ceo-sundar-pichai-shares-a-few-success-lessons-2684661.htm

them, and no matter what they do, they can never win—so why even try! In psychology, this feeling is termed 'learnt helplessness'. Nothing is more dangerous for a company than having employees who don't give a damn about it! It is your responsibility to reward merit and denounce self-seeking behaviour.

- **Improve team working experience**

Much of the times employees work in teams. If an employee has a bad experience while working as member of a team, it means she had a bad experience with the company. To engage employees, ensure that the teams work in harmony—they communicate among themselves, extend help to each other and show mutual trust and respect.

- **Infuse a feeling of trust**

Lack of trust in an organization breeds politics. Employees tend to give politically-correct answers rather than reveal what they actually think. For example, when an opinion is sought about an initiative, an employee may think it is noxious, but will protect her position by giving a politically-correct answer. In an environment devoid of trust it is a good strategy to avoid conflict and retribution. In such companies, employees work towards guarding their narrow self-interest and few, if any, are focused on helping the company achieve its goals.

When trust reigns supreme, there is openness in a company. This encourages employees to freely and frankly share their opinions and work together as a team to achieve the company's goals.

Will employees misuse the trust reposed in them?

Yes, some might. The solution is to follow the Russian saying that translates to 'Trust, but verify.' This means trust your employees, but also put in place a system to identify those misusing it. The enterprise should come down heavily, decisively and swiftly on these black sheep.

At Wipro, a senior person was caught padding the expense statement. He was immediately asked to leave, despite his stellar professional performance. Everybody in the company was transparently informed about the circumstances leading to the person's departure[9]. Hewlett-Packard too asked its chief executive to leave when he violated the trust reposed in him as head of the company.[10]

Now for the good news. Empirical evidence indicates that the number of employees likely to misuse trust does not exceed 5 per cent of the workforce. Now should you plan a system that will favour 95 per cent of your employees who are trustworthy or focus on the 5 per cent who may not be?

How can you know that trust reigns supreme in your enterprise? It is similar to clean air. When present, it will be experienced, but its absence gets noticed as well.

- **Demonstrate respect and care towards your employees**

This can be achieved by taking the following initiatives:

[9]   Asha Rai, 'Azim Premji, Living small, giving large', *Times of India*, 13 June 2019, https://timesofindia.indiatimes.com/business/india-business/azim-premji-living-small-giving-large/articleshow/69683975.cms

[10]   Ben Worthen and Pui-Wing Tam, 'H-P chief quits in scandal', *Wall Street Journal*, 7 August 2010, https://www.wsj.com/articles/SB100014 24052748703309704575413663370670900.

- Treat your employees as your internal customers. Give them the same attention and respect that you shower on your end customers.
- Show respect. Employees yearn to be respected. You should show respect to them through your behaviour, words and deeds. The employees in turn will show commitment and a sense of ownership towards the company.
- Boost self-esteem. Nothing will boost the self-esteem of employees more than being asked for their opinion by their boss:
  o What do you think?
  o What should we do?

Pose these questions and listen attentively—not with the intent to manipulate them but to gain from their answers.

- Honour promises. Employees trust companies that honour promises. This simple act will motivate your employees to display greater commitment and passion while doing their jobs.

- **Provide training**

Companies should invest in training their employees before expecting them to invest their time in furthering the company's objectives. But many companies are wary of investing money in training employees, believing that they might leave and the investment would be lost. But what happens if they don't?

Let me get Richard Branson to share his thoughts on this issue: 'Train your people well enough so they can leave, treat them well enough so that they don't want to.[11]'

• Give employees autonomy

Provide autonomy to people to do their jobs and trust them to do it. Do not micro-manage them. This will demonstrate that you trust them to deliver results. In such cases, employees go the extra mile to live up to the expectations of the company. After all, when you trust people they become more trustworthy.

Take a leaf out of Apple, LinkedIn, Microsoft and 3M playbook and allocate 15–20 per cent as 'me time' to employees during which they can devote time to their own projects.[12]

• Discourage fear of failure

When employees feels that even for a miniscule mistake, the system will throw them under the bus, the brain interprets the work environment as threatening and unsafe. Now the employees are focused on surviving in the 'hostile' work environment by taking actions to protect their self-interest. Your job as a leader is to create a workplace where there is no fear of failure. Demonstrate it with your actions. This will compel employees to take initiatives which will benefit the company.

---

[11] Richard Branson's Twitter Handle: https://twitter.com/richardbranson/status/449220072176107520?lang=en

[12] Alex Hill, Liz Mellon, and Jules Goddard, 'How Winning Organizations Last 100 Years', *Harvard Business Review*, 27 September 2018, https://hbr.org/2018/09/how-winning-organizations-last-100-years

- **Give honest and actionable feedback**

When employees are given honest and actionable feedback it shows that you care for them.

- **Provide reward and recognition**

There is a mistaken belief that only money will motivate employees to perform. This hypothesis may be partially true. Offering recognition (read: non-financial rewards) can also motivate employees to give their best at work. Therefore, it is prudent to have a judicious balance of both to motivate employees.

Financial rewards are already offered in companies. Let us put the spotlight on recognition because there are manifold advantages associated with it:

- It can be dispensed all year round.
- It costs a pittance to execute it.
- It makes employees feel that you care about them.
- It instils a sense of pride in them.

There are multitudinous ways in which you can shower recognition on your employees.

Here is a partial list to get you started:

- Celebrating birthdays/anniversaries
- Showing appreciation in public
- Giving them time off to go on a short vacation
- Distributing gratitude cards
- Permitting them to bring pets to office on select days

- Spotlighting your best employees and their contribution on the company's website
- Organizing staff lunches
- Recognizing people's non-work achievements
- Arranging one-on-one meetings between high-performing employees and company's top brass

Instilling a sense of purpose among employees: Let us move to the second initiative required to cultivate a sense of ownership among employees: instilling a sense of purpose and connecting it to their daily work.

Let me narrate a parable told by my mother about the importance of connecting daily work to a higher purpose. This is how she related to parable to me:

'A traveller came upon three men working. He asked the first man what he was doing and the man said he was laying bricks. He asked the second man the same question and he said he was putting up a wall. When he got to the third man and asked him what he was doing he said he was building a temple'.

My mother paused here and posed a question to me: 'All three men were engaged in the same job, but who do you think will do a better job?'

Without waiting for my answer she said, 'the third person, because he had discovered a purpose in his job, which will inspire him to do his job better.'

Let us come to employees. Many of them believe that they are merely doing a job to make a living. If we can link their job to a higher purpose, they can be inspired to produce better quality work.

Let me share an incident involving the US President, John F. Kennedy. He bumped into a janitor who was mopping floors at NASA headquarters, long after the normal office time.

The President enquired why was he working so late?

'Because I am not mopping the floors, I am putting a man on the moon.' he replied.

Not just the janitor, but many employees across NASA started to believe that 'putting a man on the moon' was their job, regardless of what they were assigned to do.[13]

Employees subscribing to this perspective would no longer see themselves doing a job, but working for the larger purpose of 'putting a man on the moon.'

You may say that NASA is a one-of-a-kind organization. Its mission was to put man on the moon. Therefore, finding a purpose for its people may not be challenging. Can a purpose be linked to an employee working in a company with more modest aspirations?

Let us bring Medtronic, the global leader in medical devices, into our discussion. It seeks to link its mission—contribute to human welfare by alleviating pain, restoring health and extending life—to the seemingly mundane jobs of its employees.[14]

To build this linkage, Medtronic organizes an event called the Holiday Party. On this day, patients come to the company to share their stories about how Medtronic products transformed their lives. Employees from all over the world watch this event live or via video conference.

---

[13] Henrich Greve, 'How Great Leaders Make Work Meaningful', *INSEAD Knowledge*, 13 October 2017, https://knowledge.insead.edu/blog/insead-blog/how-great-leaders-make-work-meaningful-7421

[14] Medtronic: https://www.medtronic.com/us-en/about/mission.html.

Bill George, ex-CEO of Medtronic, describes one such story:

> T.J. was the last patient to tell his story that day. Abandoning his wheelchair, he walked up the steps to the podium using just his arms' braces. T.J. told of the sixteen surgeries he'd had, all-in-vain attempts to relieve the growing spasticity and rigidity of his cerebral palsy. At the age of sixteen, he had finally had enough and refused further surgery. His body became even stiffer as the disease progressed. It took him an hour to just get out of the bed. Until the Medtronic drug pump transformed his life, T.J.'s simplest acts required Herculean efforts. Now he could get out of the bed relatively easily, walk up to the stairs of his classrooms; even his hampered speech had improved markedly.[15]

Hearing T.J.'s story filled Bill George's eyes with tears and it had a similar impact on the Medtronic employees in the room and around the world. This real story must have made its employees realize that they were not merely engaged in the mundane work of making devices, but were alleviating pain, restoring health and extending the life of people around the world.

Coming back to you: what is the purpose of your company? You have to introspect and discover it. And then share it with your employees and link it to their jobs. If you can successfully do this, then your employees will come to work, motivated and inspired by a purpose. The output they produce will be palpably superior.

---

[15] Bill George, 'Authentic Leadership: Rediscovering the Secrets to Creating Lasting Value' (Josset-Bass, 2003).

When employees are empowered, engaged and have discovered a sense of purpose in their job, they feel a sense of ownership towards the company. This will motivate them to work with unbounded energy to achieve, if not exceed, the company's goals.

Positive Employee Experience and Employee Advocates

The same factors that instil a sense of ownership also instil a positive employee experience.[16] This in turn results in positivity, bonhomie and warmth spreading across the company. People smile a lot, work better in teams and support each other. Can you ask for more?

EMPLOYEE EXPERIENCE
Factors that contribute to positive customer experience*

Meaningful work	Supportive Management	Positive work environment	Growth Opportunities	Trust in leadership
- Autonomy	- Demonstrate respect & care - Treat employee as internal customers - Show respect - Boost self-esteem - Honor promise - Open communication - Give honest & actionable feedback	- Frictionless workplace - Fair & transparent system - No fear of failure - Infuse feeling of trust - Recognition & reward	- Provide training	- Provide purpose & meaning

*Source: 2017 Human Capital Trends (Deloitte)

Additionally, employees imbued with a sense of ownership and having an enjoyable experience at work transform into employee advocates. It should be your intent to convert as

---

16 Josh Bersin, et al., 'The employee experience: culture, engagement, and beyond', Deloitte Insights, https://www2.deloitte.com/insights/us/en/focus/human-capital-trends/2017/improving-the-employee-experience-culture-engagement.html.

many employees as you can into advocates for your company and experience the myriad benefits that follow in its wake:

- They say good things about the company at almost every opportunity—both online and offline.
- They display strong loyalty towards the company.
- They help in recruitment by providing referrals.
- They amplify the company's message by posting on their social media platform.

When all these benefits are added up, they will lead to a higher revenue and lowering of costs, resulting in an improved bottom line.

Measuring the Results

You can measure the results of these initiatives through the employee Net Promoter Score (eNPS). Pose this question to your employees and do the analysis on the lines of NPS (as discussed in chapter 3). Based on your experience in the company, how likely are you to recommend the company to your friends?

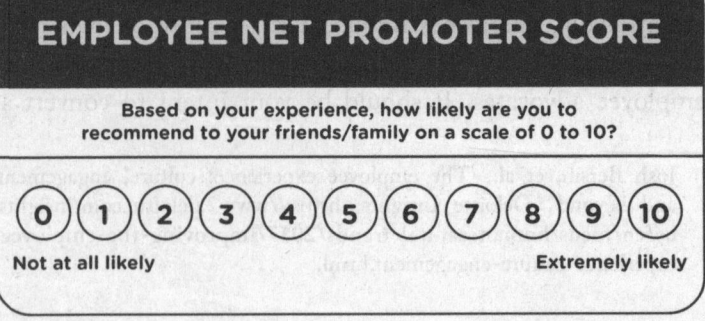

EMPLOYEE NET PROMOTER SCORE

Based on your experience, how likely are you to recommend to your friends/family on a scale of 0 to 10?

0 1 2 3 4 5 6 7 8 9 10

Not at all likely   Extremely likely

Use eNPS in conjunction with the Employee Effort Score (EES) which measures how easy/difficult it is for employees get 'help' in the company.

To measure it, pose this question to your employee: overall, how difficult was it to get the help you expected? Do the analysis on the lines of Customer Effort Score.

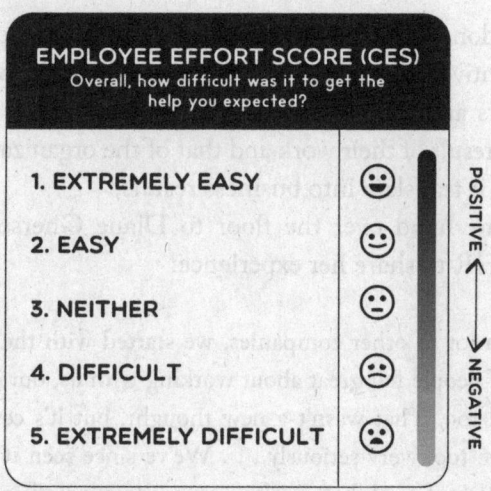

If an employee finds it difficult to get help, it indicates, in words of Warren Buffet, that ABC—arrogance, bureaucracy and complacency—has taken root and it leads to business decay.[17] Committed employees will feel suffocated. In that case, in the words of Mark Zuckerberg, 'They will use your Internet to look for a new job.'[18]

---

[17] Noah Buhayar, 'Buffet Says Next Berkshire CEO Must Fight Arrogance, Decay', Bloomberg, 28 February 2015, https://www.bloomberg.com/news/articles/2015-02-28/buffett-says-next-ceo-must-fight-decay-complacency-at-berkshire

[18] Read 20+ Motivational Quotes by Mark Zuckerberg, https://quotesdownload.com/mark-zuckerberg-quotes/

Insight: to keep your company in robust health, ensure that 'ABC' does not set in and work towards maximizing eNPS and minimizing EES.

Does Engaging Employees Make for a Sound Business Case?

Research done by Gallup indicates that, 'Engaged employees are more attentive and vigilant. They look out for the needs of their co-workers and the overall enterprise, because they personally 'own' the result of their work and that of the organization.'[19]

Does it translate into business results?

Let me hand over the floor to Diane Gherson, IBM's Head of HR to share her experience:

> Like a lot of other companies, we started with the belief that if people felt great about working with us, our clients would too. That wasn't a new thought, but it's certainly one we took very seriously . . . We've since seen it borne out. We've found that employee engagement explains two-thirds of our client experience scores. And if we're able to increase client satisfaction by five points on an account, we see an extra 20 per cent in revenue, on average. So clearly there's an impact. That's the business case for the change.[20]

---

[19] John Baldoni, 'Employee Engagement Does More than Boost Productivity', *Harvard Business Review*, 4 July 2013, https://hbr.org/2013/07/employee-engagement-does-more

[20] Lisa Burrel, 'Co-Creating the Employee Experience', *Harvard Business Review*, March-April 2018, https://hbr.org/2018/03/the-new-rules-of-talent-management#co-creating-the-employee-experience

How Can You Apply These Learnings?

Here is what you should do:

- Invest your time in selecting the 'right' employees. Trust and provide them with autonomy and actionable feedback.
- Identify, in advance, the behavioural traits that you wish them to exhibit. Invest in their training so that they acquire these traits. Reward and recognize them every time they display them.
- The rewards and recognitions have to be speedily delivered
- Run your own version of 'The Offer' and 'Pay to Quit' to weed out the disgruntled employees.
- Treat your employees as you would treat your best customers by providing them with respect and care.
- Do not hesitate to show the door to customers who misbehave with your employees.
- Build a network of commitment among your employees.
- Infuse a sense of ownership among employees:
  - Empower and engage them.
  - Introspect deeply to instil purpose and meaning, and link this to their jobs.

- Deliver an enjoyable employee experience.
- Maximize Employee Net Promoter Score and minimize Employee Effort Score. This will help you cultivate and nurture employee advocates.

Postscript

Let me share with you how the Indian Army treats its personnel.

In the Cadets' Mess at the National Defence Academy, a table for one is set with its chair leaning forward onto the table, waiting to be occupied. It is a mark of respect for those alumni of the academy who are listed as missing in action or have been taken prisoners of war. It signifies hope that they will return one day. The placard on the table reads[21]:

'The table set is small, for one, symbolizing the frailty of one prisoner against his oppressors.

The single rose displayed in a vase reminds us of the families and loved ones of our comrades-in-arms who keep their faith awaiting their return.

The Red Ribbon tied so prominently on the vase is reminiscent of the red ribbon worn upon the lapel and breasts of thousands who bear witness to their unyielding determination to demand a proper accounting of our missing.

The candle is unlit, symbolizing the upward reach of their unconquerable spirit.

The slice of lemon is on the bread plate, to remind us of the bitter fate.

There is salt upon the bread plate—symbolic of the families' tears as they wait.

---

[21] POW-MIA, 'You Are Not Forgotten', National Defense Academy, https://www.nda.nic.in/cadets-mess.html

The glass is inverted, they cannot toast with us this night.

The chair—it is empty. They are not here.

Remember all of you who served with them and called them comrades, who depended upon their might and aid and relied upon them, for surely, they have not forsaken you.

Remember them until they come home . . . ' [22]

This symbolic gesture lets the troops know that the army cares about them. Knowing this they are more willing to give it their all, knowing they will be honoured and remembered, even when they are no more.

Let us talk about you. How do you treat your employees? On par with defence forces? Or less? The answer lies in our heart.

---

[22] Abhishek Saksena, 'Army has kept this table ready for the past 45 years, waiting for those who didn't return in 1971', Lifestyle, 11 May 2016

RULE 6

Create Sales Consultants

What you plant now, you will harvest later.

—Og Mandino

Are you familiar with the new way of selling?

'Sell more and more,' did you say?

That is the old way of selling! The new way of selling builds on the above theme of selling more and more but encompasses much more.

It recommends:

- Building, nurturing and deepening the relationship between the customer and your brand at every moment of truth—when your customer comes in touch with your brand
- Not attempting to monetize this relationship at each and every transaction; doing it over the lifetime of the relationship
- Delivering an excellent customer experience

Therefore, the job of the salesperson is not merely to sell, but to be an authentic sales consultant (hereafter referred to as 'consultant') who establishes and deepens relationships with customers at every touch point and ensures that they reach their 'objective', and in the process, gain financially or non-financially, if not on both counts.

Financial gain would be in the form of money, for example, by making customers aware of the discounts and offers, while non-financial gains would be in terms of convenience, peace of mind, excellent customer service, customized solutions, time-saving, etc.

In this new role of a consultant, all the time they have acted as the customer's, not the company's ambassador, and many a time may end up recommending a competitor's brand. So be it.

A question may pop up in your mind: 'Is my consultant working for my company or my customers and competitors?' The answer is simple: All of us, be it the top management or a consultant, work neither for our company nor our competitor. We all work for our customer.

All this reads well on paper. Does any company follow this counter-intuitive axiom? Well, Taj Group does.

It insist that its employees must act as the customer's, not the company's ambassador. Of course, employees are on Taj payroll; but if they protect the Taj's interest ahead of customers then this move could be counter-productive, especially when they have to interact with guest. 'Trainees are assured that the company leadership, right up to the CEO, will support any employee decision that puts guest front and centre and that shows that employees did everything possible to delight them,' observe Rohit Deshpande and Anjali Raina.[1]

---

[1]   Rohit Deshpande and Anjali Raina, 'The Ordinary Heroes of the Taj', *Harvard Business Review*, December 2011, https://hbr.org/2011/12/the-ordinary-heroes-of-the-taj

Bringing Reciprocity and Likability Principles into Play

You may be wondering whether such acts of generosity towards customers and competitors ever pay off. They will, because you are pressing into service the reciprocity and likeability principles and in the process, earning the trust of your customers.

The reciprocity principle states that whenever you do good to somebody, it creates a favourable predisposition in the other person to reciprocate your gesture. By this logic, when a salesperson assumes the role of a consultant and advises a customer without any ulterior motives, the salesperson wins their trust, goodwill and gratitude. As a result, the customers will invariably return to them with business whenever the need arises.

The likeability principle, on the other hand, states that we tend to do business with the people we like. If someone is striving to protect our interests, will we not like them? If there was an opportunity to do business again, would we not choose them over others? Of course we would!

Apple Retail

Are you wondering whether any company has prospered following this seemingly illogical strategy?

Yes, there is Apple Retail. It has become the world's most profitable retail store following this counter-intuitive strategy.

Apple Retail was set up with the strategic intent, not to sell Apple products, but to establish and deepen the relationship between the company and its customers. And, more importantly, repair any relationship that might have broken when, perhaps, a MacBook crashed or an iPad failed to boot.

Here is how I experienced this strategy in action.

A business assignment took me to Silicon Valley. A day into the trip, panic gripped me when my MacBook Air, in which my presentation was saved, stopped responding.

I called up a friend who was based in San Francisco and shared the tragedy that had befallen me. 'Without the presentation I will not be effective and may lose the deal,' I told her dejectedly.

'No need to panic. Drive down here to San Francisco and visit an Apple Retail. They can help you,' she said calmly.

Locating the Apple Retail was easy. Upon entering, I was approached by a person dressed in a T-shirt and armed to the teeth with tech gadgets. 'Can I help you, sir?' he asked.

'Yes,' I said. 'My Apple laptop has crashed and I need to get it working.'

'No worries, sir,' he said confidently. 'Just go up the stairs to the Genius Bar. They'll it get it going.'

Every Apple store has a Genius Bar, manned by 'geniuses': they are not salespersons but high-calibre consultants. The geniuses have extensive technical know-how to troubleshoot most problems that may jeopardize the company's relationship with the customer.

Climbing a winding glass staircase I saw a wall emblazoned with the words 'Genius Bar'. There was a long counter—the kind I have seen innumerable times gracing bars across the world. Behind it sat people wearing blue T-shirts and a smile; they looked confident, knowledgeable and approachable.

'How can I help you?' I heard a voice say.

I looked in that direction and saw that a 'genius' was trying to attract my attention.

'Yes, I need help. My Apple laptop has crashed,' I said.

'No worries, can I have it?' the 'genius' said, resting his elbow on the bar top and leaning forward.

I took it out from my bag and placed it before him.

He started to examine it. 'Got it!' he soon muttered under his breath. Looking up, he said, 'Please have a seat. I need fifteen minutes to get her going.'

'Are you sure?' I asked incredulously.

'As sure as sunrise!' he said confidently.

As the minutes ticked by, my apprehensions started to grow again, approaching a crescendo as the fifteen-minute deadline loomed.

Then, the 'genius' appeared—a smile on his face and my laptop nestled safely on his palm.

'Done!' he said. 'It's as good as new.'

Much to my relief, the computer was now responding to my command.

'How much do I owe you?' I asked him.

'Zilch—it's still under warranty,' he said with a smile.

I felt a huge sense of relief: not only was my computer working but Apple itself had informed me that it was under warranty.

'Thank you' was all I could say, my faith in Apple becoming stronger.

'Godspeed,' he said, as I made my way down the winding staircase.

As soon as I reached the bottom of the staircase, the person who had initially greeted me materialized almost miraculously. 'All good?' he asked and all I could do was nod.

'Hang on, sir,' he said. 'You will love the experience.'

Apple Store has a transparent look and is designed to re-create modern-day town square. Customers visit it not merely to shop but to hang out, be inspired and learn skills. Today Apple offers free hands-on-sessions focused on photograph, video, music, coding, app development, art, design and more.[2] No wonder the *New York Times* concluded that Apple stores were '[turning] the boring computer sales floor into a sleek playroom filled with gadgets'.[3]

While 'hanging out' at the store, I checked out the latest version of the iPhone. I realized that I needed to upgrade and ended up buying it.

As I walked out of Apple Retail, it became clear to me that Apple did not make any attempt to sell its products to me. But their consultants honestly strived to 'repair' the fractured relationship by quickly repairing the product; in the process they strengthened the relationship between Apple and me, and also invoked in me a sense of gratitude, goodwill and trust. So much so that I ended up buying a new phone.

Apple seems to believe in monetizing the relationship with its customers over a lifetime. So far, I have bought two iPads, two iPods, five iPhones and three Mac Books!

Was my experience at Apple Store an exception? Or were the stores designed to deliver this experience to every customer?

---

[2]   Press Release, Newsroom, Apple Inc. 29 January 2019, https://www.apple.com/in/newsroom/2019/01/apple-announces-new-today-at-apple-sessions/

[3]   Stephane Clifford, 'Apple Store Chief to Take the Helm at J.C. Penny', *New York Times*, 14 June 2011, https://www.nytimes.com/2011/06/15/business/economy/15shop.html

Let me hand the floor to Ron Johnson, former retail chief of Apple to weigh in on this:

> 'People come to the Apple Store for the experience—and they're willing to pay a premium for that. There are lots of components to that experience, but maybe the most important—and this is something that can translate to any retailer—is that the staff isn't focused on selling stuff, it's focused on building relationships and trying to make people's lives better. That may sound hokey, but it's true. The staff is exceptionally well trained, and they're not on commission, so it makes no difference to them if they sell you an expensive new computer or help you make your old one run better so you're happy with it. Their job is to figure out what you need and help you get it, even if it's a product Apple doesn't carry. Compare that with other retailers where the emphasis is on cross-selling and upselling and, basically, encouraging customers to buy more, even if they don't want or need it. That doesn't enrich their lives and it doesn't deepen the retailer's relationship with them. It just makes their wallets lighter.'[4]

Disney Store

While strolling along the streets of San Francisco, I noticed a Disney Store and was drawn towards it. Upon entering, I was greeted by a smiling sales associate (read: consultant)

---

4   Ron Johnson, 'What I learned Building the Apple Store', *Harvard Business Review*, 21 November 2011, https://hbr.org/2011/11/what-i-learned-building-the-ap

who said, 'Call me when you need assistance,' and left me to explore the treasures stacked in the store. Not once was I tailed by a cast member, anxious to make a sale.

I wanted to buy a T-shirt for my teenage son but could not make up my mind about the design and size. I beckoned the sales associate over and she helped me out very efficiently and pleasantly.

While paying my bill, I got talking to her about her job. She told me, 'Our job is to create "magical" moments for guests of all ages.' Did you notice that she did not even mention sales? Disney Store puts customers' interests ahead of the company.[5]

I know what's on your mind: Apple takes on, metaphorically, gravity-defying stunts and pulls them off. Disney has mastered the art of crafting magical moments like no other company. It may be risky to emulate these marquee companies.

Let me share with you an example of a technology company that has succeeded in evoking reciprocity and likability principles, and built trust with its customers.

It has in its portfolio, a range of financial products which are designed to cater to every kind of financial need. Like any business, it also receives customer complaints. Upon receiving one, it assigns its best engineer to resolve it, with dual objectives:

- Customers are delighted because 'a competent and senior resource' has been assigned to troubleshoot.

5 Barbara Farfan, 'Disney Store Values and Mission Statement', *Balance Small Business*', Updated 23 September 2018, https://www.thebalancesmb.com/disney-mission-statement-2891828

Being subject-matter experts, they quickly rectify the issue. This strategy ensures that Intuit wins the trust and loyalty of its customers.

- From the company's perspective, the engineers gain first-hand understanding of problems with any product. After rectifying it at the customer's location they come back and work out a strategy to eliminate the problem at the root itself, so that, in the future, customers do not face this problem. As more and more glitches get eliminated from the product, it becomes better and better. Satisfaction and trust in the company keep rising, as does its revenue.

Sephora

Businesses such as Apple and Disney may be amenable to having salespeople act as 'consultants'. What about other industries, such as beauty and fashion? Can this strategy be applied?

Take Sephora, a beauty store owned by LVMH (Moët Hennessy–Louis Vuitton), which has a retail presence in India as well. Sephora has beauty advisors (not salespeople) on its rolls. The beauty advisors act as consultant: they listen with the intent of understanding the customer's requirements, and offer personalized tips and suggestions, make-up lessons and beauty treatments to empower customers to put their best face forward. She does not try to push their range of products.

How do you think this makes the customers feel? A sense of gratitude that their interests are being prioritized before the company's. This would lead to building of trust between the customer and Sephora and it brings the reciprocity and likeability principles into play. Next time they have to buy beauty products, who will they consult or reach out to for advice? Undoubtedly Sephora's beauty advisors. Which store will they buy the products from? Most likely Sephora.

This reads well on paper, but has it delivered on the ground?

Sephora was named 'Retailer of Year' at the 2018 World Retail Congress.[6]

Zappos

All the stories chronicled here are of physical stores. Can this strategy be extended to e-commerce companies?

Take Zappos, an e-commerce company which is a part of Amazon. The company's mission is to provide the best customer service possible. In pursuit of this mission, it has embraced concepts that would seem counter-intuitive. Employees act as consultants to customers. They are not given any standard script to pitch to the customers but are encouraged to be themselves so that they sound genuine. And they are free to spend as much time as required to help customers make the right choice. They are advised not to cross-sell or upsell merely to increase the value of the sale. They are there only to recommend what is in the interests of the customers.

---

6   'Sephora named Retailer of the Year', LVMH, 25 April 2018, https://www.lvmh.com/news-documents/news/sephora-named-retailer-of-the-year/

The downside of following this strategy: they have a returns rate of 37 per cent,[7] when the average returns rate for an e-tailer is in the region of 18–20 per cent and in single digit for B&C and mom-and-pop stores. This has the power to burn a hole in the company profits.

Zappos is not fazed because it believes the heavy cost it incurs in 'returns' is an investment in ensuring that each of its customers becomes its customer for life. Over the lifetime of the relationship, Zappos will monetize its investment. What has Zappos subtly done? It has put the reciprocity and likability principles into play, and in the process earned the trust and loyalty of its customers. No wonder repeat purchase at Zappos is over 75 per cent: for every 100 customers, seventy-five return to Zappos with repeat business.[8]

Tanishq

I can sense many of you feeling that this counter-intuitive strategy may find resonance in the western world, but is likely to tank in India.

Reality seems to indicate otherwise. There are a host of Indian companies which follow this strategy and have established themselves in the market.

---

7   Tony Hsieh, 'Zappos's CEO on Going to Extremes for Customers', *Harvard Business Review*, July–August 2010, https://hbr.org/2010/07/how-i-did-it-zapposs-ceo-on-going-to-extremes-for-customers

8   Languatics Contributor, 'Delivering Happiness. Why At Zappos It's Your Birthday Every Day', *Forbes*, 31 May 2012, https://www.forbes.com/sites/languatica/2012/05/31/delivering-happiness-why-at-zappos-its-your-birthday-every-day/#13b660685f00

Let us move to another Tata Group company, and let me share with you our experience with Tanishq, a respected and trusted jewellery brand from the Tata Group. A Tanishq showroom resembles a five-star hotel. It has well-appointed furnishings, marble floors and elegant display windows adorned with masterpieces of jewellery.

Upon entering the store, we are customarily greeted by a salesperson and escorted to the counter where we will be serviced. A waiter, wearing white gloves, comes with a tray holding glasses of water and also takes orders for beverages.

With pleasantries out of the way, the salesperson subtly transforms into a sales consultant and poses open-ended questions to understand our requirements. What kind of jewellery are we looking for? What is the occasion for buying it? Based on their initial understanding, they present the first round of curated options to us.

While showing the options, they engage in a conversation to gain deeper insights into our likes and requirements. Based on that, they present the second round of curated options. This is closer to what we have in mind. At this stage they engage in further discussions to home in on our specific requirements and come back with a third round of curated options. Most often, in the third round they hit the bullseye.

The staff member (read: consultant) clears away other options so that the chosen piece has the stage all to itself. Then my wife is requested to try it on. A woman staff member assists her in putting it on and a mirror is placed in front of her to see the magical transformation.

Many a time we have postponed the decision to purchase the selected item or decided against buying it. Not once have we noticed a frown cross any of the faces of the staff. They politely support our decision and enthusiastically invite us to visit again.

But we depart with a feeling of guilt. Through their behaviour and helpful attitude, the staff had pressed into service the reciprocity and likability principles. Whenever we have such requirements, we tend to make our way towards Tanishq.

Bottom line: the new way of selling is not to sell, but to build and deepen relationships with customers at every touch point, and in the process set into motion the reciprocity and liability principles. In due course you would have earned the customer's trust and loyalty. Chance are bright that they will seek you out when they have the relevant requirements.

Lifebuoy

Yes, the strategy of transforming salespeople into consultants seems to work for technology, high-involvement product categories and e-commerce companies. Can it also yield results with a dull category, such as soap?

Let us take the case of Unilever's Lifebuoy soap. In 2010, the company drew up a Sustainable Living Plan. 'The essence of the plan,' explained Paul Polman, the then chairperson and architect of the plan, 'is to put society and the challenges facing society smack in the middle of the business.'[9]

Every year more than two million children under the age of five die of infections like diarrhoea and pneumonia. For the

---

[9] Marc Gunther, 'Unilever's CEO Has a Green Thumb', *Fortune*, 23 May 2013, https://fortune.com/2013/05/23/unilevers-ceo-has-a-green-thumb/

past ten years, Lifebuoy soap has tried to help prevent these deaths by teaching children the simple act of washing hands with soap at key occasions.[10]

In the entire process, Lifebuoy does not attempt to sell itself; its focus is on improving the health and well-being of the children. But by educating children about the benefits of maintaining good health, they win the trust of the family and subtly bring into play the principles of reciprocity and likability. The benefits for Lifebuoy are clear: parents of these children will be positively predisposed towards the brand that is inculcating a good habit in their children and ensuring that they remain healthy. Next time parents have to buy soap, which brand are they likely to be positively predisposed towards? Of course, Lifebuoy soap.

What Do Good 'Consultants' Do Differently?

In the role of a trainer, I get opportunities to train salespeople to deliver results. In every company a small group of sales people almost always deliver results. I am fascinated to know why this is the case. When I dig deeper, I notice that there are certain traits that they all share. Here is what I discover:

They do not attempt to sell to customers. They believe in building strong emotional relationships with them. They achieve this by not selling products or services to their customers, but providing with them piece of mind and comfort. They believe that they are not salespeople but consultants and their job is to help their customers achieve

---

[10] 'Help a Child Reach 5', Lifebuoy, https://www.lifebuoy.in/mission/help-a-child-reach-5.html

their business goals. Should things go wrong, the customers are confident that the consultant will not desert them but will be by their side to help them overcome the adversity.

Does it sound surreal? Can a company sell 'comfort'? Take Progressive Corporation for instance. It is a provider of car insurance in America. 'Progressive does not sell car insurance. It sells comfort: the comfort of knowing that if you have an accident, they will be at the scene, ready to write a check.', explains Harry Beckwith in his book *What Clients Love*[11], and goes on to say great salespersons do not sell products or services but satisfaction.

In addition, these consultants do a few other things which are shared by Joseph Curtis in an article in the Harvard Business Review, 'The 5 Things All Great Salespeople Do'[12]:

- **Own everything:** Even if it is not their fault, they believe it is their responsibility. This mindset is termed as 'internal locus of control'—a belief that power resides inside us not outside us. It is co-related with success at work, higher income and greater health outcomes.
- **Resourceful:** When encountering difficulties, they lean on their ingenuity to come up with a solution.
- **Experts:** Sales is less about selling and more about leading with high level of confidence, which in turn

[11] Harry Beckwith, 'What Clients Love: A Field Guide to Growing Your Business', (Business Plus, 2010)

[12] Joseph Curtis, 'The 5 Things All Great Salespeople Do', *Harvard Business Review*, 18 December 2018, https://hbr.org/2018/12/the-5-things-all-great-salespeople-do

comes from knowledge and experience—in short, by being an expert. Expertise leads to confidence which leads to building of trust culminating in sales.

- **Help others:** They are 'givers' and regularly share and pass on their knowledge to their colleagues without an agenda or quid pro quo. This endears them to their colleagues who go out of there of way to extend help.
- **Move quickly:** They move with purpose, speed and determination.

B2B Selling

So far we have focused on B2C selling. Let us shift the focus to B2B selling.

B2B buyers have changed. They are better informed and in no mood to be sold things. Instead, they desire the salesperson to transform into a consultant and help them:

- Acquire deeper insight into their industry
- Understand emerging trends in their industry
- Make sense of the information swirling around and about the industry
- Become knowledgeable about the innovations in their industry
- Know more about the competitive environment
- Understand how these products and services will create value for their own business

This requires consultants to constantly update their knowledge and acquire a deep understanding of the industry of their customers so that they can inform and educate them. This can be achieved if consultant follows the following practices:

- Constantly upskills to remain relevant and competent.
- Comes well prepared for every meeting.
- Is armed to the teeth with relevant data and information.
- Shows care and empathy for customers.
- Is an active listener, with the intent of understanding buyers' issues and challenges, and not simply giving them an answer.
- Poses questions to better understand the requirements.
- Aims to provide customized solutions.
- Provides ironclad guarantees or outcomes. In the unlikely case the guaranteed outcome is not entirely delivered, the shortfall will be made good.
- Politely refuses the order if there is an iota of doubt that the promised outcome cannot be delivered.
- Always keeps the interests of the customers ahead of the company's.

What Should You Do to Convert Your Salespeople into Consultants?

You should bring about a change in your mindset and embark on a journey of transforming your salesperson into consultants. The consultants should:

- Be an ambassador of customers and protect their interest even at the cost of the company's interest.
- Help companies reach their business goal.

- Not strive to sell products or services but build deep emotional relationships with customers.
- Not attempt to monetize at each and every transaction; doing it over the lifetime of the relationship.
- Win the customer's confidence and trust, and inspire confidence and hope.
- Empower them to take decisions.
- Invest in training them so they are always updated.
- Motivate them to imbibe excellent work ethics.
- Reward and recognize them when they display these behavioral traits.

By following these guidelines, some business will be lost; but in the process, the trust of customers will be won and the reciprocity and likability principles would be called into play. Next time the customer has business requirements, who will they reach out to your company? Of course, you! Did you notice that instead of you running after the customer they are seeking you out? What a refreshing change!

I know what's on your mind: should I take the risk and follow this advice? Do you have a choice, in this day and age?

LEADERSHIP

LEADERSHIP

RULE 7

Transform into an Admired Leader

It is better to lead from behind and put others in front, especially when you celebrate victory when nice things occur. You take the front line when there is a danger. Then people will appreciate your leadership.

—Nelson Mandela

Do you consider yourself to be an admired leader? Of course you do because you are highly competent.

- When your enterprise faces an issue, you take the initiative to propose a solution.
- When your colleagues approach you with a problem, you offer very effective solutions.
- You are task-driven and do not brook any nonsense or incompetence from your colleagues.
- If you spot any professional weaknesses among your colleagues, you do not hesitate to correct them, then and there.

But despite your high level of competence, perhaps your colleagues are not willing to be led by you? They do not wish to affiliate or engage with you, and worse, they resent you!

Legions of professionals face this very problem.

Let me share the root cause of the problem you face: you.

To resolve this conundrum, let me share a graph. The x-axis represents competence, while the y-axis represents warmth.

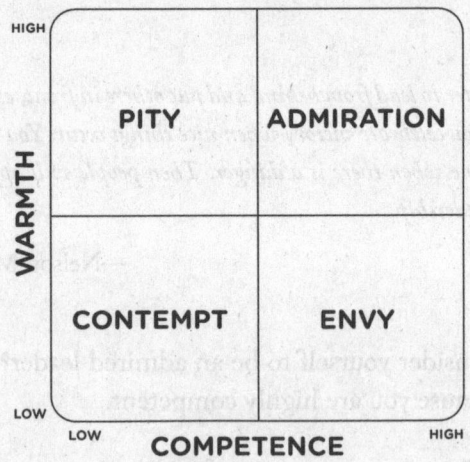

Place yourself on this graph[1]. Your traits indicate that you are high on competence, but low on warmth. Hence, you occupy the 'envy' quadrant.

Envy is an emotion that generates animosity; it causes pain, unhappiness and resentment towards the envied person. It also generates a feeling of inferiority in the person experiencing this

1 Amy J.C. Cuddy, Matthew Kohut, and John Neffinger, 'Connect, Then Lead', *Harvard Business Review*, July–August 2013, https://hbr. org/2013/07/connect-then-lead

emotion. So strong is the feeling that at times it culminates in a display of hostile behaviour towards the envied person. That is what is happening to your colleagues. They envy you, so you generate all the above emotions in them. Therefore, they do not wish to be led by you.

These traits that you possess in abundance will do justice to a manager whose key responsibility is to control and direct employees to achieve the objectives of the enterprise.

Now let us revisit the graph. A manager who is high on competence but low on warmth is envied, while a leader who scores high on both warmth and competence is admired.

So what should you do?

Simple. Move from the 'envy' to the 'admired' quadrant.

You are already high on competence. Acquire skills that will help you score high on warmth and you will transform into an admired leader.

This sounds too simple. Is there any success story to lend credence to this recommendation?

Microsoft was led by Bill Gates, and later by Steve Ballmer. Both were high on competence but had well-earned reputations for being hard taskmasters who expressed their displeasure in public. It was not uncommon for people to be rebuked by Bill Gates during a meeting: 'That's the dumbest idea I have heard.'[2] Take Steve Ballmer now, who was described by Paul Allen, co-founder of Microsoft, in his 2011

---

[2] Tanza Loudenback, 'Bill Gates's Best Quotes on Success and Innovation', *Inc.*, 6 February 2016, https://www.inc.com/business-insider/best-bill-gates-quotes.html

book, *Idea Man*, 'I thought, this guy looks like an operative for the NKVD (the secret police of the U.S.S.R.). He had piercing blue eyes and a genuine toughness.'[3]

In the graph, they would find a place in the 'envy' quadrant.

During Steve Ballmer's stewardship, Microsoft's stock moved more sideways and companies such as Apple, Alphabet and others were effortlessly overtaking it.[4]

In 2014, Satya Nadella took over the mantle of leadership from Ballmer. He was an unlikely choice to lead an iconic American company. Born and schooled in Hyderabad, he earned a degree in electrical engineering from the Manipal Institute of Technology, India. Paying heed to the clarion call of the 1980s—'Go west, young man'—he travelled to the US and got an MS degree in computer science. In 1992, he joined Microsoft and made a career in the company.

During his tenure he must have won Bill Gates's deep admiration. Upon Nadella's elevation, Gates said in a prepared statement, 'Satya is a proven leader with hard-core engineering skills, a business vision and the ability to bring people together.[5]

Nadella brings people together by being an empathetic communicator. He forms emotional connections with people

3   Kurt Eichenwald, 'Microsoft's Lost Decade', *Vanity Fair Hive*, 24 July 2012, https://www.vanityfair.com/news/business/2012/08/microsoft-lost-mojo-steve-ballmer

4   Kurt Eichenwald, 'Microsoft's Lost Decade', *Vanity Fair Hive*, 24 July 2012 https://www.vanityfair.com/news/business/2012/08/microsoft-lost-mojo-steve-ballmer

5   Samantha Sharf, 'It's Official: Microsoft Names Satya Nadella Its Third CEO', *Forbes*, 4 February 2014, https://www.forbes.com/sites/samanthasharf/2014/02/04/its-official-microsoft-names-satya-nadella-its-third-ceo/#72e5139c4efd

by appearing vulnerable. This was evident in the mail he sent
to employees upon taking charge:

> I am 46. I've been married for 22 years and we have 3
> kids. And like anyone else, a lot of what I do and how I
> think has been shaped by my family and my overall life
> experiences. Many who know me say I am also defined
> by my curiosity and thirst for learning. I buy more books
> than I can finish. I sign up for more online courses than
> I can complete. I fundamentally believe that if you are
> not learning new things, you stop doing great and useful
> things. So family, curiosity and hunger for knowledge, all
> define me.[6]

No wonder Nadella finds a place in the 'admired' quadrant!

Do 'Admired' Leaders Win in Today's 'Wild' World?

A question must have arisen in your mind. Nadella seems like
a 'nice' guy. But don't nice guys finish last? After all, Silicon
Valley is dominated by aggressive, brash, combative and, at
times, autocratic barons. More importantly, do nice guys
deliver numbers?

Nadella's performance says a lot. In 2018, he was rated
the best CEO in the US based on ratings by employees.[7]
Under his watch Microsoft has become the world's third

---

6   Microsoft site: https://news.microsoft.com/2014/02/04/satya-nadella-
   email-to-employees-on-first-day-as-ceo/.
7   Daniel Herborn, 'Microsoft's Satya Nadella tops list of USA best CEOs',
   CEO Magazine, 12 December 2018, https://news.theceomagazine.com/
   news/microsofts-satya-nadella-tops-list-of-usas-best-ceos/.

most valuable company.[8] Nice guys do win and deliver numbers.

I can almost hear many of you saying that Satya may be an exception. So let me invoke another Indian-born professional. Born and brought up in a middle-class household in Chennai, he now leads Google.

There is no doubt that Sundar Pichai, CEO of Google, is extremely competent. He would not have been elevated by Larry Page and Sergey Brin or accepted by peers as their leader. What makes Pichai's elevation stand out in Silicon Valley is that he is known to be 'shy', 'self-effacing', and unfailingly polite and affable. This is in sharp contrast to warlords of Silicon Valley, like Steve Jobs, Larry Ellison and Travis Kalanick, famed for their aggressive style of leadership.

The winds of change are sweeping across Silicon Valley too. The baton is being passed to humbler, warmer, friendlier leaders. At Apple it is Tim Cook, at Microsoft it is Satya Nadella, at Google it is Sundar Pichai. Therefore, you can be reassured that being an 'admired' leader will get you to pole position.

Strategies of 'Warm' Leaders

What strategies has Pichai deployed to earn this reputation? They are like him: simple, uncomplicated but effective.

- He lets his work speak.
- He does not monopolize the limelight but shares it with his team.

---

[8] The World's Most Valuable Brands, 2019 Ranking, *Forbes*, https://www.forbes.com/powerful-brands/list/

- He favours cooperation and collaboration over confrontation.
- He communicates in a 'conversational' style that helps him build emotional connections with people.
- He maintains equanimity. 'There is not much difference between an enthusiastic Sundar Pichai and a quiet, thoughtful Sundar Pichai.'[9]

The combination of competence and warmth has earned him 'admiration' from a large section of people he leads at Google and around the world. It is not surprising that Sundar Pichai finds himself occupying the 'admired' quadrant.

You might surmise that being 'warm' may work in tech companies, and that too in Silicon Valley. Nothing could be further than the truth. Even in India this strategy has delivered results.

Take Dhirubhai Ambani, for example. He founded Reliance Industries, which today is ranked among India's most valuable company.[10] He possessed one quality that endeared him to his people. It was genuine warmth which he radiated when he met people.

'*Kya Dost* . . . (hey, buddy . . .)' was the way he greeted everybody. Regardless of class, creed or religion. And that

---

9   Dieter Bohn, 'Sundar Pichai says the future of Google is AI. But can he fix the algorithm?' The Verge, 4 October 2017, https://www.theverge.com/2017/10/4/16405174/ceo-sundar-pichai-interview-google-ai-artificial-intelligence-interface.

10 'BT 500: India's Most Valuable Companies', *Business Today*, 18 November 2018, https://www.businesstoday.in/magazine/indias-most-valuable-companies-2018/bt-500-india-most-valuable-companies/story/286951.html

was truly how he felt. Physical proximity came naturally to him. He would without a second's hesitation slip his arm around our shoulder and walk a few meters, if he wanted to discuss anything with us,' recalled late A.G. Krishnamurthy, founder CMD of Mudra Communications[11] (now christened DDB Mudra).

Putting an arm around people in a friendly manner, also called supportive touch, leads to positive outcomes. It results in reduction of the stress hormone—cortisol and a release of the cuddle hormone—oxytocin—which promotes trust behaviours.[12]

How Can We Become 'Warm' Leaders?

We should start by bringing about a change in our mindset and making a habit of the behaviours discussed below.

- **Serve your people:** Start believing that your job is to serve your employees. Therefore, you should be available for them whenever they require you. Periodically, ask people what challenges they are facing. Once you know them, put in sincere effort to either reduce or eliminate them.
- **Lead with compassion:** You should lead with compassion by forming meaningful relationships with your employees and empowering them so they are able to achieve their potential. This you can do by

---

[11] A G Krishnamurthy, Dhirubhaism (Tata McGraw Hill, 2007)
[12] Michelle Trudeau, 'Human Connections Starts With A Friendly Touch', NPR, 20 September 2010, https://www.npr.org/templates/story/story.php?storyId=128795325

asking people how you can contribute towards their well-being and growth.

- **Help others succeed:** 'As a leader it's less about trying to be successful (yourself), and more about making others succeed.' said Sundar Pichai on a visit to his alma mater.[13] At regular interval ask people what you can do to help them. Put in sincere effort to help.

- **Practice active listening:** Listen to people with the intent of understanding them and not replying immediately. Also, do not listen in complete silence. Punctuate it with a 'yes' or 'hmm' to indicate that you are indeed listening and not merely hearing. If you have not understood a point, ask your colleague to explain it again. At the end, summarize important elements of the conversations to make sure you have understood what was sought to be communicated to you.

- **Have non-violent conversations:** Be compassionate while having conversations with your employees. Punctuate your conversations with 'Please', 'May I?' and 'Thank you'. Refrain from accusing, blaming or finding fault with others, or proving yourself right. They too will respond in a similar vein.

- **Apologize when you are in the wrong:** Most people believe that they will be perceived as a wimp if they apologize. But I believe that if you apologize when

---

[13] Devjyot Ghoshal, 'Sundar Pichai at IIT Kharagpur: When a shy Indian engineer returned to his alma mater as Google's CEO', Quartz India, 6 January 2017, https://qz.com/india/878842/sundar-pichai-at-iit-kharagpur-when-a-shy-indian-engineer-returned-to-his-alma-mater-as-the-ceo-of-google/.

you have committed an error, you come across as someone who is trustworthy.

Here is what I do to determine if an apology is warranted. I review the mistake and if I realize that I have committed it inadvertently, I immediately and unconditionally apologize. Most people notice the genuineness of my intention, accept it and we move on. But if I have committed a mistake or caused harm knowingly, I not only apologize but make good the damage caused.

Let me share an example to illustrate this point. I had made a commitment to my vendor that the payment would be released on a specific date. For unforeseen reasons it had to be deferred.

When we made the payment, we self-penalized and paid the vendor interest for the number of days the payment was delayed. By following this strategy, I was able to strengthen the trust between the vendor and our company. They forgot the lapse but remembered our act of generosity.

- **Keep your ego in check:** Never allow your ego to surface because it gives you a false sense of superiority. Experience has taught me that everybody knows more than me in some way or the other and that I can learn from them.

- **Appreciate, but only in deserving cases:** Draw inspiration from Sir Alex Ferguson. He had to manage multi-millionaire football stars like Cristiano Ronaldo, David Beckham and Wayne Rooney among others. To motivate them he used two words: 'Well done'. He believes that there is nobody in the world who does not like to hear these two words. 'Those are the two best words ever invented. You don't need to use superlatives.' believes Sir Alex.[14] But use it sparingly and in deserving cases only. Excessive use diminishes its value.

Does appreciation work in corporate environment? Dan Ariely, a Duke University professor did an experiment, among factory workers, in a factory located in Israel. The workers were offered three reward options for improving productivity—receiving a $30 bonus, a pizza voucher, or a 'Well done!' complimentary text message from the boss. '. . . while a bonus resulted in a spike in worker productivity, it then declined to below what it was before the bonus was offered. Gratitude and complements are better motivators,' Ariely say. 'Acknowledgment is a kind of human magic.'[15]

- **Make people feel special:** You can achieve this by:
  o Knowing them as people
  o Focusing on their strengths
  o Treating them as they want to be treated
  o Being courteous to them
  o Giving credit where it is genuinely due
  o Being patient with them

- **Demonstrate that you care:** Let me share with you how I demonstrated to my team that I cared for

[14] Anita Elberse, 'Ferguson's Formula', *Harvard Business Review*, October 2013, https://hbr.org/2013/10/fergusons-formula
[15] Michael Skapinker, 'Review–'Payoff' by Dan Ariely', *Financial Times*, 10 November 2016, https://www.ft.com/content/934209e2-a736-11e6-8b69-02899e8bd9d1

them. I was the President of J.K. Helene Curtis. On Sunday mornings, around 11 a.m., I would call Sales Managers. As soon as they realized that I was on the phone, they would start updating me on business. I would immediately interrupt them, 'I have called you, not to discuss business, but to find out about you and your family.' Hearing this they would invariably say that they and their family are doing well. After exchanging some more pleasantries, I would disconnect. Each phone call would last for may be three minutes. Since I made these calls on Sunday, hence my wife could overhear my conversation.

'Do these phone calls serve any purpose?' She would ask me.

'Of course, they do.' I would reply. But I could see from her expression that she did not believe me.

'How would you feel if Mr Gautam Singhania, our CMD, called on a Sunday morning, not to discuss business, but to enquire for our family welfare?' I asked her.

'Delighted,' she said, 'After all he is such a busy man. And if he takes time out, that too on a Sunday, then it shows he really cares about us,' she replied.

'For my team member, I am their Gautam Singhania . . .' I told her. 'Their family too feels that the company cares about them.'

Needless to say, the salespeople would work with renewed vigour.

A word of caution—do this to demonstrate genuine care and not to manipulate them to work harder.

- **Use positive body language:** Let me share a secret with you. Non-verbal communication (NVC) is more impactful than verbal communication. People subconsciously pick up NVC and form opinions based on it. So, make a conscious effort to learn the basics of body language so that you do not send out any unintended messages. Let me share a few tips on body language to come across as a warm person.

  o **Eye contact:** Try to maintain eye contact with the person you are speaking to. This makes you seem more honest.

  o **Hands:** Keep your palms facing up when making a point. This indicates that you are making a request for your ideas to be heard and accepted.

  o **Pointing a finger:** Do not do it during a discussion or while making a point. It is tantamount to accusing a person.

  o **Speak slowly:** When you speak at a fast pace you run the risk of being incoherent and appearing nervous. Make a conscious effort to speak slowly. This will make you appear more confident.

  o **Smile:** Make it a point to smile when engaging with people or having a conversation because it makes you appear more approachable, likeable and confident.

Strategies for Building Competencies

You need to follow a multipronged approach to build competencies. But here is the rub. You can opt to learn a multitude of competencies all at once only to realize that you may have gained mastery in none. Alternatively, you may choose to focus on attaining mastery in one competency at a time, moving slowly but steadily.

- **A 'Growth' Mindset:** In a VUCA (Volatile, Uncertain, Complex and Ambiguous) world, competency comes with an expiry date. Therefore, the advantage rests with people who opt for being lifelong learners. They believe that no matter how much they know, they need to know more. This hunger for learning ensures that they keep on acquiring competencies which will keep them relevant and effective.

  This mindset is popularly referred to as the 'growth' mindset. I practice the growth mindset by following the 1 per cent rule: every day I strive to be 1 per cent better than I was yesterday. For that, every day I set aside a minimum of one hour every weekday, or five hours a week, for deliberate learning. This is popularly called the five-hour rule. It is followed by Warren Buffet, Oprah Winfrey and Bill Gates.

  If you too follow this rule diligently, then in due course, the law of compounding will set in and you will realize that you have accumulated a treasure trove of knowledge. It will give you the confidence to thrive in the VUCA world.

  In contrast is the 'fixed' mindset, which tries to get people to believe that 'I know it all' and there is no further need to acquire new competencies. This mindset can prove to be fatal. Shun it.

- **Using Time Wisely:** Get comfortable saying 'no' to many demands on your time. This will free up your time and you can focus on things that really matter. Next, put the time that you have saved to good use. To understand the value of time, seek inspiration from Warren Buffet. He was once asked if there is anything money cannot buy. He replied, 'Time!'[16] What is true for Warren Buffet is true for you. Learn to spend your time wisely to build competencies.

- **Digital Strategy:** It involves:
    - o **Video strategy:** Curate a list of videos you wish to watch on YouTube, be it TED Talks or other videos. Be on guard that you do not fall victim to binge-watching of content that will merely entertain you.
    - o **Social media strategy:** Craft a robust social media strategy in which LinkedIn figures prominently. Remember, social media can be addictive. If you are not disciplined, you can end up wasting precious time.
    - o **Reading strategy:** Buy books on Kindle that will keep you ahead. Carry your Kindle with you and immerse yourself in it whenever you find time. Download more books than you can finish! Surrounding yourself with reading material in whichever manner is a good way to push yourself to read.

---

[16] Barnaby Lashbrooke, 'You Cannot Buy Time, But What If You Could?' *Forbes,* January 24, 2019, https://www.forbes.com/sites/barnabylashbrooke/2019/01/24/warren-buffett-thinks-you-cannot-buy-time-but-what-if-you-could/#28c9a58c5fd7

- **MOOCS (Massive Open Online Courses) strategy:** Sign up for online courses that will help you proactively build competency. Sign up for more courses than you can complete.
- **Seminars and training programmes:** Make an annual plan of the seminars and training programmes you plan to attend. Also, become a member of professional bodies of your industry and make a conscious effort to network and gain insights about your industry.
- **Reverse mentoring:** I invite young people with whom I am associated—my students, younger people in the organization where I work—to teach me new competencies, particularly digital competences. I must admit that I have gained enormously. You too should embrace reverse mentoring.
- **Get a coach:** Change is difficult. A good coach can be of great help. They do not guide, nor lead, nor push, or nor pull. They will pose good question that can challenge you and also keep you on course.[17]
- **The company you keep:** Strive to be in the company of people more knowledgeable than you. In their company, be an active listener and observer. In the process you will be putting the law of entropy into play. The law states that heat transfers from hot to cold; in your case knowledge and wisdom will get transferred from them to you.

---

[17] Richard E. Boyatzis, Melvin Smith, and Ellen Van Oosten, 'Coaching For Change', *Harvard Business Review*, September-October 2019, https://hbr.org/2019/09/coaching-for-change

- **Diversity index:** Make a conscious effort to meet people from diverse professions and backgrounds and those who hold views contrary to yours. This ensures that you are constantly challenged. It will help you be comfortable in uncomfortable situations so you get a chance to be more creative since you are exposed to so many different ideas and viewpoints.
- **Willingness to kill your own darlings:** If I find that an idea that I strongly believed in has outlived its utility or is not delivering results, I have no hesitation in 'killing' it. The ability to kill your own darling is an important skill I have cultivated. So should you.
- **Learn from mistakes:** 'Success is a lousy teacher. It seduces smart people into thinking they can't lose,' observed Bill Gates.[18] Failure, on the other hand, is a great teacher. Learn from it. And make sure you do not commit the same mistake again. Remember to learn from the mistakes of others too. After all, life is too short to make all the mistakes!

A Word of Caution

Critically evaluate each practice mentioned here and choose those that resonate with you. Then start practising them till they become habits.

Before you adopt these practices, especially for appearing 'warm', pose an introspective question to yourself: what is your intention behind adopting these practices? Is it to

---

[18] Bill Gates, 'The Road Ahead' (Penguin Group USA, 1995)

manipulate people to serve your selfish interests or is to serve them?

If it is to manipulate them, than sooner or later your selfish motive will be uncovered and the backlash will be severe. You will lose your credibility. Once it is lost, it is difficult to earn it back.

Have I Become an 'Admired' Leader?

Let me pose a question that may be niggling you: how will you know you have transformed into an admired leader?

Request your employees to score you on two questions:

1. Do you feel good in my presence?
2. When you face a problem do you feel confident about confiding in me?

If the answer to both these questions is yes, you can certify yourself as an 'admired leader'.

Postscript:

During his childhood, Nelson Mandela was greatly influenced by Jongintaba, the tribal king who brought him up. In his court, people sat around in a circle and spoke. Only after all had spoken the king would speak. The message that young Nelson took from observing this ritual was that a leader's job is not to dictate people and tell them what they should do but to collaborate with them to form a consensus.

Years later, when Mandela had meetings in his home, people would huddle around his dining table or sometime in his driveway in a circle. Some of his more aggressive colleagues would prompt him to speed things up but Mandela would merely listen. Finally when he spoke, he first summarized every one's ideas and then shared his own—in a manner that people did not feel it was being imposed upon them.

'It is wise,' he said, 'to persuade people to do things and make them think it was their own idea.' In short, the trick of leadership is allowing yourself to be led too. This idea, he had imbibed when as a child he would herd cattle. 'You know,' he would say, 'you can lead them from behind.'[19]

The same will be true for you too. As an admired leader allow yourself to be led because the best leaders lead from behind. But your responsibility does not end here. You have to make sure that your legacy endures. For that you have to adopt a trusteeship mindset, as enunciated by Lee Kuan Yew, popularly referred to by his initials LKY, the first prime minister of Singapore and who transformed it into a flourishing First-World country: leaders must have the sense of trusteeship, that they are only temporarily in charge of the destiny of their people and that their duty is not only to discharge this trust but also to pass it on to equally trustworthy and competent hands.[20]

---

[19] Richard Stengel, 'Mandela: His 8 Lessons of Leadership', *Time*, 9 July 2008, http://content.time.com/time/subscriber/article/0,33009,1821659-2,00.html

[20] Lance Ng, 'Lee Kuan Yew on Choosing Leaders', *M*, March 2019, https://medium.com/@lancengym/lee-kuan-yew-on-choosing-leaders-49c62fdb5f34

BRAND

RULE 8

Create a Supercool Brand

A 'cool' brand is attractive, while a 'supercool' brand is irresistible.

—Rajesh Srivastava

Let us begin this conversation with a question: will creating a brand satisfy you? I guess, for most of us, the answer would be an unequivocal 'yes'.

But pause for a moment. In today's time, the companies we admire have upped their ante. Merely creating a brand does not satisfy them; they are taking it one step further by creating cool brands.

What is the difference between a brand and a cool brand? A brand merely satisfies its customers, while a cool brand makes them happy.

What is the difference between a satisfied and a happy customer? To understand the difference, consider yourself as an example. You are proficient at your job. Whenever your company needs to engage in a strategic negotiation, perhaps it is you who is entrusted with the responsibility. You ensure it is concluded in your company's favour. How do you feel at the end of the negotiation? Of course—satisfied, because you delivered on the promise.

When you reach office, your boss showers fulsome praise on you in front of your peers: 'we knew you would conclude the negotiation successfully . . . the company depends on you . . . you have a great future with us . . . we see you in a bigger leadership role in due course of time.'

What's your reaction to this praise? Your chest swells with pride, you walk tall with a smile plastered on your face! How are you feeling? Satisfied or happy? Without a doubt, happy!

And why are you happy? The effusive praise and recognition, that too in front of your peers, boosted your self-esteem and confidence. It also helped you project yourself in the eyes of your peers the way you wanted to be projected: as an important member of the company; someone the company respects and depends upon; someone who has a great future in the company.

Let's revisit this scenario to glean the learnings. When you successfully concluded the negotiation, you delivered on your promise: that you are proficient in your job. That made you feel satisfied. But when your boss praised you in front of everyone, it made you happy because it delivered two additional benefits:

- It boosted your self-esteem and confidence.
- You were able to project yourself the way you desired in the eyes of your peers.

What is true for you is also true for a brand.

Customers buy a brand based on the promise it makes to them. When it delivers on the promise, it satisfies them.

Cool Brand

A cool brand not only delivers on the promise, satisfying customers, but also scores on two additional dimensions: it boosts their self-esteem and confidence, and it helps them project themselves the way they wish to before their peers. In short, a cool brand helps us shape our identity, enhances our confidence and self-esteem, and helps us project ourselves to the rest of the world. Result: cool brands make us feel happy and good about ourselves.

Let us take BMW for instance. It promises its owners the 'joy of driving'.[1] When owners drive it, they indeed experience the joy of driving. Thus BMW delivers on a key promise it makes to its customers.

Now, how does an owner feel when she is sitting in her BMW? More confident or less confident? Of course, more confident. And when her peers see her sitting in the BMW, what has she silently communicated about herself to her peers? 'I can afford a BMW. I have class. I know how to appreciate the finer things in life.' Who did the talking on her behalf? The brand, BMW. And because it did it efficiently and effectively, BMW has earned the right to be labelled as a cool brand.

Let us measure BMW on three attributes that form the DNA of a cool brand and see where it stands:

- **Deliver on the promise:** Owners indeed experience the promise held out by BMW—the joy of driving.
- **Boost self-esteem:** Help the customers feel happy by boosting their self-esteem and confidence.

---

[1] BMW Site: https://www.bmwdrivingluxury.com/driving-luxury/joy-of-driving

- **Assist in projecting desired image:** Assist the customer (read: owner) in projecting themselves the way they desire in the eyes of their peers.

Indeed it does—that too, without saying a word. Who does the talking on their behalf? BMW. And because BMW scores high on all three parameters, it qualifies as a cool brand.

Since you now know the secret recipe to transforming your brand into a cool brand; make sure it scores high on all three parameters.

A word of caution: a cool brand may not be cool universally. What is cool to you may not be cool to others. Take Salman Khan for instance. He is considered cool and his many fans affectionately call him 'Bhai'. But for others, he may not be cool. The lesson for us: do not get upset when a section of the target audience refuses to acknowledge your brand as cool.

Keep another point in mind: a cool brand comes with a shelf life. What is cool for one generation may not be cool for the following ones. Take cigarettes for instance. In the 1950s and 1960s, smoking cigarettes was considered cool. In the twenty-first century, however, it is no longer cool and in fact, is frowned upon.

What Should You Not Do to Become a Cool Brand?

Let us take the example of Google Glass.[2] It was expected to be the next game changer like iPhone. But sadly, it did not live up to the expectations.

---

[2] Umair Haque, 'Google Glass Failed Because It Just Wasn't Cool,' *Harvard Business Review*, January 30, 2015, https://hbr.org/2015/01/google-glass-failed-because-it-just-wasnt-cool

This happened despite Google investing resources to create buzz and hype around it. It ran advertorials in fashion magazines, got models to sport it during Fashion Week, and handed it to influencers.

But people perceived these initiatives as trying to 'buy' coolness. After all, it is so uncool to buy or manufacture 'coolness'. If 'cool' has to be 'purchased or manufactured' then the product is not worthy of being labelled as 'cool'.

Bottom line: Cool has to be earned. Do not try to buy it. It may backfire.

What Should Brands Do to Remain Cool?

Let us take the example of Nike. It has managed to remain cool across decades. What marketing strategy has it pursued to achieve this distinction?

Nike has consistently pursued a celebrity endorsement strategy by signing up leading sports stars who are the epitome of coolness for their generation. A partial list of the Nike roster of sports stars across decades includes Carl Lewis, Jackie Joyner-Kersee, Sebastian Coe, Michael Jordan, Tiger Woods, Rafael Nadal, Roger Federer and Maria Sharapova. Among football stars, its roster has included Ian Rush, Luis Figo, Eric Cantona, Ronaldo Nazario in the past, and more recently, Wayne Rooney, Sergio Ramos, Neymar, Cristiano Ronaldo, among others. In India, it has sponsored the kit and apparel of the national cricket team.

Since sports has an inherent coolness attached to it, Nike has reinforced its relevance by picking the best ambassadors through the ages.

Supercool Brand

Let us continue this conversation with a follow-up question: will creating merely a cool brand make you happy? Or do you desire to create a supercool brand?

I hear many of you saying 'supercool brand!' Let me share the DNA of a supercool brand.

Let's look at Tesla.

In a short space of time it has unleashed a torrent of innovation. Powered by technology, it has captured the world's imagination. A partial list includes:

- **Autopilot:** This feature offers assistance to the active driver. It can control the accelerator, brakes, and the steering wheel. It can even change lanes on highways.[3]
- **Sales:** It is focusing on direct-to-customer sales by migrating to selling online. In the process, it is side-lining dealers. [4]
- **Gallery:** Tesla has galleries for showcasing its products and educating its customers.
- **Supercharger:** They are a Tesla charging network. It will serve to charge Tesla cars and reduce 'range anxiety'.[5]

---

[3] Mark Hogan, 'These are the 11 coolest features of Tesla Model S,' CNBC, 17 November 2017, https://www.cnbc.com/2017/11/17/tesla-model-s-best-features.html

[4] Jeff Dyer and Hal Gergersen, 'Tesla's Innovations Are Transforming The Auto Industry,' *Forbes*, 24 August 2016, https://www.forbes.com/sites/innovatorsdna/2016/08/24/teslas-innovations-are-transforming-the-auto-industry/#27f96e3319f7

[5] Supercharger: https://www.tesla.com/supercharger

- **Over-the-Air Updates:** It offers software upgrades over-the-air just like smart phones do.
- **Home Energy Upgrades:** You can produce as well as store clean energy to power your home and charge your car day and night.[6]
- **Key:** It is shaped like a miniature version of Model 3.[7]
- **Giga Factory:** At full capacity it will be the world's largest producer of lithium batteries.
- **Autonomous Cars:** 'When true self-driving is approved by regulators, it will mean that you will be able to summon your Tesla from pretty much anywhere. Once it picks you up, you will be able to sleep, read or do anything else en route to your destination.' Says Elon Musk.[8]

The crowning glory is that it offers 'clean' transportation.

Traditional car companies led by General Motors, Ford, Toyota and others, continue to mainly build vehicles which have a harmful impact on our planet.

Does 'clean' transportation resonate with buyers? Maybe not with older people. But the new generation of customers strongly support sustainability and are often at loss on how to engage in activities through which they can support this cause. When they come across a brand that is sincerely supporting this cause, they vote for it with their wallets as they did for Tesla Model 3.

---

[6] Tesla site: https://www.tesla.com/models/design#payment

[7] Key: https://www.tesla.com/support/model-3-key-fob

[8] Robert Ferris, 'Elon Musk says: "It's not Tesla vs Uber. It is the people vs Uber"', CNBC, 27 October 2016, https://www.cnbc.com/2016/10/26/elon-musk-says-its-not-tesla-vs-uber-it-is-the-people-vs-uber.html

When Tesla announced the launch of Model 3 in March 2016, an affordable EV, no less than 4,50,000 buyers paid $1000 refundable deposit.[9] This enabled Tesla to garner $450 million, which translates into potential revenue of over $15 billion, provided no order gets cancelled.

What about Wall Street? How does it view Tesla? In April 2017, it overtook General Motors to become the most valuable car company in the US (since then, its share prices have fallen).[10]

What has Tesla done differently to reach pole position? The majority of cars across the world are powered by internal combustion (IC) engines. They exude carbon monoxide, nitrogen oxide and hydrocarbons gases into the atmosphere, aggravating the greenhouse effect, acid rain and climate change. A Tesla is an EV (electric vehicle) and is powered by a battery that does not discharge pollutants.

Tesla, like other automobiles, transports people but because it does not pollute, it is perceived as a 'clean' car that promotes sustainability. It is this aspect that has earned Tesla bragging rights as not just a 'cool' but a 'supercool' brand.

A supercool brand sports an additional layer: it is associated with a cause that resonates with the customers and other stakeholders.

---

[9] Samuel Gibbs, 'Whatever happened to that $35000 Tesla Model 3 you still can't buy?' *Guardian*, 25 May 2018, https://www.theguardian.com/technology/2018/may/25/tesla-model-3-tax-credits-elon-musk-buy

[10] Tim Higgins, 'Tesla Tivals GM as the Most Valuable Auto Maker in U.S.,' *Wall Street Journal*,' Updated 10 April 2017, https://www.wsj.com/articles/tesla-overtakes-gm-to-become-most-valuable-u-s-auto-maker-1491832043

This strategy is popularly called 'do well by doing good', and this is the way it plays out in a customer's mind. On learning that Tesla is offering clean transportation, a thought is set in motion: I need to buy a car and if by buying a Tesla I can contribute to saving the planet, that too without inconveniencing myself, then why not?

There are four attributes that form the DNA of a supercool brand. Tesla possesses all the attributes:

1. **Deliver on the promise:** It provides 'clean' transportation.
2. **Boost the customer's self-esteem and confidence:** Owning a Tesla indeed boosts the owner's confidence and self-esteem.
3. **Assist in projecting desired image:** By supporting Tesla, people project themselves as conscientious and as someone who cares for the environment, which is what they desired to be seen as in the eyes their peers.
4. **Is associated with a cause:** Tesla is inexorably linked to clean transportation.

Any brand or business that scores high on the four points mentioned above can earn this title. Let me introduce TOMS Shoes, a for-profit company started in the US in 2006. It is engaged in designing and selling shoes, but with an interesting twist. When you purchase a pair of shoes from TOMS, you actually purchase two pairs: one for yourself and another to be given to an impoverished child.

TOMS Shoes have embedded the 'do well by doing good' strategy into the product itself. On learning about the cause that TOMS is associated with, a buyer is likely to think: I have to buy a pair of shoes, and if by buying TOMS I can be of help to an impoverished child, that too without inconveniencing myself, then why not? Buyers experience self-efficacy and confidence that their actions will have a meaningful impact.

'With every product you purchase, TOMS will help a person in need. The premise is simple, but the potential to help others is huge,' it says on the TOMS website.

Let us quickly evaluate TOMS on the four attributes that form the DNA of a supercool brand:

1. **Deliver on the promise:** TOMS footwear is well designed and stylish, plus it is associated with a remarkable cause.
2. **Boost the customer's self-esteem and confidence:** It does so, coupled with a feeling of doing the right thing.
3. **Assist in projecting desired image:** In the eyes of the customer's peers, TOMS helps in portraying their customers as compassionate and caring indivisuals with a big heart.
4. **Is associated with a cause:** It is associated with a social cause of providing footwear to an impoverished child.

TOMS has transformed into a supercool brand by associating itself memorably with a social cause. Perusing the strategy of 'do well by doing good' has certainly assisted TOMS in recording a steady revenue growth.

Take Warby Parker for instance.[11] It was launched in 2010, 'with the objective of offering designer eyewear at a

---

[11] Warby Parker website: https://www.warbyparker.com/history

revolutionary price, while leading the way for socially conscious businesses.' It has seamlessly integrated social purpose into the sales strategy—when you buy a pair, you actually give a pair to somebody in need. In 2015 it was valued at $1.2 billion.[12]

What does this indicate? In the case of parity products, among which customers believe only minor differences exist and therefore they can readily be substituted, customers are likely to opt for a product from a company that is associated with a cause that resonates with them. Lesson: companies should choose to get associated with a cause.

TOMS and Warby Parker are examples of pursuing 'do well by doing good' of brands where the 'good' part was not a part of the product. It was an external thing. Are there examples of this strategy where it is strongly related to the product?

Take Brita for instance,[13] a water purification brand, which sells tap water filters giving water of great taste and purity. Slowing sales made the team decided to embrace the 'do well by doing good' strategy.' It decided to offer an alternative to 'bottled water'—'pure' water from Brita tap water filters could be filled into reusable bottles. It was easy on the pocket because it obviated the need for buying bottled water, which after consumption ended up in a landfill. This strategy got traction because customers were getting two desirable benefits—clean water at economical rates and that too, without harming the environment. Sales went sky-high.

---

[12] Douglas MacMillan, 'Eyeglass Retailer Warby Parer Valued at $1.2 Billion', *Wall Street Journal*, 3 April 2015, https://blogs.wsj.com/digits/2015/04/30/eyeglass-retailer-warby-parker-valued-at-1-2-billion/

[13] Omar Rodriguez Vila and Sunder Bharadwaj, 'Competing on Social Purpose,' *Harvard Business Review*, September–October 2017, https://hbr.org/2017/09/competing-on-social-purpose

Motivation for Supporting a Supercool Brand

Let me now address the elephant in the room: what motivates customers to support brands and businesses associated with a cause?

Customers look upon them as an extension of themselves: by supporting them, they feel they are supporting themselves and acting in their own self-interest. In addition, as mentioned earlier, self-efficacy kicks in and gives them the confidence that their actions will have a meaningful impact. Therefore, brands and companies should support a cause, so that the association can awaken empathy and self-efficacy among customers.

Many of you would be thinking that 'empathy' is an altruistic concept and a spent force, particularly in today's hyper commercial world. People assume that the only sound that makes people dance is that of money.

Consider the Swiss-born political philosopher Jean-Jacques Rousseau's (1712–1778) perspective on empathy and assess if it works today. Rousseau believed that all humans were born with empathy that the rise of consumerism has led to the recession of these qualities, if not the extinction. But, deep down, empathy still resides. It just needs to be awakened: supercool brands succeed in awakening it.

Does Altruism Really Sell?

This makes for great reading, but is there any research data or findings to back this interesting hypothesis?

2017 Cone Communications CRS Study concluded that 87 per cent of the people would vote with their wallet and buy a product based on a company's support of a cause that strikes a chord with them. Another Cone Communications study found that 85 per cent of consumers would switch over to a brand associated with a cause. The number is even higher for millennial consumers.[14]

Independently, the 2015 Nielsen Global Corporate Sustainability Report which polled 30,000 consumers in sixty countries across the globe concluded that 66 per cent of the global consumers are willing to pay more for sustainable brands—up 55 per cent from 2014. While 73 per cent of the global millennials to pay extra for sustainable offerings—up from 50 per cent in 2014.[15]

Transforming into supercool brands works best when companies authentically believe in the cause and voluntarily adopt it and not as a gimmick, or an opportunity to exploit people's emotions and boost sales.

Therefore, brands and companies—if they embrace a cause with an honourable intention—can lay the foundations for establishing an emotional relationship with the customers and building customer preference.

Green Washing

What happens if a brand or company wishes to take advantage of this strategy and makes false claims about its association with social or an environmental causes? The backlash that

---

[14] CONE, A Porter Novelli Company, 2017 Cone Communication CSR Study, http://www.conecomm.com/research-blog/2017-csr-study.

[15] 'Consumers-Goods' Brands That Demostrate Commitment to Sustainability Outerform Those That Don't,' Nielsen, 12 October 2015, https://www.nielsen.com/in/en/press-releases/2015/consumer-goods-brands-that-demonstrate-commitment-to-sustainability-outperform/

would follow when their nefarious intentions are exposed would be crippling.

Take Volkswagen for instance: it claimed that its cars delivered high performance with excellent fuel economy, an emission so squeaky clean as to rival electric hybrids like Toyota Prius. This was not true. A 'cheat software' had been installed which ensured that their vehicles passed emission norms. When VW was caught green washing[16] a global scandal—dubbed Green Gate—erupted and captured international headlines. It has resulted in the company taking a hit of $25 billion in fines, penalties, and restitution levied by US authorities![17]

Is VW an isolated case? Of course, not. The rogues' gallery is crowded and you should take a pledge that you will never join it.

Employee Engagement

A business that embraces a cause with honourable intentions does not only get customers' support by being voted for with their wallet, but can also hope to experience an increase in employee engagement, a significant reduction in attrition rate, and an increase in revenue.

What Are the Takeaways for You?

The crux of the discussion on cool and supercool brands has been consolidated in the table below for your benefit. Here is

---

[16] Reviewed by Will Kenton, 'Greenwashing', Investopedia, Updated 18 April 2019, https://www.investopedia.com/terms/g/greenwashing.asp

[17] Roger Parloff, 'How VW paid $25 billion for Dieselgate—and got off easy', *Fortune*, 6 February 2018, https://fortune.com/2018/02/06/volkswagen-vw-emissions-scandal-penalties/

a golden opportunity for you to create a preference for your brand and business, command a premium price and increase employee engagement at work. Go ahead and transform your brand into a supercool brand.

You can then put your feet up and watch your brand and business take an upwards trajectory!

BRAND // COOL BRAND // SUPER COOL BRAND				
DESCRIPTION	Deliver the promise	Boosts self-esteem and confidence	Assists the buyers in projecting themselves the way they desire in the eyes of their peers	Associated with a cause
BRAND	✓	NIL	NIL	NIL
COOL BRAND	✓	✓	✓	NIL
SUPER COOL BRAND	✓	✓	✓	✓

WORKPLACE

WORKPLACE

RULE 9

Transform Your Workplace into a Fun Place

There is little success where there is little laughter.

—Andrew Carnegie

In the modern-day workplace, roles are reversing. Employees are no longer working for the company; it is the company that is working for them.

Sounds quixotic? Some of the world's most admired companies have adopted this strategy with aplomb and are reaping the benefits. These companies are transforming the 'workplace' into a 'fun place', ensuring their employees experience 'bursts of happiness' while at work.

What Are the Benefits?

Empirical evidence suggests that children learn best and tend to be more imaginative when they are playing, having fun or are generally in a happy state. This principle also applies to adults: our learning ability and power of imagination heads northwards when we are in a relaxed, playful and a happy mood. Hard research also corroborates this empirical evidence that happy employees are more productive (by 12 per cent and, in some cases, by up to 20 per cent than the control group)[1].

Has any company adopted this ostensibly unbusinesslike strategy and experienced these benefits?

Google has adopted this strategy. It has replaced a formal office atmosphere, which can be intimidating, with a fun ambience that enhances learning, creativity and productivity of Googlers—as it calls its employees.

I believe it drew inspiration from kindergarten (KG) classes, where classroom walls, desks and chairs are splashed with primary colours—red, yellow, green and blue—to make it appear less intimidating and also to unleash the creativity of the toddlers.

Were we not at our creative best in KG? So, Google uses oodles of bright primary colours to give its campus—the term it uses to refer to its office complex—a pre-school feel. It has turned its campus into a 'fun place' so that Googlers can unleash their creativity.

Further, Google has tried to provide for most of the amenities that employees usually work and earn for, like food stations that offer a wide range of options, gyms, hair salons, sauna, yoga classes and everything you might expect in luxury hotels. Except that the employees are not expected to pay for these.

The presence of these alluring amenities at its colourful campus makes Googlers happy and puts them in a relaxed state of mind. This leads to building trust, deepening and strengthening of relationships, and better team work among

---

[1]   Barry Chignell, 'Six reasons why fun in the office is the future of work,' CIPHR, 22 May 2018, https://www.ciphr.com/advice/fun-in-the-office/

them. At a deeper level, the fun and playful ambience imparts a lethal blow to the silo way of thinking and working.

There's another bonus. When employees spend more and more time in office, they are more likely to 'collide' with each other. Such interactions, referred to as 'office collision' or 'inadvertent encounters', lead to exchange of ideas, which can prompt creative solutions to vexing problems. In exceptional cases, ideas for new businesses could also emerge from these collisions.

Has any other organization benefited from 'inadvertent encounters'?

Pixar, arguably one of the world's most creative organizations, believes that part of its creativity springs from the way its office buildings are designed to facilitate 'inadvertent encounters'.

Ed Catmull, former president of Pixar describes the idea behind it:

> Our building, which is Steve Jobs' brainchild, is another way we try to get people from different departments to interact. Most buildings are designed for some functional purpose, but ours is structured to maximize inadvertent encounters. At its centre is a large atrium, which contains the cafeteria, meeting rooms, bathrooms and mailboxes. As a result, everyone has strong reasons to go there repeatedly during the course of the workday. It's hard to describe just how valuable the resulting chance encounters are.[2]

---

2   Ed Catmull, How Pixar Fosters Collective Creativity, Harvard Business Review, September 2018, https://hbr.org/2008/09/how-pixar-fosters-collective-creativity

No wonder Pixar's chief creative officer exclaimed, 'I've never seen a building that promoted collaboration and creativity as well as this one.'[3]

Urban Physics

What Steve Jobs did intuitively has sprung up as a new discipline with a fancy name, 'urban physics', which seeks to blend two disparate branches of knowledge—physics and urban planning—in a holy alliance.

By leveraging the principles of urban physics, office spaces can be designed to enhance productivity, creativity, teamwork, transparency and more.

- **Productivity:** It has been found that employees, at their busiest, yearn for coffee to keep the work momentum going. So, for enhancing productivity, coffee dispensers/cafeterias are located at the heart of the work area.

  You may design standing-only conference rooms. The time of meetings reduces without loss in quality of engagement. In fact, it increases collaboration and creative output.[4]

---

[3]   Jeff Miller, 'The science behind how Steve Jobs designed Pixar's office,' *Inc.*, 22 August 2017, https://www.inc.com/jeff-miller/3-ways-to-design-an-office-for-collaboration-not-c.html.

[4]   Shereen Lehman, 'Standing meetings may improve group productivity,' 21 June 2014, Reuters, https://www.reuters.com/article/us-psychology-group-meetings-productivit/standing-meetings-may-improve-group-productivity-idUSKBN0EV29V20140620

- **Creativity:** The presence of natural sunlight, greenery, the sound of falling water and the liberal use of primary colour facilitate creativity. Take Groupon for instance. It uses 'tiki huts' which liberally use forest motifs to create a vicarious feeling of forests to ignite creativity.

Collaboration and Teamwork

Common areas should be embellished with amenities and facilities so that employees find reasons to visit them often. This facilitates 'office collisions' among employees of different divisions and results in serendipitous encounters which results in collaboration, increased learning and ultimate innovation.[5] This will also result in breaking down of the silo mentality and ways of working.

- **Exchange Ideas:** Provide white-board and marker pens along with Post-It pads. This will make it easier for people to congregate around white-board to exchange ideas.
- **Transparency:** The presence of glass subconsciously indicates transparency to stakeholders. Leaders sitting in transparent offices or cubicles appear more approachable. Therefore, office spaces should be designed by using lots of glass.
- **Foster a family feeing:** At home, a family sits down and has a meal together accompanied with free-flowing

---

[5] Jennifer Magnolfi, 'Why Apple's New HQ is Nothing Like the Rest of Silicon Valley,' 26 June 2017, *Harvard Business Review*, https://hbr.org/2017/06/why-apples-new-hq-is-nothing-like-the-rest-of-silicon-valley

conversations. This builds family bonding. Plan the dining area so that people can sit together, have food and conversations. This is likely to forge a family-like bond among people.

- **Increase wellness and happiness:** Serotonin[6], is a chemical which is widely recognized as a wellness and happiness chemical. Its production increases when we are exposed to natural sunlight. Therefore, you must design spaces in a way that lets in ample sunlight. It will boost well-being and happiness of people.

A Good Mood is Contagious

Companies are also realizing that a good mood is contagious and can spread from one person to another.

Not convinced? What do you do when a baby smiles at you? Smile back, of course. So the mood of the people providing a service is also contagious. Psychologists label it as emotional contagion[7]—the phenomenon of having one person's emotions and related behaviour directly trigger similar emotions and behaviours in other people.

Bottom-line: Moods of people can also go viral and therefore the mood of people providing a service is also contagious, that is, if an employee is happy, then, other

---

6   James McIntosh, 'What is serotonin and what does it do?' *Medical News Today*, 2 February 2018, https://www.medicalnewstoday.com/kc/serotonin-facts-232248

7   Sigal Barsade, 'Faster than a Speeding Text: 'Emotional Contagion' at Work', *Psychology Today*, 15 October 2014, https://www.psychologytoday.com/us/blog/the-science-work/201410/faster-speeding-text-emotional-contagion-work

colleagues will feel likewise, as will customers interacting with them.

Other research studies also allude to the importance of inducing laughter in a company. Findings by the world's best universities, which include MIT, Wharton and London Business School, conclude that 'laughter relieves stress and boredom, boosts engagement and well-being, and spurs not only creativity and collaboration but also analytic precision and productivity'.[8]

No wonder companies wish to create a conducive ambience to facilitate laughter and happiness. In some companies, employees are even encouraged to bring pets to office. It is believed that the presence of a pet increases laughter and happiness, which enhances productivity and creativity.

You may be wondering if Googlers misuse these perks. Of course, there would be a few black sheep who do. But the vast majority do not. This is because Google selects people who display 'Googliness': a mash-up of passion and drive.[9] Hence, the majority of Googlers only take advantage of the perks to improve their performance.

Bringing Nature Inside the Office

Another strategy increasingly used by companies to boost productivity is to bring nature inside the office. They create

[8] Betty-Ann Heggie, 'The Benefits of Laughing in the Office,' *Think with Google*, 16 November 2018, https://hbr.org/2018/11/the-benefits-of-laughing-in-the-office

[9] Holly Finn, 'Missions That Matter,' July 2011, *Think with Google*, https://www.thinkwithgoogle.com/intl/en-gb/marketing-resources/micro-moments/missions-that-matter/

gardens and mini forests and simulate waterfalls inside the office area; office designs also ensure that ample sunlight streams into the workplace. Prime locations in offices are now the bright, sunny areas, rather than the spaces in the corner. The combination of sunlight, greenery and the sound of nature inside the office de-stresses employees and improves their productivity.

Steve Jobs conceptualized Apple Park, the corporate headquarters of Apple, to look less like an office and more like a park. Around 80 per cent of the nearly 200-acre site is devoted to parkland. Apple Park consists of green spaces with thousands of trees.[10] As employees move around the campus, they can build relationships[11] with rest of the team, share ideas with each other, and explore opportunities to collaborate among themselves.[12] Walking through the campus can also improve cognition and creative thinking of the employees.[13]

Do Indian Companies Follow This Strategy?

You might be thinking that such over-the-top and seemingly wasteful strategies can only be pursued by the big purse Silicon

---

[10] Jennifer Magnolfi, 'Why Apple's New HQ is Nothing Like the Rest of Silicon Valley,' *Harvard Business Review*, 26 June 2017, https://hbr.org/2017/06/why-apples-new-hq-is-nothing-like-the-rest-of-silicon-valley

[11] Lynda Gratton and Tamara J. Erickson, 'Eight Ways to Build Collaborative Teams,' *Harvard Business Review*, November 2007, https://hbr.org/2007/11/eight-ways-to-build-collaborative-teams

[12] Carol Kinsey Goman, '8 Tips for Collaborative Leadership, *Forbes*, 13 February 2014, https://www.forbes.com/sites/carolkinseygoman/2014/02/13/8-tips-for-collaborative-leadership/#151d9a805fd9

[13] Florence Williams, 'The Nature Fix: Why Nature Makes Us Happier, Healthier, and More Creative,' (W. W. Norton & Company, Reprint edition, 2018)

Valley companies. Not true. This thinking is also finding favour among Indian companies.

Flipkart's head office has a cricket pitch, a basketball court, a mini-golf course, gyms and many other facilities.[14] HCL has introduced Genie, a concierge service for its employees. It helps employees with their routine duties, such as fixing up appointments, paying utility bills and running errands. It also doubles up as an entertainment guide.

Dealing with Uncivil Behaviour

But all efforts at transforming a workplace into a fun place will come to naught if companies do not keep a check on the display of uncivil behaviour indulged in by a handful of people working in the organization.

Here is a partial list of what constitutes uncivil behaviour:

- Inconsiderate words, deeds or actions
- Interrupting a conversation
- Withholding information
- Clique formation
- Harassment, bullying and physical violence

If left unchecked, this contagious disease will gradually spread its tentacles across the company and cause irreparable harm. A poll of 800 managers and employees in seventeen industries who have been at the receiving end of workplace incivility

---

[14] 'Check out photos of Flipkart's cool new headquarters', *GQ*, 11 April 2018, https://www.gqindia.com/content/flipkart-new-headquarters-bangalore.

concluded that nearly everybody who is affected responds in a negative way[15]:

- 80 per cent lost work time worrying about the incident
- 66 per cent said their performance declined
- 78 per cent said their commitment to the organization went down
- 25 per cent admitted to taking their frustration out on customers

In extreme cases, employees may decide to leave the company. Rampant prevalence of uncivil behaviour has tangible costs associated with it.

'A 2007 study published in the Academy of Management Journal reports workplace incivility costs companies $14,000 per employee because of lost productivity and work-time. This study wasn't referring to outright bullying or a threatening behaviour. Instead, the researchers examined incivility-less of misconduct, like making derogatory remarks, ignoring co-workers and a condescending tone. Perhaps, even a more disturbing study published in 2016 in the Journal of Applied Psychology reports that incivility is contagious. Just as kindness can be 'paid forward,' so can rude behaviour,' observes Amy Morin. [16]

---

[15] Christine Porath and Christine Pearson, 'The price of incivility,' *Harvard Business Review*, January–February 2013, https://hbr.org/2013/01/the-price-of-incivility

[16] Amy Morin, 'Your Rude C0-Workers Cost Your Company an Extra $14000 Per Employee, According to Science,' *Inc.*, 12 December 2016, https://www.inc.com/amy-morin/your-rude-co-workers-cost-your-company-an-extra-14000-per-employee-according-to.html

What should you do when you witness uncivil behaviour? Mete out the same treatment that you would when you spot a cockroach: just snuff it out, then and there. Do not show leniency. If you ignore it, it will spread and give birth to a stressful and toxic work environment.

Psychological Impacts on Employees

According to the Harvard School of Public Health, a stressful work environment causes psychological changes in employees due to the secretion of two hormones:

- Cortisol: Its presence causes stress.
- Adrenaline: Its presence puts people in a 'fight' or 'flight' mode.

The presence of these two hormones among employees causes stress and makes them display hostile behaviour. Presence of cortisol depletes serotonin, the well-being and happiness chemical. This leads to fall in productivity, a decrease in team spirit, detachment from work and increases stress.

On the other hand, if there is laughter and fun at a workplace then it can potentially lead to release of three types of hormones:

- Oxytocin: This leads to building of trust and increases generosity among people.
- Dopamine: This is a pleasure hormone which increases motivation.
- Endorphins: This triggers positive emotions and diminishes painful feelings.

These three hormones foster improved team-work , increased productivity, better collaboration, enhanced creativity and more.[17]

Bottom line: ensure that stress in the work environment is reduced if not eliminated; laughter and fun should abound at the workplace.

Benefits of a Fun Workplace

Here's a partial list of the benefits of pursuing this strategy of keeping employees happy:

- Lower attrition rate
- Emotional bond between the company and its employees, making it difficult for competition to poach them
- Improved attendance
- Increase in productivity
- Improved communication and collaboration among employees
- Increase in creativity and lateral thinking among the employees
- Boosts creativity
- Builds trust
- Employees reciprocate the company's gesture by taking care of its interests
- Happy employees become advocates of the company

---

[17] Sara Rimer, 'The biology of emotion—and what it may teach us about helping people to live longer,' Harvard T.H. Chan, School of Public Health, 2011, https://www.hsph.harvard.edu/news/magazine/happiness-stress-heart-disease/

- Happy employees make customers happy, and they in turn become brand advocates
- The cost of hiring (replacement) is high; this expense is reduced
- The danger of departing talent leaving with intellectual property of the company also gets mitigated
- Improved job satisfaction
- Criticism of the company and a negative buzz created by departing employees gets reduced

Transforming workplaces into fun places has so many advantages that companies now look at it as a strategy and are reaping the benefits. So, go ahead and embrace this strategy and your company too will experience the benefits that accrue from it.

What Can You Do to Create a Fun Workplace?

Here are some steps you can take to transform your workplace into a fun place:

- Bring nature inside the workplace
  - Design your office so that there is ample natural light.
  - Put potted plants throughout the office.
  - Install an artificial waterfall if space permits. The sound of falling water will de-stress your employees.

- Office ambience
  - Liberally use primary colours: red, blue, green and yellow. This will make your office appear more playful.

o   Allocate space for collaborative work.
o   Have common areas to encourage 'inadvertent collusion'.
o   Serve healthy meals or snacks.
o   Encourage employees to decorate their work area in a manner that makes them feel happy.

- Celebration
  o   Celebrate birthdays and work anniversaries of your employees.
  o   Celebrate their success.

- Encourage employees to express gratitude.
- Whenever you notice uncivil behaviour, stamp it out then and there.
- Be a role model for your team to emulate.

COMMUNICATION

RULE 10

Low-Cost, High-Impact Communication

The single biggest problem in communication is the illusion that it has taken place.

—George Bernard Shaw

How do you create awareness, interest and desire among your customers regarding your brands? Advertise on television, in the press, on the radio, in the cinema or the ambient media? But are customers noticing your advertisements or running away from them? Surely you would want them to see your advertisements. For that, you will have to understand the factors that cause customers to ignore and even avoid your communication.

Here's an example. You have a fine product and you want to advertise it so that the whole world, metaphorically speaking, knows about it. So you create a TVC extolling the benefits of your brand and decide to advertise it during one of the world's biggest carnivals: the FIFA World Cup. In consultation with your media buying agency, you decide that your TVC will appear during the World Cup final whenever a penalty kick is to be taken. Your reasoning seems logical: the penalty kick in a final match would have viewers glued to the TV screen, and if your TVC is telecast at that moment, it is bound to be seen by a spellbound global audience.

Bingo! Such an opportunity presents itself. As Cristiano Ronaldo prepares to take the penalty kick, your TVC is telecast.

Now, step into the viewers' shoes. How would they feel? Absolutely frustrated and disappointed. Many would curse your brand because it has intruded into their lives unsolicited and uninvited at a critical point in the match. They want to see Ronaldo take the penalty kick, not your TVC. Many among the audience may even take a vow never to touch your brand. This is just one of the reasons why customers shun ads.

Why Are People Turning Away from Advertisements?

- **One-way communication:** Today's customers want to engage with the brand. In fact, they wish to co-create brand communications. But most current ads are a one-way communication, with no opportunities for customer engagement.
- **One-dimensional communication:** Most ads extol only the positive features of their brands. None give a balanced view. Today's customers reject these biased, one-dimensional communications in favour of balanced communications which assist them in making an informed decision.
- **Mass communication:** Unfortunately, most ads are designed as mass communication meant for mass audiences. Today's customers desire customized/

personalized communication that are tailor-made for them as individuals.

- **Not optimized for context and location:** Most communications are not context-based or location-specific. For example, a potential customer may be sitting at home in the evening, waiting to have dinner. At this moment, he sees a TVC for shaving foam. For the viewer this TVC will be a blind spot and will do precious little for aiding product recall because it does not fit into the context of what the customer is thinking at the moment.
- **Putting the company's interests before the customers':** A majority of ads do this. Customers vehemently reject this approach. They desire that their interests should be kept ahead of the company's myopic motive of merely selling their products.

Strategies for Attractive Communication

As a custodian of business, what strategies should you deploy to ensure your customers seek out your communications? Simple: reduce or eliminate the traits listed above and replace them with the following:

1. Put customers' interests before your company's.
2. Strive to provide a two-way platform for the customer to engage and co-create the brand communication along with you.
3. Strive to customize and personalize the communication for every customer.

4. Make your communication context-based and
   location-relevant for the customer.

If you adhere to these guidelines, chances are customers will
seek out your communications.

Let me share examples of successful communications that
follow these principles.

- **Native content:** Let's take an automobile company.
  Just before the onset of the monsoon, it wants
  owners to get their cars serviced. Merely advertising
  in newspapers may not be effective. It creates a
  newsletter titled '5 Ways to Drive Safely During
  the Monsoon' and puts it out in the public domain.
  The link is likely to interest customers because the
  title indicates that the information will be useful to
  them. Result: they click on the link which displays
  the promised content. The fifth point in the list urges
  them to get their cars serviced, with a link directing
  them to the automobile company's web page offering
  the servicing facility.
  This approach works because the content is
  contextually relevant: car owners are already primed
  for safety during monsoon, so more people are likely
  to sign up for getting their cars serviced. Now is the
  automobile company running after customers, or is it
  the other way around?
- **Offers and schemes:** Let's stay with the same
  automobile company. Nine months have elapsed
  since the monsoon offer. Now it wants car owners to
  get their vehicles serviced again. Merely advertising

is likely to get a poor response. A communication is released 'offering' free servicing to the first 5000 car owners who register; everyone else who registers will also get a 25 per cent discount. The response is likely to be good, because it is in the interest of the car owners to register for servicing. Again, instead of the company running after customers, it is the customers who will run after it.

- **Rewards and loyalty programmes:** Many companies have a formalized strategy for enrolling customers in their reward and loyalty programmes. These programmes are designed to secure customer loyalty for their business. My Starbucks Rewards offers a free drink, while Encircle the loyalty card of Titan offers a discount during the birthday month. February tends to be a good month for me.

  These rewards and loyalty programmes are similar to golden handcuffs. Take my case. I was enrolled into the Jet Airways loyalty programme, Jet Privilege. Each time I flew Jet Airways, I earned free miles. This was a reward I got for displaying loyalty. The more I flew with Jet Airways, the more points I accrued, which I redeemed for free tickets and a host of gifts. On many occasions, even though Jet Airways' itinerary was not convenient or the ticket was expensive, I still insisted on flying it, due to the allure of free points.

- **Dynamic advertising:** This seeks to serve customized advertisements to a customer. It is gaining in popularity because the online marketplace is cluttered with advertisements. Therefore, for an ad to be noticed by potential customers, it needs to make a connection. That can happen if it is customized to be in sync with the current interest of the customers.

Dynamic advertising extracts information through web scrapping, aka web harvesting, about the likes and dislikes of individuals from multiple sources including social media. It serves communication that matches things that are 'liked' and refrains from serving things that are 'disliked'. Customers seek out these communications because they are about things that are of interest to them. Not surprisingly, dynamic advertising garners better returns on investments.

Writes Sunil Gupta in *Harvard Business Review*:

'Red Roof Inn realized that flight cancellations in the US left 90,000 passengers stranded every day. Imagine the emotions of a typical passenger at that moment—it perhaps starts with frustration and anger at the airlines and then turns toward the need to find a place to stay overnight. Recognizing this, the marketing team of Red Roof Inn developed a way to track flight delays in real time that triggered targeted ads for Red Roof Inn near airports. Ads that said, "Stranded at the airport? Come stay with us!" captured the consumers at the right moment, which resulted in 60 per cent increase in bookings compared to other campaigns.'[1]

---

[1]   Sunil Gupta, In Mobile Advertising Timing Is Everything, Harvard Business Review, 4 November 2015, https://hbr.org/2015/11/in-mobile-advertising-timing-is-everything

- **Geo-fencing:** Geo-fencing uses global positioning system (GPS) or radio frequency identification (RFID) to set up a virtual boundary. Anytime a device enters that zone, it triggers a text message or email to the device. I experienced it when, unknown to me, I entered the geo-fenced location and got a message on my smartphone: 'Please look to your side and you will notice us. We make delicious, natural, homemade ice creams. Step in to enjoy it. To make it taste even sweeter, we have a special 25 per cent discount waiting for you.'

  The communication was location-specific and it was customized for me.

- **Deliver a pleasurable experience to invoke reciprocation and likeability principles:** Take Charmin. It markets toilet paper. Research shows that people, especially women, face a problem during a day out because of inadequate restrooms in several areas—including Times Square, New York. So, Charmin had set up mobile restrooms in Times Square that anyone could use.[2] And when they used the restroom, they also ended up using a Charmin product. Because the product was good, they ended up not only having a positive perception about it, but from a behavioural science perspective, it also invoked feelings of reciprocation and likeability among them. The next

---

[2] 'Charmin Restroom Opens in Times Square this Holiday Season', Business Wire, 6 December 2017, https://www.businesswire.com/news/home/20171206005330/en/Charmin%C2%AE-Restrooms-Opens-Times-Square-Holiday-Season

time they buy toilet paper, you know which brand they would seek out.

- **Earn goodwill:** In the US, Uber and Lyft offered free rides on Election Day to make it convenient for voters to go out and exercise their right.[3] Let's shift our discussion to India. Do brands here also display altruism? In 2017, rains brought Mumbai to a standstill, leaving a multitude of Mumbaikars stranded. Ola stepped in and offered a free shuttle service across the worse affected areas of Mumbai; Uber too introduced Uber Pool Rides and suspended the draconian surge pricing; FB activated its Safety Check feature, which allowed FB users to mark themselves safe.[4]

  Why do companies consciously engage in these altruistic activities? When someone helps you in your moment of crisis, don't you feel a sense of gratitude towards them? Will you not speak well about this good samaritan to your family and in your social circle? You will have similar feelings towards businesses that extend help in moments of need. Next time you have to take a ride, who are you likely to give business to? Ola and Uber or a third party? My guess is to the company that helped you. Your family and your social circle too are likely to follow suit. Acting

---

[3] 'Uber, Lyft giving free rides to voters on election day', CBS New York, 8 October 2018, https://newyork.cbslocal.com/2018/10/08/uber-lyft-giving-free-rides-to-voters-on-election-day/

[4] 'Mumbai rains: Uber, Ola offer free rides, Facebook activates Safety Check', BGR, 30 August 2017, https://www.bgr.in/news/mumbai-rains-uber-ola-offer-free-rides-facebook-activates-safety-check/.

on humanitarian grounds helps businesses create brand advocates and reap the benefits that it provides. A word of caution: if a business offers humanitarian service with the dishonest intent of converting people into their brand advocates, such a move boomerangs when they are exposed. Before you deploy this strategy, pose a question to yourself: what is my intention of doing this 'altruistic' activity? If the intention is honourable—that is, to help people—go ahead and do it. If it is to win brownie points, shun it.

- **Support the local community:** Customers prefer businesses that support the local community. For example, you have to buy a bottle of jam and you have two brands vying for your wallet; both of them have a similar brand appeal and are priced at par. But of the two, only one bottle has a sticker that reads 'Low Food Miles'[5]: an indication that the distance the food has travelled before reaching consumers is low, therefore, it would have been produced locally. Chances are you will opt for the bottle with the 'Low Food Miles' sticker; by buying it, you too are showing support for the community where you reside and also voting for a cleaner and fresher product.

- **The power of sampling:** A leading FMCG company in India, dealing in packaged atta (wheat flour), took a decision to source high-quality wheat directly from farmers in Madhya Pradesh. Good quality wheat would result in good quality atta. They were confident

---

5   Food Miles, Wikipedia, https://en.wikipedia.org/wiki/Food_miles

that once the product entered a household, it would do its own marketing and compel customers to purchase it. To generate trials, the company decided to distribute free samples to potential households. Their surmise was correct. Upon trial, people saw its superior quality and began purchasing it.

What if your product is expensive and is not amenable to being distributed as a 'free' sample? For example, furniture. IKEA is the world leader in selling ready-to-assemble furniture. They 'sampled' their furniture by placing their sofas at a Paris metro station.[6] The aim was to showcase the durability of their sofas while also getting people to experience it. If people experience the sofa and like the experience, then when they are in the market to buy one, they are more likely to opt for IKEA.

- **Generate goodwill:** In Mumbai, an appliance company had launched a range of products, including microwave ovens, targeted at working women. They needed to create awareness and goodwill among them. The appliance company noticed that a large number of working women in Mumbai faced a problem commuting every day between V.T. (now Chhatrapati Shivaji Maharaj Terminus) and Nariman Point, the central business district in Mumbai. They decided to run a bus service only for women. In the morning, it would ferry them from CSMT station to

---

[6] Jesus Diaz, 'Ikea turned a Paris subway station into a showroom, and it's glorious, Fast Company', 10 May 2019, *Fast Company,* https://www. fastcompany.com/90346968/ikea-turned-a-paris-subway-station-into-a-showroom-and-its-glorious

Nariman Point; in the evening back to CSMT. This service was complimentary. The interior of the bus had advertising messages educating the commuters about the company, its range of appliances and the utilities offered.

What purpose did this free bus service serve? Countless working women found the complimentary bus service very advantageous. Subliminally, they would have felt a sense of gratitude and goodwill towards the appliance company.

- **Head-to-head comparison:** At every opportunity educate your customers about your products so that if there is ever a head-to-head comparison among brands, your brand would win.

A luxury carmaker followed this strategy. It started collecting data about people staying in the neighbourhood. Based on this survey, it sent out invites to people with the potential of buying its product, inviting them to visit their experience centre. The invitees were lavishly entertained. A salesperson took the stage and explained to the guests the various features and benefits of their vehicle and how it scores over others.

You must be wondering—if the guests were not in the market for a luxury car, why is this company squandering its scarce marketing resources? A company cannot predict when people will enter the market to buy a luxury vehicle. But it can proactively educate them so that whenever they do, they would choose that brand.

- **Be a good corporate citizen:** Customers like to support businesses that are actively engaged in initiatives for the betterment of the community and the planet.

  Diageo, the global alcoholic beverages company, runs a national campaign 'Diageo Road to Safety'[7], with the strategic intent of preventing drunken driving, underage drinking and excessive drinking. Maruti Suzuki, India's number one car company, runs the Maruti Driving School[8] that teaches drivers how to drive safely. This strategy generates goodwill towards the company and its products among customers.

- **Replace a negative image with a positive one:** Many companies inadvertently acquire an image that is detrimental to their future business prospects. They desire to purge it.

  McDonald's is facing a unique challenge. Mothers care about what their children eat and are concerned about obesity. The fast food served at McDonald's is widely perceived to cause obesity. If this perception continues unabated, the future of McDonald's would be in peril. Realizing this, McDonald's is offering a healthy menu. It wishes to create awareness about this among mothers. If McDonald's were to make claims about the healthiness of their food, the believability would be low. However, if real mothers said the same thing, believability would be far higher.

---

7 Diageo, Partnering for Road Safety-India, 25 May 2018, https://www.diageo.com/en/in-society/case-studies/partnering-for-road-safety-india/

8 Maruti Suzuki, Maruti Driving School, 1 August 2019, https://www.marutisuzuki.com/more-from-us/maruti-driving-school

Acting on this idea, a few years ago, McDonald's launched Moms' Quality Correspondents. Mothers from real families, representing different backgrounds, visited McDonald's kitchens and shared their opinions about the quality of foods and ingredients served by the chain.[9] When real mothers say good things about McDonald's, other mothers are more likely to believe them. This might set in motion the change in perception that the company desires.

- **Be associated with a cause:** There is inherent goodness in all of us and we desire to do something for the benefit of others, but often we do not know how to go about doing it. Companies have taken this pain point of customers on board and are taking steps to resolve it.

  P&G is a leading FMCG company, including in its portfolio Ariel, Gillette, Head & Shoulders, Whisper and more. Research conducted by it indicated that education is a cause that many of its consumers are very concerned about, so much so that they are exploring ways in which to support it. In 2005, P&G launched the Shiksha Campaign to enable consumers to contribute towards the cause of educating underprivileged children through the simple act of buying Gillette, Ariel, Whisper, or Pampers products. Each time these products are

9   John Schmeltzer, 'McDonald's seeking moms' approval', Chicago Tribune, 11 June 2007, https://www.chicagotribune.com/news/ct-xpm-2007-06-11-0706090068-story.html

bought, a part of the money goes towards providing education to underprivileged children.[10]

When a business gets associated with a cause, customers see a golden opportunity of routing their assistance through the company. They buy the company's products, confident that the company will donate part of the sales proceeds to the cause. Therefore, by helping the company, customers are indirectly helping the cause.

Other Innovative Ways to Engage Customers

Till the 1970s, customers were exposed to fewer advertisements in a day. This figure has shot up to upwards of thousands per day.[11] Today's customers are petrified of unsolicited advertisements, therefore, they change the channel when they see one. What should you do to ensure that your communication is noticed by customers?

- **Integrating the brand message into the content:** One solution for this seemingly intractable problem is to integrate the brand message into the content in a manner that when people attempt to skip the brand message, they also skip the content. Let me share innovative ways to achieve this goal.

---

[10] P&G, Social Responsibility Programs in India, P&G, https://www.pg.com/en_IN/sustainability/social_responsibility/social-responsibility-programs-in-india.shtml

[11] Oksana Tunikova, How Many Ads Do You Actually See Daily?, StopAdBlog, 6 April 2018, https://stopad.io/blog/ads-seen-daily

o **Brand placement:** When I was working at a beverage company, we tied up with a music channel to place our brand and the advertising message on the backdrop against which artists were to perform. When viewers were viewing the performance our brand and the message was always in the background. You too should intelligently place your brand message so that it is present in every frame.

o **Brand integration:** The product can seamlessly be integrated with the content so that it does not appear to be an advertisement. In the film *Koi . . . Mil Gaya*, Bournvita was seamlessly integrated into the content.

o **Branded entertainment:** Content can be created with the intent of entertaining the audience and not advertising the brand. Coke Studio is an excellent example of this. It is an enjoyable programme, in the course of which, the brand also gets serious advertising mileage.

• **Guerrilla marketing:** The essence of guerrilla marketing is that it produces a high decibel buzz with minimal expenditure. Take the case of a pencil cell battery company, which hired the back panel of a bus and put up a visual showing two batteries. When people saw this advertisement, it appeared to them that the bus was powered by two simple pencil cells. This campaign always brought a smile to people's faces.

Intel's tagline for the longest time has been 'Intel Inside'. So when they signed a shirt sponsorship deal with FC Barcelona, the logo of Intel was placed on the inside of the shirts. Although the placement reduced visibility, its execution being in sync with its tagline made it a unique and quirky idea, which enthralled people. The entire deal made waves on the playing field as much as outside it.

- **Use of 'alternative media':** Traditional companies built brands leveraging five traditional media vehicles:
  o Television
  o Press
  o Radio
  o Cinema
  o Ambient media

But these advertising vehicles are starting to lose steam because of the following reasons:
  o **Overflow:** These traditional forms of media tend to be non-discriminating. As a result, an advertising broadcast ends up reaching people for whom it is not intended. For example, take women's hygiene products: the advertisements for these products when broadcast on TV also end up reaching men.
  o **Expensive:** Relatively large budgets are required to run marketing campaigns on these vehicles.
  o **Longer time:** Advertisements are broadcast over mass media and therefore, the opportunity of seeing the ad every time it is broadcast is low. Hence it has to be run over an extended period of time before a customer sees it enough number of times to be influenced by it.

o **No guarantees:** Media owners demand payment for merely broadcasting the advertising. They do not give any assurance that the communication will be seen by the target group or of its efficacy.

No wonder, in recent times, TV and print growth is dwarfed by the growth of digital media. 'Growth in screens and internet broadband penetration, coupled with falling data rates led to more consumption of content and increased time spent on digital media. Advertisers shifted expenditure to the digital medium.'[12]

Media & Entertainment (INR in Bilions)									
Segment	2016		2017		2018		2020 (Est)		CAGR
	INR Billion	%	INR Billion	%	INR Billion	%	INR Billion	%	%
TV	594	45	660	45	734	44	862	42	9.8
Print	296	23	303	21	331	20	369	18	5.7
Digital Media	92	7	119	8	151	9	224	11	24.9
Others	327	25	391	26	444	27	577	29	
Total	1309	100	1473	100	1660	100	2032	100	11.6

Realizing the drawbacks of traditional advertising vehicles, new age companies such as Apple, Tesla, Google, Facebook and Twitter have adopted alternate media vehicles to create awareness, interest, desire and action.

These vehicles are:

• **Buzz, or word of mouth:** When customers and other stakeholders speak about brands and businesses, the believability is much higher. In addition, they do not need to be paid in order to spread the good word.

---

[12] 'Re-imagining India's M&E sector', FICCI and EY, March 2018, http://ficci.in/spdocument/22949/FICCI-study1-frames-2018.pdf

- **Public relations (PR):** When the media, which includes TV, newspaper and e-papers, gives brands and businesses organic coverage via news reports or reviews, the believability is higher. Genuine PR requires no money to be spent.
- **Events:** This offers an excellent opportunity to engage customers in a deeper way. For example, an alcoholic beverages company can ensure that its brand is sampled.
- **Digital media:** Content created can be digitally distributed and viewed on screens. Digital media is of three types:
  - o **Own media:** They help businesses build long-term relationships with their customers. These are completely under the company's control and, therefore, suffer from a drawback: their believability or credibility is low. The following vehicles are part of this type of media: company website, mobile site, app, blog posts and social media channels like LinkedIn, Facebook, Twitter, YouTube and Instagram.
  - o **Paid media:** Companies pay a third party to display advertisements on their channel. Also, paid influencers are roped in to promote the company's agenda. This channel may suffer from a lack of credibility, clutter and lower response rates.
  - o **Earned media:** It is akin to online buzz (word of mouth). Here people review, rate, share experiences, share content, mentions, reposts and reviews, and offer recommendations for others to

refer to before taking decisions. This channel has high credibility and costs very little.

Let me share how Steve Jobs used alternate media to build Apple.

On 9 January 2007, Steve Jobs organized an event to announce the iPhone. He introduced it to the world saying, 'Apple is going to reinvent the phone.' This announcement got people talking about it (**buzz**); press people present at the launch event gave it wide coverage in the media (**PR**); and it set the digital world on fire.

As you would have observed, Apple leaned on alternative advertising vehicles to create interest, awareness, desire and action about iPhone among customers. And they did this with minimum expense.

B2B Communication Strategies

For B2B businesses, a variety of options are available for engaging with their customers. Here is a partial list of initiatives that deliver excellent dividends:

- Organize company-sponsored events to educate customers about your company, its products and achievements.
- Carry out these digital initiatives:
  o Organize webinars and webcasts.
  o Create video content.
  o Publish white papers, e-newsletters and blogs.
  o Post articles on the company website.
  o Present your company's story as a case study.

- Create employee advocates and motivate them to put out posts.
- Social media: Draw out a robust social media strategy. LinkedIn, Twitter, YouTube will be most effective for B2B. The challenge for you is to consistently create engaging content and publish it once a day or at least once a week.
- Seek out experts to advocate for the company.
- Get recognized as an industry leader.
- Ensure your people are invited as keynote speakers so that they can project your company as a leader.
- Advertise in industry journals and magazines.

What Should Be Your Strategy for Effective Communications?

Here are a few more recommendations for you:

- Reduce dependence on traditional media vehicles and embrace alternative media vehicles.
- While crafting your communications, keep customers' interests at the centre of every decision. This should always take precedence over the company's interests.
- Create a balanced communication so that customers can rely on it to make decisions.
- Your communications should offer an opportunity to customers to engage with the brand.
- Educate your customers about your products.
- Ensure that the 'voice of customers' is brought inside the company, is heard and acted upon.

- Offer opportunities to customers to engage in a dialogue with you.
- Lean on technology to create and deliver customized, contextualized and location-specific communications. This would ensure that these resonate with them.
- Get your customers to opt to receive communications from you.
- Get your customers to talk about your brands and the press to write about it.
- Explore opportunities for brand integration, branded entertainment and guerrilla marketing opportunities.
- Generate sampling opportunities for your brand.
- Generate goodwill about your product among your target group by putting reciprocal and likability principles into play.
- Have a robust digital strategy. Go in for own, paid and earned media.
- Associate your business with a cause, be it social or environmental. Choose a cause that is in sync with your business.

If you execute these strategies faithfully you will discover that customers, instead of running away from your communications, will actively seek them out and, most importantly, act upon them. Mission accomplished!

A question must be worrying you: can the results of these initiatives be measured? Not directly, but they would be reflected in:

- Increased revenues

- Improvement in:
  o Customer retention and loyalty
  o Lead generation and quality of leads

- Increased traffic to company website and greater time spent on the site
- Increased engagement of customers with the company

If you can draw up a detailed plan and execute it, it will create awareness, interest, desire and action among your customers. The acid test of this plan is whether customers reach out to you. It is seen that when customers discover and reach out to companies, the conversion rates (to those companies) are higher.

SUPPLY CHAIN

SUPPLY CHAIN

RULE 11

Embrace Omnichannel

I want to shop anytime, anywhere, on a device of my choice; even when I am on the move.

—Voice of a Customer

Till recently, buyers were influenced by brand advertisements or word of mouth, which motivated them to visit bricks-and-mortar stores to buy a particular brand. In the store, the salespeople further educated the buyer about the brand. Based on inputs from these myriad sources, the buyer purchased the brand. The buyer pursued a perfectly linear way of buying.

Let us come to the millennials: those born between 1982 and 2000. They are on the way to becoming the most dominant group. They are armed with smart devices and addicted to social networking sites. Perennially connected to the internet, they are ever-ready to share their experiences with the rest of their tribe, who in turn take decisions based on their feedback. And when it comes to shopping, the millennials—also called the 'screen generation' given their proclivity for always staring at the screen—want to shop at a time and on a device convenient to them.

Non-Linear Shopping

This is how a millennial shops: She is on Facebook and sees a post from her friend about a wonderful jacket by Zara. She likes what she sees and starts researching on the Zara jacket online. As a first step, she checks out the reviews and ratings. Here, too, she reads positive reviews of the jacket.

At the next opportunity, when she is passing a Zara store, she steps in to check out how the jacket looks and feels on her. She likes herself in the jacket. While still at the store, she takes out her smartphone and goes to a price comparison site. She discovers that the jacket is available at a promotional price on Amazon. She places an order on Amazon from her smartphone and the payment is debited to her credit card, the details of which are with the site. The jacket is delivered to her home in two days. This buying process is non-linear.

Traditional retail stores are troubled by this non-linear buying behaviour. They contemptuously refer to such buyers as 'fit lifters' because they check out the fit and size in a bricks-and-mortar store, but order online, reducing the physical store to merely a showroom.

Non-linear shoppers start their shopping journey on one channel and continue across multiple channels, till the shopping process is completed. This process is also called the omnichannel shopping.

A partial list of the multiple channels through which they can navigate is given below:

- **Own channel:** Websites, mobile sites, blog sites, digital catalogues, email, social media channels (Facebook, LinkedIn, Twitter, Instagram, Pinterest,

YouTube); webinars, podcasts, sharing customers stories, engagement with advocates and detractors and bricks-and-mortar stores

- **Earned channel:** Mentions, shares, reposts, user-generated content, advocacy, reviews and ratings
- **Paid channel:**
  o Online advertising: Display and banner advertisements, paid influencers, brand ambassadors and affiliates, paid content promotions, native content, social media advertisements
  o Offline advertisements: On TV, press, radio, outdoor and ambient media
- **Other digital channel:** Price comparison sites, e-payment gateways
- **Offline channel:** Presence in non-owned bricks-and-mortar stores, buzz (word of mouth), referrals, PR, events, co-branding and more

The multiple channels through which a customer can undertake her journey can be looked at as multiple lanes on an expressway. Consider yourself: you want to travel from Point A to Point B using an expressway. You may start your journey in one lane and, depending on the traffic and other conditions, seamlessly move across lanes till you reach your destination. That is what the technology-savvy customers of today desire. Armed with a smart device and eternally connected to the internet, they want to seamlessly navigate through multiple channels, depending on their mood, device and other factors.

Many businesses have turned a blind eye to this change in shopping behaviour. This, of course, does not change reality.

Ignoring this change is detrimental to the long-term health of their business.

Businesses that wish to remain relevant have taken serious note of this tectonic shift in shoppers' behaviour and are adapting their business models to offer an omnichannel shopping experience. To achieve this, they need to integrate multiple channels through which a shopper comes in touch with a business so that regardless of which channel the shopping journey commences from, it can smoothly be completed on any other channel, in a manner that it delivers a pleasurable customer experience.

A word of caution: omnichannel does not mean a mere presence on different channels: that is just a starting point. The soul of omnichannel is to ensure that shoppers can seamlessly navigate between channels and have a memorable customer experience.

Is Omnichannel for Real?

I can sense a question niggling you: is omnichannel shopping for real or is it a question of crying wolf?

A survey referenced by Harvard Business Review[1] indicates that:

- 73 per cent of the shoppers had used omnichannels while shopping.
- 7 per cent shopped exclusively on online channels.

---

[1]   Emma Sopadjieva, Utpal M. Dholakia, and Bert Benjamin, 'A Study of 46,000 Shoppers Shoes That Omnichannel Retailing Works', *Harvard Business Review*, 3 January 2017, https://hbr.org/2017/01/a-study-of-46000-shoppers-shows-that-omnichannel-retailing-works

- 20 per cent shopped exclusively in bricks-and-mortar stores.

Omnichannel shopping is here to stay!

This reads good—really good—but what about India? Has omnichannel made inroads here too?

PwC's Annual Global Retail Survey 2016[2], which tracked consumer behaviour across retail channels, concluded that 'Indian consumers today are moving with pace towards the omnichannel way of life.' The report adds that a new breed of hyperconnected Indian shoppers expect businesses to provide an omnichannel shopping experience. The report has also busted a myth about Indian shoppers: that they are highly price-conscious. Indians shoppers are shopping online primarily because of convenience (65 per cent) and then price (31 per cent).

Online to Offline

A dominant trend in omnichannel shopping that seems to be gaining currency is seamless amalgamation of the online and offline experiences, giving birth to O2O: Online-to-Offline channel. Shoppers can order online and get the product/s delivered offline and vice versa.

In India, Zomato and Swiggy are poster children of the O2O model: orders can be placed online at our favourite

---

[2] PwC, 'Indian consumers moving towards omnichannel way of shopping: PwC', PWC India, 10 February 2016, https://www.pwc.in/press-releases/2016/indian-consumers-moving-towards-omnichannel-way-of-shopping-pwc.html

restaurant and Zomato or Swiggy will collect and deliver it offline to us.

The strategy is not restricted to retail. Many industries, including hospitality, are adopting this strategy.

For business, I had to travel to Bengaluru and was put up at the Marriott. On arriving at the hotel, I was greeted at the reception and escorted to my room. Once I was comfortable, the representative pulled out an iPad and proceeded to check me in. Look closely: the process of checking in started offline, but it was completed online. The entire process was seamless and delivered a flawless experience to me as a customer.

Even pharmaceutical industries seem to have been captivated by this strategy. A startup has launched an app that offers the user a virtual consultancy with a doctor, whose prescription goes straight to a pharmacy, which then delivers the prescribed medicines directly to the home of the patient.

Bricks and Clicks

E-retailers have realized that neither pure e-commerce nor pure bricks-and-mortar stores will deliver a desirable customer experience. The answer lies in adopting a hybrid version: the bricks and clicks (B&C) model. In the B&C model, a business has its presence both in the online space and the traditional physical store. The best thing is that the two channels are complementary: the weakness of one channel is the strength of the other. They have a symbiotic relationship.

Online & Offline: Symbiotic Relationship		
Statements	Online	Offline (Brick & Mortar)
Convenience of Shopping	High	Low
Personalised Recommendation	High	Medium to low
Range on Offer	High	Medium to low
Carry Purchase Back Home	Delivered at Destination	Carry Yourself
Stand in Queue to Make Payment	Low	Medium to High
Investment in Real Estate	Low	High
Touch & Feel the Merchandise Prior to Purchase	Low	High
Wrong Merchandise Dispatched	Medium	Low
Damaged During Delivery	High	Low
Discrepancy Between What is Stated & Received	Possible	Low

Realizing the power of the B&C model, in 2017 Amazon acquired a stake of 5 per cent in Shoppers Stop, a leading departmental store chain in India.[3] Many of the benefits listed in the table above are likely to accrue to Amazon. In addition, it will give Amazon shoppers the showroom experience, so that they can touch, feel and try fashion brands and accessories before buying. In addition, shoppers can place an order online and can collect it offline at a designated Shoppers Stop outlet. In short, the offline store can also work as a mini fulfilment centre.

Studies indicate that when shoppers come to collect their merchandise from the store, they tend to make additional purchases, setting the cash register ringing—once again.

Let us shift our focus to Lenskart.com, which aims to offer quality eyewear products at affordable prices. For that it has set up its own manufacturing facility and eliminated retailers; it is servicing customers directly. Lenskart has gained traction in the marketplace by adopting the 'hybrid plus' retailing

3 ETMarkets.com, Shoppers Stop to sell 5% stakes to Amazon unit; shares surge 20%, 25 September 2017, https://economictimes.indiatimes.com/markets/stocks/news/shoppers-stop-to-sell-5-stake-to-amazon-unit-shares-surge-20/articleshow/60822441.cms

model. It has a strong online presence plus physical stores, and it also offers home visits by opticians (at a nominal rate) for conducting eye tests.[4]

Moving on to D'Mart, arguably India's most valuable retailer. It has also embraced the omnichannel strategy and put into play the O2O model. D'Mart Ready stores occupy 'tiny' real estate across Mumbai. These stores act as mini fulfilment centres: shoppers can order online and collect their order from a D'Mart Ready store. D'Mart can also deliver it home—but for a fee.[5]

Becoming Omnichannel-Compliant

Omnichannel retailing is here for good and businesses need to embrace it to remain competitive. Here is a partial list of aspects that can help businesses become omnichannel-compliant:

- **Omnipresence:** Be sure to be present across multiple channels and ensure that a shopper can seamlessly navigate across various channels and still have an enjoyable customer experience.
- **Convenience:** Enable the shopper to shop anytime, anywhere, even on the move. They should have the convenience of starting their shopping journey on a channel of their choice and the flexibility of completing the shopping journey on another channel of their choice. Your job is to make the navigation

---

[4]   Lenskart site: https://www.lenskart.com/HTO/
[5]   DMart Ready, https://www.dmart.in/dmart-faq

across channels seamless and still deliver an amazing customer experience. This can get shoppers to display loyalty towards your business; the converse is also true.

- **Wide range of merchandise:** Shoppers feel good when they know they can find what they are looking for. So, plan to stock a large range of merchandise, but offer recommendations in chunks of not more than seven options at a time. Otherwise decision fatigue will grip the shoppers and they may postpone the buying decision.

- **Personalized recommendations:** Shoppers prefer personalized recommendations. Therefore, they are not averse to businesses collecting and warehousing their personal data based on which they can make personalized recommendations. However, as a responsible business, you must have a robust security system in place to ensure personal data is not compromised, especially that relating to credit cards. A breach can severely dent the trust between you and the shoppers.

- **Sporadic deals:** To whip up a shopper's shopping appetite, make offer deals. How much and how often to offer is exclusively your prerogative. A word of caution: do not give deals all the time as the shoppers can become addicted to it and their loyalty will be towards deals and not your business. If that happens, the moment you withdraw deals, shoppers will cease to buy from you.

- **Presence on reviews and ratings sites:** Many shoppers commence their shopping journey by checking out sites with reviews and ratings. Make sure these are easily accessible from your site. Also, encourage shoppers to put out reviews, ratings and experiences they have had with your brands/business. If the reviews are negative and the ratings are adverse, take them as feedback and work towards removing the problem that caused the adverse feedback at the root itself, so that over time, your offerings become progressively better and better.

- **Ease and speed of shopping:** This feature is of paramount importance to shoppers, because many are cash-rich and time-poor. They abhor waiting. You should embellish your sites with processes that ensure ease of shopping. Amazon's 1-Click Ordering, for instance, is easy, convenient and saves a great deal of time.

- **No delivery charges:** Shoppers dislike paying delivery charges, because when they go to a bricks-and-mortar store and make purchases, they do not pay themselves to carry the merchandise back home. Therefore, when shoppers are charged separately for delivery, it ignites a feeling of resentment. It would be advisable not to charge the shoppers separately for delivery.

- **Ease of return:** Shoppers like to do business with those who provide ease of return. This situation can arise due to a plethora of reasons:
  o Product received did not match the description given on the site.
  o It arrived in a damaged condition.
  o The wrong item was delivered.
  o It took an inordinately long time to arrive.

As you would notice, most of the reasons for returns are due to mistakes on the part of the seller.

Take my case: I had ordered a book on Amazon. On receiving it, I realized that the wrong title was shipped. To return it, I had to state my reason from a menu offered to me and was asked about the time the return pickup could be arranged. At the appointed time, a person came and collected the book, and the value of the book was credited back to my credit card account.

Bottom line: put in extra effort to ensure that wrong orders are not delivered: it is frustrating. But should this happen, the return process should be seamless and painless.

- **Tracking order:** Shoppers feel good when they can track the order right from the time it is processed to the date of dispatch and the likely date and time of delivery. Make sure that you provide this facility: it will remove suspense and make the shopping experience more pleasurable.

- **Shopping experience:** A business should always strive to deliver a pleasurable shopping experience that earns the loyalty of the shoppers. The converse is also true: if a shopper has a couple of bad experiences, she may move on. Make sure to reduce the risk of a bad experience.

- **Use of technology:** Artificial Intelligence-assisted voice search—Amazon's Alexa, Google's Home, Apple's Siri—is taking root. You too should enable this facility in omnichannel shopping and lean on other technology to deliver a fantastic customer experience.

- **Touch point:** Every touch points a shopper comes in contact with should be designed to deliver an amazing customer experience.

Offline/Physical/B&M store: To deliver shopping experience, keep these in mind:

o **Sales consultants, not salespersons:** Shoppers desire to be educated and informed about the products and services. Invest resources in educating your sales team so that they transform into authentic sales consultants whose aim is to assist shoppers make up their minds about what is best for them.

o **Education and sampling:** Physical stores can offer facilities to try/sample products prior to purchase: this significantly reduces post-purchase dissatisfaction. Make sure these facilities are exceptional.

o **Personal finance:** Brick-and-mortar stores can offer tailor-made finance packages to meet an individual shopper's requirements. See how you can make it easier, financially, for customers to make purchases.

What Should Be Your Omnichannel Strategy?

Some of you may own a store or a small business, and you may be wondering whether you can apply these concepts. Here's how:

- Build a mobile app with the following features:
  o It should greet the customer by name, be configured to meet each customer's requirements, and aim to gratify them as quickly as possible.

- o It should be easy to navigate and discover the merchandise on the app.
- o It should be easy to place orders.
- o It should incorporate the facility of tracking orders.
- o Payments should be easy to make and secure.
- o It could incorporate 1-Click ordering.

- Occasionally, offer deals.
- Make recommendations based on past purchases of each of your customers.
- Announce a reward/loyalty programme.
- Do not charge separately for delivery.
- Adapt to your customer's pace. For example, let the customers set up the time for delivery and abide by it.
- Educate customers about your products.
- Offer as wide a range as possible.
- Offer a 'wish list' feature. Once a customer puts an item on the wish list, go the extra mile to source and deliver it at no extra cost.
- Offer unconditional guarantees and ease of return. This will de-risk buying decisions and customers are likely to buy liberally, assured by the fact that if they need to return it will not be a challenge.
- Let your customer know that you are grateful to them for giving you their business.
- When customers visit your stores, you and your salespeople should:
  - o Greet them enthusiastically, with a smile

    o   Act like sales consultants. The job is not to sell but to advise customers on what is best for them and in their interests.

Is the Future Omnichannel?

Will the dominance of omnichannel retailing continue in the near term? According to Jack Ma, a new format—New Retail—will make its presence felt: 'The boundary between offline and online commerce disappears as we focus on fulfilling the personalized needs of every customer . . . this will be made possible through the integration of online, offline, logistics and data across a single value chain.'[6]

To give you a preview of what New Retail will look like, permit me to introduce Alibaba's Hema supermarket chain. Hema carries curated items ranging from fresh food to grocery sourced from across the world and—hold your breath—has fine dining located inside the store.

In the store, a shopper needs only a smartphone to navigate: every product in the store has a product tag that can be scanned to get a comprehensive idea about it. Shoppers can scan barcodes, make payments via the Hema app, and set up a delivery time for the merchandise to be delivered at home.

Shoppers can also order online via the Hema mobile app and get things delivered at home for free, in merely thirty minutes, provided the delivery address is within a three-mile radius.

---

6   Jon Bird, 'Alibaba's "New Retail" revolution: What Is It, And Is It Genuinely New?', *Forbes*, 18 November 2018, https://www.forbes.com/sites/jonbird1/2018/11/18/alibabas-new-retail-revolution-what-is-it-and-is-it-genuinely-new/#7782c52c6ad1

Through the app, Hema is able to record an individual shopper's behaviour and, based on that, offer personalized recommendations and promotional offers. Shoppers can also order food which is freshly cooked and served in food booths located inside Hema.

Amazon is not far behind: it has launched the Amazon Go retail store with the objective of creating a shopping experience with no lines and no checkouts.

What Should Be Your Strategic Response?

You will have to accept the fact that buyer behaviour is changing. Omnichannel retailing is here to stay, and it offers a new angle for gaining a competitive advantage. So board this train—before it is too late.

BUSINESS STRATEGY

RULE 12

Better before Cheaper: Revenue before Cost

The bitterness of poor quality remains long after the
sweetness of low price is forgotten.

—Unknown

Do you want me to share the simple rules that can guide you
in making decisions to build a valuable business?

'Go on,' I hear you say.

First, let me give the floor to the experts.

In an article in the *Harvard Business Review*, Michael E.
Rayon and Mumtaz Ahmed laid out the three rules for achieving
enduring success in business, based on their study of 25,453
companies over forty-four years. These rules are applicable
across industries because they are distilled from analysing a
wide cross-section of companies from diverse backgrounds.

All these companies consistently pursued seemingly
elementary rules.[1]

---

[1] Michael E. Raynor and Mumtaz Ahmed, 'Three Rules for Making a
Company Truly Great', *Harvard Business Review*, April 2013, https://
hbr.org/2013/04/three-rules-for-making-a-company-truly-great

Rule 1: **Better before cheaper.** In other words, compete on differentiation instead of price.

Rule 2: **Revenue before cost.** That is, prioritize increasing revenue over reducing cost.

Rule 3: **There are no other rules.** So to change anything, you must follow rules 1 and 2.

If there are only two actionable rules, then why have a third rule? We remember things better when they are in chunks of three. Take the English language. There is: good, better, best; or grey, greyer, greyest. By having a Rule of Three, our recall ability of the rules is likely to be better!

The rules neither dictate specific behaviour nor are they general strategies. They are fundamental concepts, using which, companies attain greatness over many years.

Has any company of recent vintage that we love and admire embraced these rules?

Singapore Airlines

Take Singapore Airlines (SIA) which is renowned for its legendary service. It has embraced all the three rules.[2]

Let me share some of the practices adopted by SIA.

- **New aircraft for better flying experience:** SIA invests heavily in buying new aircraft. In 2009, the age of

---

[2] Loizos Heracleous and Jochen Wirtz, 'The Globe: Singapore Airlines' Balancing Act', *Harvard Business Review*, July–August 2010, https://hbr.org/2010/07/the-globe-singapore-airlines-balancing-act

its fleet was an average of seventy-four months old, compared with the industry average of 160 months. New aircraft, which come with state-of-the-art technology and fittings, provide customers with a better on-board experience compared with other airlines that fly older and dated aircraft.

- **Training and retraining its employees:** SIA invests heavily in training and, more importantly, retraining its employees. Fresh recruits are provided with four months of intensive training, which is twice as long as the industry average of eight weeks. This comprehensive training ensures that the staff is able to deliver a memorable experience to the guests each time they come in touch with the airline.
- **More staff on each flight:** A normal SIA flight has more cabin crew compared with other airlines. This ensures better quality service.

These practices would indicate that SIA is guided by the Rule of Three while taking business decisions. No wonder it has earned international acclaim for its service.

Has SIA financially benefitted by embracing these rules? Indeed, by pursuing the Rule of Three, SIA has strengthened its financial parameters. Here's how:

- **Depreciation of aircraft:** Depreciation of new aircraft results in tax shield, which lowers its taxable income and increases its cash profit correspondingly. Moreover, SIA depreciates these new aircraft over fifteen years, not twenty-five years as is the industry practice, thus lowering its taxable income further.

- **Lower-priced aircraft:** Remember, SIA invests heavily in buying new aircraft and hence places regular 'large orders' for airplanes. It pays for these acquisitions in cash; therefore, it is able to negotiate a better deal from the aircraft manufacturer, which results in cost savings.
- **Repair and maintenance cost:** Since its aircrafts are new, the repair and maintenance bills for 2008 were 4 per cent of the revenue, which is lower compared with other airlines, where such expenditure ranges from 4.8 per cent to 5.9 per cent. The lower repair and maintenance costs translate into tangible benefits in the form of fattening of the bottom line.
- **More time in the air:** Because the aircrafts are new, they spend more time in the air: thirteen hours, as against the industry average of 11.3 hours. Remember, an airline makes money when the planes are in the air and not when they are parked on the ground.
- **Fuel cost:** Fuel is a major cost component for an airline. Since SIA's planes are new, they consume less fuel per air miles flown, compared with competitors' planes, which are of an older make and hence guzzle more fuel. Lower fuel consumption means more margins which, in turn, results in a healthier bottom line.
- **On-time departures and arrivals:** Since the planes are new, a majority of flights take off and land on time. There are few disruptions in schedule—a trait that is valued by frequent flyers who go out of their way to offer their business to SIA.

- **Better guest experience on board:** New aircraft, on-time departure and arrival, few deviations from schedule, better trained airhostesses, more staff per flight—all these act in unison to deliver a memorable and unforgettable experience to each of the guests on board. The next time they have to fly, they naturally choose to give their business to SIA, which results in the airline having a healthy top line and an equally robust bottom line.

Park Avenue Deodorant

During the course of my career, I too have intuitively followed the Rule of Three and have reaped rich dividends.

As I have mentioned, I used to work with J.K. Helene Curtis, a Raymond Group company dealing in personal care products for men. These products were marketed under the brand name Park Avenue. I was entrusted with the responsibility of growing the business.

As a first step towards reviving the company's growth, I wanted to get rid of the non-moving stock lying in our godown. This would free up space in the godown, as well as get us some salvage value, no matter how meagre, which could be deployed in our business.

I requested our production head to give me the complete list of non-moving stock lying in our godown, mentioning the quantity and 'age' of stock (number of days the stock was lying in the godown). Shortly, he sauntered into my room and handed over a computer printout containing the information. I glanced at the list and noticed that a significant quantity of deodorants had not moved for a substantial amount of time.

'Why have the deos not moved?' I asked him.

'*Mujhe kya pata—mera kam hai deo banana. Aur isi baat ke liye toh aap ko rakha hai?*' (I don't know the reason—my job is to get deo manufactured. And isn't that the reason they have appointed you?) He replied cheekily, with a small smile on his face.

I felt insulted: how dare he speak to me so impertinently? But I quickly realized that he was bluntly telling me the truth.

Moreover, I reasoned, if I lose my cool, word would get out in the office that I am prone to getting provoked. Many people would deliberately provoke me and then sit back and enjoy themselves.

I smiled feebly and requested him to get me a sample of the deodorants from the non-moving stock lying in our godown.

In no time the production head was back with a sample deodorant. 'How did you get it so fast?' I asked him. Our godown was at least ten kilometres away.

'Sir, I had anticipated this request and therefore I had brought a single sample of all non-moving and slow-moving stock,' he replied, with a smile hovering on his face.

It was then that I realized that he had a naturally smiling demeanour and he was not smirking at me.

Taking the deodorant from him, I sprayed it on my wrist to sample it. It had a mildly medicated fragrance that did not appeal to me and I spontaneously burst out, 'Even I would not buy it!'

Hearing this, he let out an uproarious laugh, which I guess he must have been controlling for a long time. I too gave him company, but weakly.

Once he regained control of himself, he asked simply, 'Why?' My spontaneous reaction must have intrigued him.

'The fragrance doesn't appeal to me. It has a harsh smell,' I murmured more to myself than to him.

He left the room and I began to ponder as to why the deodorant had such a harsh fragrance. There had to be a reason and I needed to discover it. Only then would I be able to come up with a strategy to gain traction in the market.

As I started researching, the puzzle started to unravel. In cold countries, like Russia, where the temperature hovers near zero, people avoid bathing. This leads to body odour which is very pungent. To mask it, a deodorant is liberally sprayed on the body. Therefore, the deodorant has to have harsh fragrance—after all, diamond cuts diamond!

But in India, we have a bath daily. In fact, as a child, my mother would not let me have breakfast until I had had a bath. What was true for our household was playing out in many households across the country. Therefore, body odour caused due to the absence of bathing would not be a pain point of customers here. But India presented a great opportunity for the deodorant category if it could be suitably modified to suit local requirements.

I looked at the stats: 65 per cent of Indians were below the age of twenty-five. Young people of opposite sexes wish to socialize and get closer to each other. Unpleasant body odour, caused due to sweating, can rear its ugly head at these moments of truth and drive a couple apart.

I knew a large pay-off awaited me if I could mask this foul smell and replace it with a mood-enhancing fragrance! If I succeeded, young men would give my brands a thumbs up.

I started collecting insights into how to resolve this challenge—from my past as well as the experiences of other companies. Let me take you back to the 1990s, when I was based in Calcutta during my stint with United Spirits (now Diageo), an alcoholic beverage company.

Wanting to set the alcoholic beverage market on fire—after all, I was young then—I decided to pose a very basic question to alcoholic beverage connoisseurs: what will make you drink 'more'?

Many tipplers candidly confessed that they enjoyed their drink, but when they got back home at night and got closer to their wives, their alcohol breath would invariably lead to a harsh exchange of words.

'Remove the smell and we will enjoy ourselves more', they shared with us.

Based on this insight, we launched a vodka with a promise: 'Now you can get a little closer . . . it leaves no trace.' We left the tag line incomplete by design.

The vodka got traction in the market place. I was elated.

Also, I had noticed that Colgate had captured a sizable share of the toothpaste market in India, based on the promise that it fights tooth decay and bad breath.

So this was the insight I armed myself with as I focused on the deodorant market: a disagreeable odour is indeed a problem with Indian customers and by eliminating it, I could win customers' votes. The market leader in this category was Unilever's Axe. It promised its customers the magical power of the 'Axe effect': women would be drawn in hordes to any man who had sprayed himself liberally with the Axe deodorant. The promise of the brand seemed irresistible.

However, whenever I enquired about the Axe effect with young men who used the deodorant, they would respond with an embarrassed smile, which tacitly implied that this effect had eluded them. Therefore, I concluded, it was a case of a tall promise that had not delivered to the ground.

I was now getting closer to formulating a winning strategy. I had to mask the 'offensive' odour of the deodorant and replace it with a fine fragrance, so that when young men wore it, went out on a date and the couple came closer, the fragrance would enhance the mood and encourage them to stay close.

My strategy was to change the rules of the industry: by selling deodorant not as deodorant but as fragrance.

To achieve this goal, I had to source superior quality fragrance that would deliver on the promise. I posed simple, open-ended questions to myself:

Q: Where is the world's finest fragrance available?
Answer: France.

Q: Where in France is it available?
Answer: Nice.

Q: Which company in Nice has a formidable reputation for fine fragrance?
Answer: Robertet, a family-owned fragrance house that has been in the business since 1856.

We decided to get in touch with them. As luck would have it, they had an office in India. Based on our insight into

Indian customers, we shared our requirements with them for a fragrance. It should be 'sweet, strong and long lasting'.

Hearing our brief, Team Robertet made an observation: fragrance should be mild, because it is worn for oneself; if the fragrance is strong and a customer wore it to office, then it may offend co-workers.

'That's the point,' I said. 'In India, fragrance is worn for others to notice. Therefore, if people wear a fragrance and no one notices it, then it is a waste of money.'

Robertet understood our requirement and submitted some samples. We made our choice from the samples submitted and substituted the harsh medicated fragrance with double the dosage of fine French fragrance.

In 2003, we launched a 'New' Park Avenue deodorant with the promise of 'Come closer'.

The Park Avenue deodorant witnessed galloping sales and so did the category. In 2002, the deodorant category was estimated to be less than Rs 100 crore. In 2017, it was estimated to be in the region of approximately Rs 3380 crore[3], a jump of over thirty-times. Today, there are over 100 brands of deodorants in the market and 'fragrance' has become an industry standard.

Let's look at the Park Avenue deodorant through the lens of the Rule of Three:

---

[3] Varuni Khosla, 'How Indian family businesses are taking on MNCs in deodorant industry', *Economic Times*, 9 October 2018, https://economictimes.indiatimes.com/industry/cons-products/fashion-/-cosmetics-/-jewellery/how-the-family-businesses-are-taking-on-the-mncs-in-the-deodorant-industry/articleshow/66127812.cms

- Rule 1: We strived to make it a better product by embellishing it with two-times the French fragrance which was imported from a leading fragrance house in France.
- Rule 2: We ignored the ballooning input costs. We regarded it not as a cost we were loading into the product, but as creating value that customers would love and in return for which give us repeat business. And they did.
- Rule 3: There is no other rule!

Indian Premier League (IPL)

Are there any more examples of Indian brands that successfully followed the Rule of Three and won our hearts and minds?

IPL, the Twenty20 cricket league, launched in 2008, followed the rules and has won our hearts and mind.

- **Rule 1: No expense was spared to create a world class product.**
  - It signed-up the best players from around the world
  - It acquired state of the art technology to enhance viewing pleasure. Every match is covered with multiple cameras to cover every move of the players and many a time of spectators, too. These cameras are of varied types - ultra-motion cameras, Spidercam—they enhance viewing experience.
  - Attractive animated graphics add value to the live broadcast

o   High octane entertainment is staged inside the stadium by having cheer girls gyrating to lively music.

- **Rule 2: It has multiple revenue sources.**
  o   Broadcasting right, including digital media rights
  o   Gate revenue
  o   Sponsorship deals of team, jersey and more
  o   Sale of Merchandising
  o   Prize money
  o   Brand value of IPL and of each team is heading northwards.

- **Rule 3: There is no other rule.**

In just over a decade, IPL has become a multi-billion dollar brand. In 2018, Duff & Phelps had valued it at $6.3 billion (from $5.3 billion in 2017).[4]

The Rule of 3 does work in India and deliver results.

Other Companies

There are many more companies across the world, and in India, who adhere to the Rule of Three.

Let us start with Apple. Since its inception it has been an ardent follower of this rule. It believes in making its product so good that it enriches the lives of its customers.

---

[4]   Gaurav Laghate, 'No stopping brand IPL; valuations soars to $6.3 bn, *Economic Times*, 8 August 2018, https://economictimes.indiatimes.com/news/sports/no-stopping-brand-ipl-valuation-soars-to-6-3-bn/articleshow/65319443.cms

Here is my analysis of the iPhone.

- Rule 1: Apple has invested considerably to make the iPhone a great product. It is powered by smart and powerful chips, and has excellent screen resolution, a long battery life and a high-definition camera. With all these features, Apple delivers an incredible performance and experience to its customers.
- Rule 2: Apple does not look upon the above features as adding costs, but as adding value which customers find useful and are happy to pay for. iPhones are premium-priced, which boosts the revenue of the company.
- Rule 3: There is no other rule.

Apple follows the Rule of Three for every product in its repertoire. Therefore, each product delivers an amazing experience to customers. This has given birth to the Apple 'ecosystem'. Once a customer buys one Apple product, he or she inadvertently enters the Apple ecosystem and starts buying other products of the company because every Apple product is smartly integrated with each other. For example, I can ask Siri to play a song from Apple Music on my iPhone. This leads Apple to have captive customers who tend to buy products from the Apple stable, giving it a distinct advantage. For example, iPhone users buy iPads followed by Apple Watches and so on.

By following the Rule of Three, Apple has ensured that it is ranked among the world's most valuable company.

Let us examine Xiaomi, a smart phone from China. It is valued at $54 billion.[5] Did it also follow the Rule of Three to build a formidable reputation?

Let me share my insights into the strategy[6] followed by Xiaomi in its formative years.

- **Sold online:** In the initial years its preferred channel of sale was online. By choosing this distribution strategy, Xiaomi eliminated distributors and retailers from the distribution chain. Result: they saved the margin money that would have lined the pockets of channel partners.

- **Manufactured limited quantity:** This strategy put the behavioural science principle of the 'scarcity effect' into play: anything that is scarce becomes more valuable. People would wait to get their hands on it.

- **Relied on social media and buzz (word of mouth) to create awareness:** Xiaomi leaned on social media— owned and earned to create awareness. It believed that its product's superior quality would delight its users who in turn will spread the good word about the brand. It saved substantial money by eschewing traditional advertising.

---

[5]   Yuan Yang and Louise Lucas, 'Xiaomi valued at $54bn as IPO falls short of original goal', *Financial Times*, 29 June 2018, https://www.ft.com/content/12daa23e-7b59-11e8-bc55-50daf11b720d

[6]   Steven Millward, 'These 10 ingredients are the recipe to Xiaomi's secret sauce', Tech in Asia, November 2014, https://www.techinasia.com/10-strategies-xiaomi-secret-sauce;

John Dudovskiy, 'Xiaomi Marketing Strategy: hunger marketing in action', Research Methodology, 28 May 2018, https://research-methodology.net/xiaomi-marketing-strategy-hunger-marketing-in-action/

- **Reduced inventory-carrying cost:** Since limited quantity was produced, it incurred lower inventory carrying costs compared to other smartphone brands.
- **Spent less money on liquidating non-moving stock:** Since limited quantity was produced, hence the stock invariably got sold out. Therefore, little money was spent to liquidate non-moving stock.
- **Premium Product and attractive price do the marketing:** Xiaomi believed that premium product offered at attractive price would do its own marketing.

Here is my analysis: Xiaomi saved money by perusing the strategies mentioned above. It did not allow the saving to fatten its bottom line but ploughed it into making Xiaomi a better product and offering it at an extremely attractive price. Xiaomi counted upon the product and price to do marketing on its behalf.

This strategy pursued by the company turned out to be effective. It can be referred to as 'Hunger Marketing'. Xiaomi sought to create 'hunger' for its product by simultaneously focusing on two aspects: create shortage and aspiration among people to own it. Shortage was created by manufacturing in limited quantity and many a time putting it on 'Flash Sales'; aspiration was created by offering premium quality at attractive prices. This combination made it irresistible for people!

This strategy earned Xiaomi a place in the Guinness World Records of having sold 2.1 million phones within twenty-four hours.[7]

---

[7]   PTI, 'Xiaomi sells 2.11 million in 12 hours; sets Guinness record', *Economic Times*, 10 April 2015, https://economictimes.indiatimes.com/news/international/business/xiaomi-sells-2-11-million-phones-in-12-hours-sets-guinness-record/articleshow/46866312.cms?from=mdr

Xiaomi entered the Indian market in 2014, drawing upon the strategy discussed above. It partnered with Flipkart and put its phone on flash sales: discount or promotion offered for a short period of time. When sales opened, large number of buyers logged on to Flipkart website, trying to be the lucky ones to get their hands on it. The high volume of traffic caused the site to crash[8] in minutes but it made Xiaomi a recognizable brand name in India.

Did Xiaomi conform to the Rule of Three?

- Rule 1: It invested its resources in making Xiaomi a better product.
- Rule 2: Xiaomi did not focus on the cost. Due to its attractive price, it attracted people in droves and sold in large numbers (earned revenue). Yes, the margin per phone was thin, but it made money on the turnover.
- Rule 3: There is no other rule!

What's in It for You?

If you wish to build a business where customers offer their business to you, adopt the Rule of Three and watch your business grow from strength to strength.

---

[8] Danish Khan, 'Flipkart crashes temporarily after Xiaomi's Mi 3 goes on sale', *Economic Times*, 23 July 2014, https://economictimes.indiatimes. com/tech/internet/flipkart-crashes-temporarily-after-xiaomis-mi-3- goes-on-sale/articleshow/38889525.cms

RULE 13

Pivot to Unlock Growth

If you are not embarrassed by the first version of your product, then you've launched too late.

—Reid Hoffman

Business history is littered with examples of the initial strategy of an enterprise invariably failing. Successful enterprises don't give up when their initial strategy proves ineffective. They pivot as many times as required, till they hit upon a successful strategy: either by chance, through superlative thinking or from a competitor's mistake or by sheer luck. Once the successful strategy is discovered, the enterprise drops anchor.

Implied in this approach is an axiom: it is unwise to put all resources—financial and non-financial—into the initial strategy. Enterprises should hold back sufficient resources for subsequent strategic pivots they might have to undertake along the way till the successful one is identified. An enterprise, therefore identifies and places a bet on the best initial strategy and invests sufficient resources to make it a success. But it also holds back enough resources in case the initial strategy does not work out and the enterprise has to pivot to arrive at another strategy.

Enterprises that ignore the pivot strategy could make mistakes at a great cost to themselves and their shareholders.

Are there examples of enterprises that have embraced the pivot strategy to lay the foundation for business success?

Wikipedia

Wikipedia[1] leads the list. It 'pivoted' its way to becoming the world's largest collaborative, free encyclopaedia. In March 2000, Jimmy Wales, the founder of Wikipedia, launched an online encyclopaedia and called it 'Nupedia'. As was the norm then, he assembled an advisory board of experts to mentor this project. They in turn developed an intensive acceptance and editing process that included multi-step peer review process to control the content of the articles.

After twelve months, merely twelve articles were written, despite many contributors evincing interest. The strategy of having experts to control and drive the project was clearly not working. Wales needed to pivot, and quickly.

In 2001, a second free online encyclopaedia was launched where anyone could contribute. It was called Wikipedia. It operated on the principles of software industry where a collaborative approach was followed. Work released at the earliest possible opportunity and refined subsequently. This process is called 'beta testing'. Leading software companies are in a state of perpetual beta: they are striving for continuous improvements. A leading proponent of this strategy is Google.

---

[1]   Wikipedia, https://en.wikipedia.org/wiki/Wikipedia

It releases its latest software version the moment it is 80 per cent ready. And then based on user feedback, it keeps improving the software, live.

Wikipedia too released the earliest possible version of an article, letting several people work simultaneously to rapidly refine it. The new pivot got traction and Wikipedia, as we know it, was born. Nupedia, which decided to remain rigid and not pivot, shut shop in 2003.

YouTube

If you are still not convinced, let me share how YouTube pivoted its way to becoming the world's no. 1 platform for uploading and viewing videos. But that was not the initial strategy with which it was launched in 2005. To begin with, it was intended to be an online dating site—as a way for people to upload videos of where they spokes about the partners of their dreams. Its tag line was 'Tune In, Hook Up'.[2]

This strategy did not find significant traction. And as it invariably happens, the serendipitous moment arrived unannounced for the founders.

During a live performance, Janet Jackson's wardrobe malfunctioned. Millions saw it live. But Jawed Karim[3], who was at the time working for PayPal, missed it. He wanted to

[2] Stuart Dredge, 'YouTube was meant to be video-dating website', *Guardian*, 16 March 2016, https://www.theguardian.com/technology/2016/mar/16/youtube-past-video-dating-website

[3] Hugh McIntyre, 'How Janet Jackson's Super Bowl Wardrobe Malfunction Helped Start YouTube', *Forbes*, 1 February 2015, https://www.forbes.com/sites/hughmcintyre/2015/02/01/how-janet-jacksons-super-bowl-wardrobe-malfunction-helped-start-youtube/#3013ba6a19ca

watch the video but was unable to find it. He, along with his friends Steve Chen and Chad Hurley, sniffed an opportunity for a 'platform' business model, where any video could be uploaded by anyone and could be viewed by anybody from any part of the globe. They quickly pivoted to embrace the new strategy. It found not just traction, but also attracted Google's attention, and the latter purchased it for $1.65 billion in 2006 in an all-stock deal. Today, the YouTube business is valued at $ 90 billion.[4]

Airbnb

Airbnb made its debut by offering 'staying solutions' centring on conferences/conventions. But business was slow, and the founders quickly realized that the target market they were focusing on was small. It was only when they pivoted to offer 'staying' solutions to travellers on a budget—who were looking for affordable accommodation along with local experience—that Airbnb struck gold. In 2018 it was valued at $ 31 billion.[5]

Twitter

The birth of Twitter can be, traced back to Odeo—a podcasting platform where people could discover and subscribe to

[4] '#44 Susan Wojcicki', *Forbes*, March 6, 2019, https://www.forbes.com/profile/susan-wojcicki/#38e5b243ae33

[5] Biz Carson, 'Old unicorn, new tricks: Airbnb has a sky high valuation. Here's its audacious plan to earn it', *Forbes*, 3 October 2018, https://www.forbes.com/sites/bizcarson/2018/10/03/old-unicorn-new-tricks-airbnb-has-a-sky-high-valuation-heres-its-audacious-plan-to-earn-it/#7553803d6fa3

podcasts.[6] But the launch of iTunes threw a spanner in their wheels. Facing the heat, founders Jack Dorsey, Evan Williams and Biz Stone came up with the idea of a microblogging site using 140 characters where people could broadcast themselves instantly. This pivoting energized the company and laid the foundation for its global success.[7]

Today, it has become a vehicle of choice for 'revolutionaries' to mobilize people for causes. Presidents have taken to this platform to broadcast official announcements. Most importantly, it amplifies voices of ordinary people and broadcasts them across the world. It has 126 million daily active users.[8]

Facebook

The seed of FB was sown by Mark Zuckerberg while he was still a student at Harvard.

- **Initial strategy:** In 2003, Zuckerberg launched FaceMash[9], which allowed visitors to the site to

---

6   Christian Wolan, 'The Real Story of Twitter', *Forbes*, 14 April 2011, https://www.forbes.com/sites/christianwolan/2011/04/14/the-real-story-of-twitter/#3493848366af

7   Ibid.

8   Hamza Shaban, 'Twitter reveals its daily active user numbers for the first time', *Washington Post*, 7 February 2019, https://www.washingtonpost.com/technology/2019/02/07/twitter-reveals-its-daily-active-user-numbers-first-time/

9   Andrew Greiner et al., 'Facebook at 15: How a College Experiment Changed the World', CNN Business, 1 February 2019, https://edition.cnn.com/interactive/2019/02/business/facebook-history-timeline/index.html

compare students and rate them. It met with an inglorious end.

- **Pivot:** In 2004, Zuckerberg pivoted to create a website that could connect students. It was initially accessible only to students of Harvard University. Gradually it opened to students of other Ivy League schools and then to the world. Today it has 1.2 billion daily active users.[10]

Instagram

Let me share an example of a company which Facebook bought for $1 billion—only because it pivoted. 28-year-old Kevin Systrom set up Burbn 'Inc.'. It enabled users to leave messages using their smart phones that could be seen by others visiting the same location. Over time the idea evolved but another idea caught Systrom's fancy—having a mobile app that would enable users to take photos, alter them visually and share them. The app was called Instagram.[11] Rest is history.

Apple

Hold your breath, the biggest of them all—Apple—too is pivoting. iPhone, which had powered Apple into becoming one of the world's most valuable company is showing signs of slowing down. In response to this challenge, Apple is pivoting from a product (read: iPhone) company into a product + service

---

[10] Ibid, previous page's number to be added here after typesetting

[11] Lizette Chapman, 'Pivoting' Pays Off for Tech Entrepreneurs, *Wall Street Journal*, 26 April 2012, https://www.wsj.com/articles/SB100014 24052702303592404577364171598999252

that is fuelled by app and entertainment sales as much as its products.[12]

Does the Pivot Strategy Apply to All?

Is the 'pivot' strategy the prerogative of the new age technology companies? Or are there examples of non-technology companies achieving stupendous success upon pivoting?

Starbucks opened for business in 1971, retailing coffee beans. In 1982 Howard Schultz joined the company and on a buying trip to Milan experienced the way coffee was consumed in Italy: coffee bars acted as a public meeting place.[13] He got the company to 'pivot' from a retail store selling coffee beans to selling it as an experience; the rest, as they say, is history.

Is the 'pivot' strategy of recent vintage? It has been in existence, it seems, from time immemorial.

Tiffany and Co. opened for business in 1837 in New York as a stationery and fancy goods store with a $1000 advance from Tiffany's father. In 1867 Tiffany first achieved international recognition for silver craftsmanship. Over time it gained reputation as the world's diamond authority. It was pivoting from selling stationery and fancy goods to jewellery

---

12 Tripp Mickle and Joe Flint, 'Apple Pushes Beyond iPhone With Launch of TV, Finance, Gaming, News Services', *Wall Street Journal*, 25 March 2019, https://www.wsj.com/articles/apple-to-launch-new-magazine-service-called-apple-news-plus-11553534113

13 Colin Marshall, 'The first Starbucks coffee shop, Seattle—a history of cities in 50 buildings, day 36', *Guardian*, 14 May 2015, https://www.theguardian.com/cities/2015/may/14/the-first-starbucks-coffee-shop-seattle-a-history-of-cities-in-50-buildings-day-36

that won Tiffany worldwide recognition as a trusted maker of gifts that will be treasured for a lifetime.[14]

Avon is yet another example of a company that achieved success upon 'pivoting'. In the nineteenth century, its founder David H. McConnell was a travelling book-salesperson who offered beauty products as a gift to facilitate the sale of books. Much to his consternation, he observed that the customers were more interested in the free perfume sample than the books those perfumes were supposed to sell. This insight made him pivot. McConnell formulated the company's first perfume himself and recruited a team comprising only women to sell it door to door, as he believed that they had an innate passion for the products and also loved to network with other women. This business model—direct sales, or selling directly to end customers, offered women the opportunity to be the CEO of their own businesses—continues till date.[15]

You may surmise that Avon stumbling upon a successful formula may be a flash in the pan. Take William Wrigley Jr take for instance. Mr Wrigley took up a job of a salesman selling soap and baking power. To increase sales, he offered chewing gum free with the product. Lo and behold, gum proved to be more popular than soap. Wrigley jettisoned his selling career and pivoted towards manufacturing chewing gum brands.[16] Today, Wrigley is among the most recognized brands.

[14] About Tiffany & Co., http://press.tiffany.com/ViewBackgrounder.aspx?backgrounderId=33

[15] Avon website: https://www.avon.co.in/avon-in/about-us/history.html

[16] Jason Nazar, '14 Famous Business Pivots', Forbes, 8 October 2013, https://www.forbes.com/sites/jasonnazar/2013/10/08/14-famous-business-pivots/#4b2cdc7c5797

Even Marlboro had to pivot before it achieved its current cult status as one of the world's most famous men's cigarette brands. When launched in 1924, it was targeted at women and positioned as 'Mild as May'.[17] The brand sales remained in the doldrums.

With little to show for itself even after two decades of existence, Philip Morris, the brand owner, decided to 'pivot' and relaunch the brand, this time 'for men' personified by rugged cowboys. This pivot in strategy gave Marlboro the winning edge and catapulted it among the leading brands of the world, a position it continues to enjoy even today. Marlboro, the brand, is now ranked no. 23 in the Forbes list of the world's most valuable brands (2019) and its brand value stood at $ 28.5 billion.[18]

Philip Morris has once again sensed the urgency to pivot. It knows that the cigarette industry is facing a hostile environment: governments are relentlessly increasing taxes on it to bring down the menace of smoking. Offices and many public places are declaring themselves smoke-free.[19] The woes of the cigarette industry seem unending.

Before water rises above its head, Philip Morris has decided to pivot towards a smoke-free future by replacing cigarettes with smoke-free products. Why are they proactively pivoting? Because if they don't, they might be the next Nokia.

---

[17] Wikipedia https://en.wikipedia.org/wiki/Marlboro_(cigarette)

[18] The World's Most Valuable Brands, 2019 Ranking, *Forbes*, https://www.forbes.com/powerful-brands/list/#tab:rank

[19] Designing a Smoke-free Future, https://www.pmi.com/who-we-are/designing-a-smoke-free-future

Pivoting to revitalize a business is not the prerogative of companies dealing in consumer products. Even engineering and heavy equipment companies pivot to stay relevant. Let us look at John Deere, a ninety-year-old heavy equipment MNC that enjoys world wide reputation and goodwill. It sells its products mostly to farmers and construction companies.

John Deere realized that merely selling tractors and farm equipment would make it an easy target for disruption. Therefore, it decided to pivot. From the 2000s, it started embedding sensors and software to its equipment to collect data. Since then it has collected a treasure trove of data which it has analysed to gain insights into various issues relating to farmers.[20]

It is now providing customized information on weather, and seed and fertilizer usage to farmers. In addition, it has built capabilities to proactively predict when maintenance is required, so that equipment downtime can be reduced, if not eliminated. By providing these additional services, John Deere pivoted from a farm equipment company to a farm management company. By proactively pivoting, it has secured its future.

Have Indian Companies Pivoted?

Scores of Indian companies have pivoted and reached commanding heights. Here's the story[21] of how an Indian outlier pivoted its way to a leadership position.

[20] Sunil Gupta, 'Driving Digital Strategy' (Harvard Business Review Press, 2018)
[21] Harish Bhat, 'Tanishq Sets the Gold Standard' (Portfolio Penguin, 2012); and Harish Bhat, 'Tatalog' (Portfolio Penguin, 2012)

The birth of Tanishq was accidental. The parent company, Titan, had made a mark as a leading watch brand, using many imported components in its watches. In 1991, India was faced with a severe foreign currency crisis. The government advised importers to earn foreign exchange to fund their imports. This made Titan scout for opportunities to earn foreign exchange through the export route.

In Europe, they noticed an interesting phenomenon. Stores selling jewellery also sold premium watches, because much like jewellery they were also worn as an accessory. Since Titan was already in the watch business, getting into jewellery seemed a logical extension.

- **Initial strategy:** Titan decided to manufacture jewellery to export to European countries with the intent of earning foreign exchange to fund the import of components required for making Titan watches. It built a factory and hired designers to design jewellery that would appeal to European or western sensibilities.

  Two events occurred that came as a bolt from the blue and sounded a near death knell for the fledgling jewellery business. The market for gold jewellery in Europe shrank: European women began to show a preference for inexpensive steel and costume jewellery instead of expensive gold jewellery. In 1991, the Indian government announced reforms due to which the Indian economy started to move at a faster clip. IT companies and other industries in the service sector built large export surpluses and the government freely permitted imports. Overnight, the necessity to earn foreign exchange evaporated. Titan found itself straddled with a manufacturing plant, workforce and no market to sell to.

- **Pivot 1:** To utilize the factory and employees, Titan decided to enter the Indian jewellery market under the brand name Tanishq. To differentiate itself and command a price premium it decided not to launch a gold jewellery range. It reasoned that customers were aware of the gold prices. They simply had to add making and wastage charges to arrive at the price of any gold jewellery. Therefore it would be difficult to charge a price premium. Moreover, gold jewellery designs were made by a common pool of *karigars* and therefore designs were copied fast.

Based on this insight a decision was taken to launch a studded jewellery range: gems and diamonds studded into gold. Customers were not sufficiently educated about prices of gems and diamonds and therefore cannot arrive at the price of studded jewellery. This offered an opportunity to charge a price premium.

But another problem reared its head. Since 22-carat gold is soft, gems and diamonds cannot be studded into it, while 18-carat gold allows it. It was decided to launch the studded jewellery range with 18-carat gold. However, customers gave it a tepid response. In India gold is looked upon as *stridhan* (woman's wealth) and associated with 22-carat gold. Gold of 18 carats did not make the cut because it was perceived to be less precious.

- **Pivot 2:** Realizing that it had misread the market, in 1999 Tanishq pivoted away from 18-carats and launched the 22-carat gold jewellery range in Indian designs. This range resonated with Indian women and they started patronizing the store.

The team came up with a stunning idea. It was decided that Tanishq stores would have a carat metre. This instrument can measure the purity or carat of gold within three minutes without damaging or destroying the gold jewellery. A marketing campaign was launched to inform women that many a time jewellery sold in India was of lower carats than promised. They were invited to visit Tanishq showrooms and get the purity of their jewellery checked, free of cost. They were also informed that Tanishq offered 100 per cent guarantee. After all, it was a Tata company.

Women turned up in large numbers to get the purity of their jewellery checked. Much to their horror, in many cases Tanishq's warning turned out to be true. The gold was of lower carats than what the family jeweller had promised.

Hell hath no fury like a women scorned—or cheated. Many decided to transfer their loyalty to Tanishq. Sales have been robust since Pivot 2.

When Should Companies Pivot?

That is a billion-dollar question. Let me share with you a partial list of responses:

- **Small market size:** When the original target market is small (Airbnb: conference stay), do not hesitate to pivot towards a larger market (Airbnb: budget traveller).

- **Shrinking market:** When the existing market (single-screen cinema hall) is on the wane and a new market with tremendous potential is opening up (multiplex).
- **Competition:** When the market is under assault from a 1000-pound gorilla (Apple: iTunes), do not hesitate to abandon it; search for new opportunities and anchor your business to it (Twitter: Microblogging site).
- **Market reality:** When you find that a product (Avon: perfume) designed to boost sales of your main product (Avon: book) is generating more interest, build your business around the product generating the larger interest.
- **Incorrect targeting:** When you realize that you have targeted a product at a wrong segment (Marlboro: cigarette for women), pivot to position it right (Marlboro: cigarette for macho men)
- **Shifting market:** The automobile market is shifting towards clean transportation. Therefore, major automobiles companies are pivoting to launch electric vehicles. Take movie halls. The market has shifted from single screen to multiplex. Many single-screen cinema halls are pivoting to multiplex.
- **Hostile environment:** When you realize that your current business is facing hostility from all sides (Philip Morris: cigarette), pivot towards a more welcoming environment (Philip Morris: creating a smoke-free future).

- **Incorrect business model:** When the existing business model does not get traction (Nupedia), get inspiration from successful companies outside your industry and intelligently adopt their business model to suit your requirements (Wikipedia).

- **Serving a bigger market:** When you sense that you can serve a bigger market (as Flipkart did when it pivoted to include fashion in its portfolio).

- **Presenting a product in a different way:** Try to add new dimensions to existing products. Take deodorants in India, which I presented as a perfume. Today, perfume has become an industry standard and the market has witnessed explosive growth.

- **New opportunities opening up:** The world is constantly changing so make the most of the opportunities that present themselves during these transitions. For example, the size of the print media market is shrinking. Today, news, stories, and entertainment are all consumed online and on-screen. Noticing this shift, media houses are pivoting and launching online editions.

- **Selling a product as an experience:** When you feel that there is greater potential in selling your product (Starbucks coffee beans and espresso maker) as an experience (Starbucks coffee chain).

- **Inaccurate identification of customer pain point:** When the pain point you thought would set the market on fire (Tune In, Hook Up) turns out to be a whimper and, in a serendipitous moment, you experience a pain point that you surmise is one for many other people— and you provide a solution (YouTube).

- *Your product becomes irrelevant:* For example, the rotary phone. With ever increasing acceptance of mobile phones, it is becoming increasingly irrelevant.

Is Pivoting Applicable to People?

Is pivoting the sole property of the business world? Or can we also apply to our lives?

M.S. Dhoni was the goalkeeper of his school football team. It is by pivoting to cricket that he earned his fortune, reputation and the moniker 'Captain Cool'.

I can hear some of you saying that MSD is an exception. What about 'normal' people like you and I? Can we also pivot and achieve greater success in our career?

Take my case. In the 1970s, when I was growing up, boys pursued a career in engineering, while girls went in for medicine. I too followed this trend, sat for the Joint Entrance Examination (JEE), and secured a seat at IIT Kanpur.

In IIT, it was compulsory to sign up for humanities and social science (HSS) courses, along with engineering ones. The thinking behind making HSS courses compulsory is to make us well-rounded engineers. I took courses in psychology, sociology and modern art. Courses in psychology introduced me to theories of motivation, consumer behaviour and more. I enjoyed these immensely.

Upon graduation, I joined an engineering company as a graduate trainee engineer and was posted in Jamshedpur. I had to work on the shop floor surrounded by machines. I did not like it a wee bit and began to realize that I did not want to spend the rest of my life working as an engineer. Since I had loved psychology courses, I intuitively surmised that I would make a good marketer: after all, marketing involved understanding customers and designing products to meet their needs. This motivated me to take the Common Admission Test (CAT) and, as luck would have it, I secured admission at IIM Calcutta and IIM Bangalore. I opted to join the latter.

Since graduation, I have had a satisfying career during which I launched a multitude of brands, catapulted select brands to leadership positions, challenged and changed well-entrenched rules of the Indian industry, and turned around businesses. Many of these brands have survived the test of time, and even today they serve the needs of millions of people daily. For me the pivot from engineering to management made all the difference in my career. I am happy I took the decision to pivot.

If you feel suffocated in what you are doing, try to understand what makes your heart beat faster. Then take a leap of faith and pivot in that direction. By the simple process of pivoting, you may discover your life's calling—as I discovered mine.

When Should You Pivot?

In a VUCA world, change is constant. To cope with change you will have to warm up to the idea of pivoting.

There will be a multitude of reasons which will make it imperative for you to pivot. Failure to do so means that you run a real risk of being rendered irrelevant and left behind to lick your wounds.

Here is a partial list of when to pivot, for your quick reference:

- Market dynamics may be undergoing changes.
- You may wish to serve a new or larger market.

- The current market may be shrinking.
- An 800-pound gorilla has entered your market.
- New opportunities may have opened up.
- Customers are moving their business away from you.
- You wish to try a new business model.
- You desire to present your existing product in a new and exciting manner.
- Your growth becomes anaemic.
- Regulations have changed and compliance becomes a challenge.
- Market is growing and you are not.
- Your profit is shrinking.

You should bear in mind that it is unlikely that the strategy you craft to address the above challenges will immediately score a bullseye. Do not lose heart. Do a thorough analysis to determine the root cause that led to the failure of the strategy. Wiser now, focus on identifying which direction you should now pivot in order to gain traction in the market. Do as many pivots as required till you hit upon a successful strategy, and then drop anchor.

Epilogue: Once a company hits upon a successful strategy, it does look simple and obvious. Which is why armchair critics have made a profession of criticizing companies that keep pivoting their strategy till they discover a successful one. 'Why do they waste a company's scarce resources by pivoting so often, only to discover such a simple and obvious strategy?' the critics ask.

A stinging retort to such a query was delivered long ago, by the explorer who accidently discovered a continent on a voyage to discover India. Upon his return, a banquet was hosted in his honour. Many guests were not appreciative of the explorer's efforts, maintaining that anyone can set sail and accidently discover an island. Hearing this, the explorer fetched a half-boiled egg and asked his audience if anyone could make the egg stand on its head.

Several guests attempted but failed. Finally, the explorer took the egg and gave it a firm tap against the table, cracking the shell. He then balanced the egg on its head and turned around to tell the audience: 'Now anyone can make the egg stand on its head. It is no big deal after you have been shown how to do it.'

RULE 14

Nudge Your Customer to Act Your Way!

We can be blind to the obvious, and we are also blind to our blindness.

—Daniel Kahneman

Are you able to influence your customers without resorting to coercion or financial rewards? The answer for most of us would be in the negative.

There's a solution to this vexing problem: subtly 'nudge' your customers by embedding principles of behavioural science into your business, and sit back and reap rich dividends.

How Does Nudging Work?

Nudging is based on the insight that when people have to make a decision, they choose an option from possible options that are available to them. Therefore, businesses seek to understand why customers behave the way they do and what influences their behaviour. Armed with this understanding, a 'choice' is crafted and intelligently embedded in people's list of decisions to make.

People choose an option that either promotes or protects their self-interest. If people perceive the business' choice to be in their self-interest, then they will, of their own volition, opt for it. Once that company's choice is given a go-ahead, customers will behave the way the business wants, without them realizing it.

Nudging is most effective when:

- It is subtle.
- It keeps the interest of people at the centre of decision-making.
- It preserves people's freedom of choice.
- There is no coercion.
- It strictly avoids doling out financial rewards.
- It has potential of delivering beneficial outcomes

Nudging Customers to Display Desirable Behaviour

During the course of my corporate career, I have fallen back on the power of a nudge to gain a competitive advantage. For example, under my watch, Bagpiper became India's largest selling whisky. With great pride we advertised it as 'India's largest selling whisky'.

The reason we publicized this claim was to evoke in drinkers the behavioural science principle of 'social proof'.[1] When potential drinkers were informed that Bagpiper was India's largest selling whisky, they felt that a large number of people must be patronizing it and so many people cannot

---

[1] Social Proof, behaviouraleconimics.com, https://www.behavioraleconomics. com/resources/mini-encyclopedia-of-be/social-proof/

be wrong in their choice. Hence, it must be a good product. Buoyed by this confidence, more and more customers ended up trying it!

If your brand is a market leader then you too should harness the power of 'social proof'. It will reassure your base of existing customers that the choice they have made is indeed correct and instil brand loyalty in them. It will also act as a bait to draw new customers into your fold.

I am not alone in leveraging the nudge to gain a competitive advantage for my business. Leading enterprises such as Zara, OnePlus, the *Economist*, Sensodyne and Amazon have embedded the principles of the nudge in their businesses.

Zara, the global fashion house, introduced the world to 'fast fashion'. It launches hundreds of designs every year, but manufactures each of them in limited quantity. This way they are not stuck with unsold inventory at the end of the season. Since the prices are extremely attractive and the designs are trendy, there is always a rush to buy Zara clothes. Customers know that if they postpone the decision of buying a particular outfit, it is unlikely to be available later. Zara has intelligently put the behavioural science principle of 'loss aversion' into play: we fear losses twice as much as we covet a similar gain. Loss aversion is built into our DNA through the evolutionary process. When our forefathers lived in the jungle, survival, not prosperity, was their main focus. That instinct continues to drive us today. Result: in a Zara store, a buying decision is unlikely to be postponed.

You too can ensure that your customers do not postpone the buying decision by leaning upon loss aversion. Explore the possibilities of manufacturing your product in limited quantities so that your buyer knows that it is unlikely to be available at a later date. This strategy will ensure faster sales velocity, steady cash flow and lower levels of unsold inventories.

OnePlus launched its smartphone using a counter-intuitive strategy. It was made available neither at retail stores nor online, but by invitation only.[2] With this strategy, OnePlus put into play the behavioural science principle of 'scarcity effect'.[3] When something is scarce, it automatically becomes desirable.

People with invites became sought-after within their social circle. They were constantly asked for spare invites. Now, instead of the company running after customers, the customers were running after the brand: in this case, by trying to source the invite that would make them eligible for a OnePlus phone. By virtue of this strategy, OnePlus incurred near zero cost in advertising and sales promotion, customer acquisition and lead generation. Result: a healthy bottom line.

Your business too can gain from this nudge. You will have to come up with a strategy to create 'scarcity' for your product so that it becomes more desirable to customers. You can achieve this by making your product available through invites, or restrict the number of units that can be bought per purchase, or mention that just a few units are left. The strategy for creating scarcity is left to your ingenuity.

---

[2] Niranjan Born Malla, 'How To Get OnePlus one Invite—OnePlus Invitation, Detechter, https://detechter.com/get-oneplus-one-invite-oneplus-invitation/

[3] Neuromarketing Glossary, Convertize, https://www.convertize.com/glossary/scarcity-effect/

The *Economist* is arguably one of the top magazine choice of intelligent people. For its subscription offer, potential subscribers have three options (as on 22 August 2019):[4]

- Print: twelve weeks for Rs 2999
- Print + Digital: twelve weeks for Rs 3799
- Digital: twelve weeks for Rs 1799

What is the purpose of the digital subscription offer? It is a decoy that is strategically placed to give subscribers a perception that the combined 'print + digital' offer, priced at Rs 3799, is a good deal: it offers a saving of 20 per cent. And when you see a good deal, can you refuse it? Of course not!

Here is why the digital edition is a decoy. It costs the publisher a pittance, therefore the price too should be extremely low. But its high price renders the print + digital attractive.

You too can strategically utilize a decoy to enhance the appeal of the option you want your customers to choose. If you are selling a product and providing aftersales service then you can make the aftersales service the decoy so that you nudge your customers to opt for your bundled offering:

1. Product Price: Rs 1000
2. Aftersales Service: Rs 700
3. Product Price + Aftersales Service Price: Rs 1200

---

[4] The *Economist*, https://subscription.economist.com/DA/PPC/ ALLALLRDCD/ALL?gclsrc=aw.ds&gclid=EAIaIQobChMI uffe1N2U5AIVzhwrCh2yvQiJEAAYASAAEgJbpvD_ BwE&gclsrc=aw.ds

Customers, most likely, will choose Option 3, without you having to hard sell it.

Sensodyne has made major inroads into the toothpaste market. They established themselves with a series of distinctive advertisements. The ads have a real doctor recommending the brand. By following this strategy, Sensodyne has put into play the behavioural science principle of 'expert bias': we tend to be persuaded more by an expert than by a layperson. In this case, because a doctor is recommending it, we get positively persuaded by their recommendation and end up buying the brand.

Many a time you may find it difficult to influence your customers. Nudge them your way by getting an 'expert' to speak to them.

E-commerce companies come up with tantalizing offers promising the moon to their customers. But next to each of these offers, they insert a starburst that informs the potential buyer it is available 'only for one day'. Airlines are the biggest adopters of this strategy when it comes to selling seats online. Next to the attractive offer, they add this bit of info for potential fliers: 'one seat left'.

Words like 'only', 'just', 'limited', 'sale', 'now', 'left' are referred to as hot buttons in behavioural science and are used to evoke the 'fear of regret'. When customers see an attractive deal, they are compelled to buy it immediately for the fear of regret, as the deal may not be available later. But if they go to the site two days later, they are likely to find that there is still 'one seat left'. Hot buttons make us behave irrationally and we end up buying things we do not need!

Amazon is driving revenue growth with its introduction of Prime, an annual membership programme, for just Rs 999 (initially it was as low as Rs 499)[5]. It entitles members to unlimited free and fast deliveries, video streaming, ad-free music, exclusive access to deals, and more. Prime works on the behavioural science concept of 'sunk cost fallacy'. A customer who has paid Rs 999 to become a member feels that the expense has become a sunk cost: a cost that has been incurred by her and is now a dead investment. And this triggers her to behave irrationally. Anytime she has to buy anything, she opts to buy it from Amazon merely to recover the sunk cost. Result: much to Amazon's delight, it notices that a Prime member spends 2.3 times more than a non-Prime member.[6]

Offer a scheme so that customers have to pay upfront to access the basic level of the product. But to use additional features they have to pay more. Why will they opt to pay for additional features? They have already 'sunk cost' to buy the product. To protect this investment they will be tempted to incur additional expenses.

Nudging Employees to Display Desirable Behaviour

The stories narrated thus far illustrate the power of a nudge to get customers to display behaviour desired by companies. Can these principles be used to nudge employees to improve

---

[5] 'Amazon launches Prime service in India at Rs 499 per year', *Hindustan Times*, 26 July 2016, https://www.hindustantimes.com/business-news/amazon-launches-prime-service-in-india-at-rs-499-per-year/story-RDstO2EW18B0WGN1hhpTuI.html

[6] Don Reisinger, 'Amazon Prime Has More Than 100 Million U.S. Subscribers', Fortune, 17 January 2019, https://fortune.com/2019/01/17/amazon-prime-subscribers/

productivity—without resorting to coercion or doling out financial rewards?

Amazon embedded the nudge to improve employees' productivity. Empirical finding seems to suggest that if there are too many people during a meeting or in a team, productivity falls because a few members resort to social loafing: a tendency of individuals to put in less effort when they are part of a group.[7]

To overcome this, Jeff Bezos, from the early days of Amazon has instituted a two-pizza rule. This does not mean that in every meeting two pizzas are served (although that would be a good rule too)! Bezos' two-pizza rule states that the number of people attending a meeting should be restricted to the number of people that can share two pizzas. This puts a cap on the number of people attending and boosts productivity and effectiveness of the meeting.[8]

This should make you determined to ensure that team size should be kept small to avoid the malaise of social loafing creeping into your company.

Can a nudge also be deployed to get employees that are not under direct supervision to behave cordially with customers? Uber has perfected the art of getting its drivers to display civil and cordial behaviour. Uber has a rating system, where drivers are rated on a scale of 1–5. A higher rating corresponds to

---

[7]   Kendra Cherry, 'How Social Loafing Is Studied in psychology', Updated 6 November 2018, Verywell Mind, https://www.verywellmind.com/what-is-social-loafing-2795883

[8]   Alex Hern, 'The two-pizza rule and the secret of Amazon's success', *Guardian*, 24 April 2018, https://www.theguardian.com/technology/2018/apr/24/the-two-pizza-rule-and-the-secret-of-amazons-success

higher business for the driver and is extremely desirable. The way Uber uses a nudge strategy is by starting drivers off with a 5-star rating: the highest rating on the scale. Thereafter, the riders give them a rating based on the experience they have had during the ride.

Uber is counting on 'loss aversion'—people fear loss twice[9] more than a similar gain—to slay this business challenge. In practice, this means that people can be nudged into action by indicating how their behaviour will prevent them from incurring losses.

The reason it helps to start a driver off with a rating of 5 is that if his average starts falling below 5, the driver experiences the negative emotions of loss. The driver is encouraged to provide the best service possible to prevent this outcome. On the other hand, if the driver started with a rating of '0' and with the passage of time gained a rating of 3.5, he would feel the positive emotions of gain. This would lead to satisfaction and a reduced desire to provide an optimum experience for the rider.

Is a fall in rating enough to motivate the driver to be on his best behaviour? Seems unlikely! Therefore, Uber has subtly intertwined rating with earning: if the rating falls below a predefined level, the driver is offloaded from the platform. Even if he performs just enough to maintain an average rating, he will unfortunately discover that his earnings are drastically reduced within the Uber ecosystem.

Here's how that happens. Take, for instance, a location where there are multiple Ubers parked. A request comes for a

---

9   Loss   Aversion,   behavioraleconomics.com,   https://www.behavioral economics.com/resources/mini-encyclopedia-of-be/loss-aversion/

ride. Who will get the first right of refusal? The Uber driver with the highest rating. Result: the Uber system rewards drivers with the highest rating by offering them more business opportunities to increase their earnings.

Insight: drivers sign up with Uber to maximize their earnings, which can only happen if the average rating from the riders hovers around 5. To achieve this, drivers have to be on their best behaviour all the time.

As is with the drivers, the same happens with the riders: if the cumulative ratings of a rider fall below a cut-off point, then the rider too can be offloaded from the Uber platform. If, at a particular location, the demand for Uber is high, then the rider with the highest rating gets preference. This ensures that riders too are on their best behaviour.

Most appraisal systems are designed to rate employees from 1 to 5. Why not use Uber's strategy to overhaul your employee appraisal system? Start by giving every employee a 5 at the start of the year. If during appraisal an employee gets a rating less than 5—the starting score—he or she is bound to feel 'pain' at the loss. This can self-motivate an employee to perform and maintain the score at a perfect 5 or close to it.

What lesson can we learn from this? A company should design a self-correcting system—without resorting to coercion—by subtly embedding the principles of behavioural science which 'nudges' the employees and customers to display the desired behaviour.

Digital Nudge

Widespread adoption of smart devices, ubiquitous connectivity to Internet, and proclivity for consuming content and engaging in online communication is offering businesses an effective, cost effective channel to digitally nudge people. Here is how it is done:

Let us stay with ride hailing cabs and see how it deploys Digital Nudge to get drivers to drive longer hours. Its drivers are independent business owners and hence company has no control over them. This would make it difficult for them to offer service at our doorsteps whenever we require. For that it has to have to have maximum number of drivers on duty. For that they digitally nudge drivers to behave the way they want without them realizing it.

- **Binge driving:** How does Netflix get us to binge watch? By sending us recommendations just before the existing content is about to end. We click on it and continue watching. Similarly, just when a ride is about to get completed, it sends request for new rides. Drivers have signed up with ride hailing companies to maximize their earnings. That can happen when they are driving. So, they accept the next ride. And the one after that. Result: binge driving. Many a times the drivers do not get time to even take a bathroom break. For them, companies offer them a facility, when activated, will ensure that they do not receive a new request.

- **Income target:** Many drivers start their shift with an income target. When they log on, many a times, they are asked for the income target they have. When they are logging off, they receive a message—you have to earn a little more to meet your income target for the day—then two options are offered—logoff and continue driving—the latter is highlighted. Motivational researchers have found that when a tangible goal is set, then it is easy to motivate people to complete tasks to achieve the goal. The driver continues driving to meet his set income target.

- **Pricing:** When the demand in an area is high then companies may find it difficult to deliver on its promise. How does it get more drivers into the area? By putting the dreaded surge pricing on. The lure of higher earnings attracts drivers to the area.

- **Prompts:** When the company's system discovers surge in demand it puts out alerts—rush started—get to this area—demand is high. This alert motivates drivers to move to the areas of high demand.

Did you notice a common theme that runs across these nudges? They all are directed to increase the driver's income and that helps ride hailing companies deliver on its promise of providing a ride anytime, anywhere within in minutes.[10]

Can a Digital Nudge also be leveraged to prompt drivers to take decisions that are non-income enhancing? Ride hailing companies collect data of every kind. If data analysis indicates that the braking is frequent or acceleration is very rapid or they receive poor customer feedback—then an alert can be sent to driver that they may be tired and should call it a day!

Now, businesses too are using Digital Nudge to get an improved employee experience. BCG leans of digital nudge

---

[10] Noam Scheiber, 'How Uber Uses Psychological Tricks to Push Its Drivers' Buttons, *New York Times*, 2 April 2017, https://www.nytimes.com/interactive/2017/04/02/technology/uber-drivers-psychological-tricks.html?_r=0

to ensure that employees do not receive official mails during non-working hours, unless it is important. Each time a person is sending a message during non-office hours, a message props up: You are trying to send an email to BCG users outside normal office hours. Please choose one of the following options:

- Mark email as low priority
- Defer sending until next business day
- Send email as is
- Cancel (Back)[11]

This prompt does not take away the power to send the message but makes the sender assist them in displaying considerate behaviour.

Google too uses digital nudge to improve collaboration and cooperation among its employees. Laszlo Bock, Google's former head of People Operations shares how digital nudge was used to increase collaboration and cooperation among teams. A quarterly survey containing two questions was administered to every member of the team:

- In the last quarter, this person helped me when I reached out to him or her.
- In the last quarter, this person involved me when I could have been helpful to, or was impacted by, his or her team's work.

---

[11] Julia Dhar et al., 'The Persuasive Power of the Digital Nudge', BCG Henderson Institute, 17 May 2017, https://www.bcg.com/ publications/2017/people-organization-operations-persuasive-power-digital-nudge.aspx

Every person rated each other and the anonymous ranking was shared with everyone. The result showed where they fell in ranking but did not show where others fell. It prompted people to improve their behaviour. In time, Google saw improvements in cooperation and collaborations among team members.[12]

My Experiences with Nudges

Let me state upfront that during the course of my corporate career I have fallen victim to nudges—expert bias, ownership bias, illusion of attention, outcome bias and many more—which have resulted in the making of suboptimal decisions.

Let me start with how I became a victim of expert bias: the power of experts to influence people's thinking based on their credentials. At the start of my career, I was enamoured by experts. In their presence I suspended my power of judgement, and accepted and implemented their recommendations blindly. On many occasions, I found myself in hot water because the expert's advice turned out to be anything but fruitful!

One time, we were making a TV commercial (TVC) for one of our brands. The shooting was about to start when I got a call from the head of our advertising agency. He excitedly informed me that an A-list Bollywood director had expressed a desire to direct our TVC.

[12] Anil Karamchandani, 'Five smart nudges for your workplace', Livemint, 11 December 2018, https://www.livemint.com/Leisure/GsHx7pV97Dotr2jj92hRjL/Five-smart-nudges-for-your-workplace.html

Much to my delight, the director paid a visit to my office and during our freewheeling conversation he assured me he would put all efforts into making the TVC a big hit. I felt reassured and delegated all decision-making to him. In due course, the shooting of TVC was completed and I was shown a rough edit. It was an unmitigated disaster. How could an A-list Bollywood director make such an unwatchable TVC? Upon probing, I discovered that the director was in between films and had utilized the free time he had on his hands to make easy money.

But he taught me an important life lesson: I should not repose blind faith in an expert even if he or she showed willingness to take full responsibility.

On to ownership bias. Our ideas appear more appealing and valuable to us compared to other people's ideas and we fight tooth and nail to implement those. It would be wise to remember that none of us have a monopoly over good ideas. If we insist that only our own ideas should be greenlighted, it is inevitable that we will end up with suboptimal results.

To ensure I did not fall victim to this bias, I made a 'rule' to put big business decisions to the sword by having a professional dissenter in our midst. Her job was to spot as many weaknesses as possible in the decisions we took, and also to offer a radically different perspective and solutions from ours. If a suitably qualified professional dissenter could not be found, then I would get the entire team to take on the role. I would invite every member, by rotation, to frankly point out what was wrong with the decision we had all agreed upon.

This strategy paid rich dividends because flaws were detected and weeded out during the discussion stage itself.

Now for the illusion of attention. When I reached middle management, I held a mistaken belief that nothing escaped my attention. The reality was otherwise, as this experiment conducted at Harvard University proves.

In this experiment, people were shown a video of a basketball game and were instructed to count the number of times the ball was passed. In it, six people—three in white shirts and three in black shirts—were passing the basketball among themselves. While the game was in progress, a gorilla walked across the middle of the court, thumped its chest and exited; in the process, it spent as many as nine seconds on the court.

When the subjects were asked if they had noticed the gorilla, the results were shocking. It was discovered that merely half of the participants had noticed the gorilla! The others were so focused on the task of counting the number of passes that they had not spotted something as conspicuous as a gorilla on the court.

This experiment revealed that when people are single-mindedly focused on a goal, they tend to miss out on what is happening in the environment. The interesting part is that they have no idea that they have missed out on noticing the obvious things.

This experiment always reminds me that when I am single-mindedly focused on tackling a business challenge, I am likely to miss out on the most obvious facts.

To overcome this bias, I list down all the assumptions I have made while making a decision. I reach out to people I respect and seek their opinion on whether or not my assumptions were comprehensive. More importantly, I ask them to look for any important aspect I may have overlooked while arriving at the decision. This strategy has saved me from committing many blunders.

Let me narrate an instance from my days in the alcoholic beverage industry. It was an industry practice to run consumer offers during the festive season. We too followed this practice. With every bottle of whisky, we offered a free gift: a ball pen, bottle opener or a glass. Since most whisky brands also offered these items, they had ceased to excite customers. Sensing this, we decided to give out a unique utility item—a bar of soap— with every bottle of whisky.

Our past experience warned us that retailers have a habit of not passing on the offer to customers and making money by selling it in the market later. To overcome the problem of pilferage, we decided to put the soap inside the whisky carton and seal it. This, we thought, will ensure near zero pilferage by retailers.

While the team got down to executing this plan, I decided to bounce with the idea off our production head. He was, to put it mildly, aghast at our plan. He warned us that if soaps were placed inside whisky cartons, the smell of soap would seep into the whisky, rendering it undrinkable! Somehow it had not occurred to us. I thanked him for pointing it out and saving us from making a big blunder.

Finally, let's discuss outcome bias. During my corporate career, I launched a plethora of new brands. Each time my bosses judged me on how the brand performed in the marketplace (outcome), rather than the process followed to conceptualize it. When the brands did well, I was deluged with bouquets, and when it did not fare well, brickbats followed!

Is it good to display outcome bias? Unfortunately, the answer is 'no'! Because excessive focus on the outcome makes employees focus on delivering end results at all costs. In the short-term, there might be results, but in the long run, it will cause irreparable harm to the systems and processes of the company.

I discovered this bitter truth when I was catapulted to a leadership position; lo and behold, I too inadvertently fell victim to this bias.

Revenue is the lifeline of a company and, in the quest to boost it, we linked the incentives and promotion of our sales manager to sales numbers. For the sales manager, achieving the sales numbers became a question of life and death. Like a person possessed, he went about single-mindedly working towards achieving numbers. He eventually managed to deliver the required sales numbers and earned the incentives and promotion. Shortly afterwards, he left for a 'better' opportunity.

We filled his position and in due course the new sales manager brought to our attention the mayhem caused in the market by the previous sales manager. In the dogged pursuit of achieving targets, he had flagrantly dumped stocks at the distributor's warehouse and given inordinately longer credit periods without approval. He had achieved sales targets but had brutalized the system. It took us a long time to set the system right after the harm his misadventures had caused.

After this experience I focused on building robust systems and processes, and linked rewards, recognitions and promotions, to adhering to it while delivering business outcomes. This strategy ensured that in the long run, I won more victories on the corporate battlefield and had less cause for embarrassment!

Upon further self-introspection, I realized that I was plagued with many more biases that hindered my career growth and had deleterious impacts on my personal life.

Upon graduation from IIT and then IIM I inadvertently fell victim to the Dunning-Kruger effect, which means that I felt I was smarter and more capable than others. This belief, of course, was mistaken. It took me some to realize that every person I meet is better than me in some way or the other, and that I can learn from them. Now I make an effort to learn from everybody I come across and I must say I have gained hugely by adopting this mindset.

During this phase, I had become overconfident and started believing and behaving like an expert. I believed that the success I was getting was due to my merit. That, of course, was not the truth. Many a time luck plays a far more significant role than we think. I had inadvertently fallen victim to the 'illusion of skills'. Now, I follow the Greek philosopher Socrates' mantra: I know one thing and that is that I know nothing. This mindset ensures that, even today, I keep on learning no matter how much I already know.

As I rose up the corporate ladder, I started feeling that what appeals to me would also appeal to others. It took me a few tumbles to realize that I had fallen victim to the false consensus bias. Having realized this, I now make a conscious effort to ask people to tell me not what works in my idea, but what doesn't. This way I have tried to protect myself from falling victim to this bias.

During my corporate career there came a phase where whatever I did just would not deliver results. I started to develop a feeling that no matter what I did, I would never be able to succeed. And if that be the case, why even try? I had fallen victim to 'learnt helplessness'. At this point I took inspiration from Tom Watson, the founder of IBM, who advised that if you want to increase your success rate, double your failure rate. Following this advice, I was no longer afraid of failure. Over time, my success rate improved and the feeling of learnt helplessness evaporated.

Another bad habit I had picked up was to criticize people when the work they had done failed to deliver the desired results. This demotivated my team. Of course, in hindsight, everything looks so obvious and predictable. When I became aware of hindsight bias, I tried to give constructive feedback to my team. This motivated my team to take more risks and deliver better results, and my reputation as a leader took an upward trajectory.

I would recommend that you introspect and cull lessons from my experiences so that you do not fall victim to these biases. Forewarned is forearmed!

Does Nudging Have Universal Application?

Of course. Wherever human beings are involved—be it education, personal life and even the social sector—a nudge will find application.

Let us start with education. Many students fall victim to outcome bias. They tend to study with the sole objective of passing the examination. Therefore, they fritter away their time during the semester, but when the examinations are around the corner, they tend to memorize chunks of text and reproduce it in the examination. Most of them indeed pass, but what about the quality of learning and its retention? That, unfortunately, is the casualty. The students realize this bitter truth when they enter the job market and potential employers find them 'unemployable'! But, by then, it is too late.

Moving on to personal life. My mother was suffering from old age-related challenges. We took her to a doctor who, after examining her, assured us that she would get well.

As a concerned son, I asked the dreaded question, 'Doctor, what are the chances of my mother recovering fully?'

Without hesitation, he said, 'There are 99 per cent chances that she will recover completely.' We were happy with his prognosis.

As a precaution, we decided to take a second opinion. We took an appointment with a second doctor, who too had a stellar reputation but was widely regarded as being conservative in her prognosis.

After she had examined my mother, I posed the same question to her: what are the chances of recovery? Being conservative, she thought for a moment and said, 'let me put it this way: the chance of failure is merely 1 per cent.'

The two doctors had arrived at a similar diagnosis, but framed their responses differently:

- Doctor 1 put the chances of recovery at 99 per cent.
- Doctor 2 put the chances of failure at 1 per cent!

If it was you, which doctor would you go with? My mother wanted to go with Doctor 1.

My mother had fallen victim to the 'framing effect': it is not important what we say, but how we say it. Doctor 1 had framed his response positively. This is also why doctors have to pay careful attention to their bedside manners. The medicines may cure the patient but it's the right words that make them feel better.

Let us move to the social sector. In the 1990s, I was asked to lend my marketing expertise to a social organization whose mission was to create awareness about eye donation. To spread their message to a wider audience, they roped in Aishwarya Rai as their 'Sight Ambassador'.[13]

A leading advertising agency had offered to make a TVC featuring Aishwarya Rai. As a first step, they wrote a script to encourage people to pledge their eyes for donation.

The script was very impactful. In it, Aishwarya Rai looks into the camera and says, 'In a beauty contest one is asked all kinds of questions, like, "How will you continue to live after you are gone?" I will leave my eyes to an eye bank and help someone see again the wonder of our world through my eyes long after I am gone.' As per the script, the screen would then go blank and a male voice would come on and say, 'If you wish to pledge your eyes, write to . . .' with the address of the social organization appearing on the screen.

I loved the script. But I made one suggestion to nudge potential donors to pledge their eyes in larger numbers. Instead of the male voice, I proposed that Aishwarya Rai's voiceover should continue: 'If you wish to donate your eyes write to *me* at . . .'

This subtle change would get people to 'believe' they were writing to Aishwarya Rai and would nudge more people to pledge their eyes. My suggestion was accepted and when the TVC was aired the response rate of people pledging their eyes went up manifold.

---

13 Eye Bank Association of India (EBAI) website: http://www.ebai.org/

In hindsight, I wonder if my nudge was ethical. Did I mislead people into believing that they were writing to Aishwarya Rai? Since my intention was honourable, I believe the nudge was justified.

Unethical Uses of a Nudge

Let me share examples of how companies are knowingly nudging us so that they can benefit from our behaviour. They have consciously added several features to get us addicted.

Take Facebook for instance. As soon as I post anything, I am anxious to see if it has garnered any 'likes'. If it has, I experience a burst of happiness, it's because my brain releases a trace amount of dopamine, the pleasure hormone. Moreover, every 'like' increases my self-worth. Therefore, I keep checking FB because the feed is designed to be continuous and has no end. I do not know where to stop; like a junkie, I keep scrolling.

Take casinos for instance.[14] They are carefully designed to motivate people to spend (read: part with) money:

- **Colour:** Gold and red are the favourite colours of a casino: gold represents money while red stands for passion. These colours prime guests to get into the spirit of the place.

---

[14] Steven John, '9 tricks casinos use to keep you spending your money', Business Insider, 9 June 2019, https://www.businessinsider. in/9-tricks-casinos-use-to-keep-you-spending-your-money/ articleshow/69714671.cms

- **Slot machines:** Normally, they are kept near the entrance. When a person steps in, they hear the sound of a falling coin. It vets the appetite for 'gambling'.

- **Serve alcohol:** Mostly, it's the women who serve it. This is done for two reasons. Alcohol gets people to exhibit risky behaviour; in presence of women it goes up a few notches. Indulging in risky behaviour is good for the casino business.

- **Absence of windows and clocks:** This ensures that people do not get to know the 'time'. Therefore, they are in no hurry to leave.

- **Play with chips, not real money:** People experience 'pain' when they have to part with 'real' money. But it is almost non-existent when they play with chips. Therefore, gamblers gamble away more chips than 'real' money.

Is it not ironical that the world's best brains are deploying cutting-edge technology and behavioural science techniques? That they nudge us to notice advertisements we do not care about and buy things that we do not need and make us gamble away our money?

Can a Well-Intentioned Nudge Backfire?

It is prudent to keep in mind that a nudge, if poorly thought through, can backfire. Take this example of an energy company that wanted its customers to reduce the consumption of energy. It did a detailed analysis of the consumption pattern of its users and in the next round of billing sent reports comparing each energy user's consumption with the average consumption. This initiative nudged users who were consuming more energy than average to reduce their consumption; but it also nudged people who were consuming less than average to start consuming more.

How Should You Leverage the Power of a Nudge'?

You should lean on nudges to put your business and yourself in an advantageous position. Let us start with business. You should use:

- Social proof to retain customers and attract new ones
- Loss aversion to compel customers to behave the way you want them to
- Scarcity effect to nudge customers to seek out your brand and not postpone the purchase decision
- Decoys to nudge customers to choose the option that is profitable to the company
- Hot buttons to propel people into action
- Social loafing to ensure that productivity improves and every member of the team is engaged and contributing.
- Expert bias and framing effect to influence customers to opt for your brand
- Sunk cost fallacy to motivate customers to spend more money on your business
- A self-correcting system to nudge your employees and customers to behave in a desirable manner
- Digital nudge to get people to display desirable behaviour.

A partial list of biases that have the power to nudge you into making grave errors:

- Ownership bias will make you believe that your idea is far superior than the other person's; it will make you fight tooth and nail to implement it.
- The illusion of attention makes you believe that nothing escapes your attention.
- Outcome bias will make you focus on outcomes and overlook system and process.
- The Dunning–Kruger effect will make you believe that you are smarter and more capable than you really are.
- The illusion of skill will make you believe that you have considerable expertise.
- False consensus will give you the wrong impression that what we like, others will like too.
- Learnt helplessness will give you a feeling that no matter what you do, you are unlikely to succeed, so why try? This will make you give up even before trying.
- In hindsight bias, everything will seem obvious and predictable after the event.

Since a nudge has the power to influence people's behaviour without them realizing it, it is therefore incumbent upon us to use it responsibly. Take a pledge that you will not lean on it to manipulate people's behaviour for your selfish gains, but will instead utilize it to help people make better decisions.

Also, do remember that you too can fall victim to nudges. You should be alert. The best way to inoculate yourself is to be aware of them. Leverage nudges wisely for the greater good, including yourself.

RULE 15

Select Profitable Business Models

I have ways of making money that you know nothing of.

—John D. Rockefeller

'So, how do you sustain a business model in which users don't pay for your service?' Senator Hatch asked Mark Zuckerberg when the latter appeared before the US Senate's Commerce and Judiciary committees to discuss data privacy and Russian disinformation on his social networking sites.

'Senator, we run ads,' said Zuckerberg.[1]

In mere four words Zuckerberg had laid bare the business model of Facebook: how it gains competitive advantage, earns money and makes profits.

A business model defines the way a firm creates, delivers, and captures value.[2]

---

[1] Sean Burch, '"Senator, we run ads": Hatch Mocked for Basic Facebook Question to Zuckerberg', The Wrap, 10 April 2018, https://www.thewrap.com/senator-orrin-hatch-facebook-biz-model-zuckerberg/

[2] Sunil Gupta, Driving Digital Strategy, (Harvard Business Review Press, 2018)

Advertising-Based Revenue Business Model

Facebook offers us a convenient way to connect and communicate with each other. It has 2.32 billion monthly active users worldwide on its platform:[3] if it were a country, it would be the most populated in the world. For FB, we are the product that it sells to advertisers in order to make money. In 2018, FB's revenue from advertising was $54.4 billion, which is 98 per cent of the total revenue.[4] This business model is popularly called the advertising-based revenue business model.

A host of internet companies—Google, Alibaba and others—use this business model to earn revenue and make profit. These companies are ranked among the world's most valuable companies. The advertising-based revenue business model is just one among many. Successful companies have either devised their own unique business models or modified and adopted an existing business model to gain competitive advantage and earn money.

Let us run through some of the other popular business models so that you can select or switch over to the one (or ones) best suited to your business.

---

[3] Felix Richter, 'How Facebook grew from 0 to 2.3 billion users in 15 years', World Economic Forum, 5 February 2019, https://www.weforum.org/agenda/2019/02/how-facebook-grew-from-0-to-2-3-billion-users-in-15-years

[4] Tony Silber, 'Facebook Ad-Spend Growth From National Marketers Is Slowing, Intelligence Firm's Data Shows', *Forbes*, 31 December 2018, https://www.forbes.com/sites/tonysilber/2018/12/31/facebook-ad-spend-from-national-marketers-is-slowing-intelligence-firms-data-shows/#13647a661591; Note for Facebook Revenue: Fortune 500, https://fortune.com/fortune500/facebook/

Razor Blade Business Model

Look at Amazon. It sells its Kindle at prices starting in the range of Rs 6000 ($84 as on 22 August 2019). How does it make money by selling it at a bargain basement price? 'We want to make money when people use our devices, not when they buy our devices,' said Jeff Bezos, the founder of the company.[5]

Yes, you heard it right. Amazon does not want to make money when it sells Kindles, but when people buy books on their Kindle for reading. What business model is Amazon following for Kindle? The same as Gillette which sells its razors at relatively low prices, but earns money from its blades. In its honour, this business model is nicknamed the 'razor blade business model'.

This business model is also popularly called 'bait and hook': the low price of the razor is the 'bait', the customer is 'hooked', resulting in recurring sales of the blades. There are a host of companies which have adopted this business model. HP, for instance, sells its printer at low prices but earns money when it sells the ink cartridges.

Pay-Per-Use Business Model

Let us shift our discussion to another technology company making waves: Uber. Have you ever wondered how it earns money? After all, it does not own the cabs, nor does it employ the drivers.

---

[5]   Austin Carr, 'Amazon loses money on the tablets. It's all going according to plan', Fast Company, 7 July 2012, https://www.fastcompany. com/3001110/amazon-loses-money-tablets-its-all-going-according-plan

It is an on-demand ride service that connects riders (read: us) with drivers and the business model they follow is 'pay per use': pay only for the duration the service is used for. They collect a matchmaker fee from the driver.

Freemium Business Model

Look at another technology company, Dropbox. It deploys the 'freemium business model' to make profits.

The name of this business model was coined by combining 'free and premium'. As the name implies, basic services are made available for free while premium services are available against payment. From a business perspective, 'free' leads to trials because customers do not perceive any risk in it. For this model to be effective, enough access should be provided to the customers so that they can experience the value of the product. Then the paid plan should gradually be introduced.

Dropbox offers a small GB of storage space free of cost. This allows users to experience how easy it is to back up and share their files using the Dropbox platform. For additional storage space Dropbox starts charging.

Spotify, the music streaming company, also offers its basic service free, but charges for premium services. Many newspapers offer basic news free. But to get access to premium content, readers have to opt for the subscription fee.

Subscription Business Model

That brings us to the 'subscription business model'. In this model, the business charges an upfront subscription fee that has to be renewed at regular intervals, most often annually.

Customers find this model appealing because for a small price they get to access a large body of work that is constantly refreshed by the addition of new content. If customers do not like the service, they can cancel the subscription.

This business model gives the company access to the data of the subscribers which it uses to gain a deeper understanding about the subscribers to make personal recommendations. They can also monetize the data by inviting advertisers to serve targeted advertisements to its subscribers.

Companies following this model include magazines, online content streaming companies like Netflix and Apple Music, and more.

Frenemy Business Model

The old adage that competition should be trampled to death may no longer be a wise strategy to pursue. Alliance with competition can bring down costs and boost margins without, in any way, compromising the competitive advantage. This is called the 'frenemy business model'. Take automobile companies for instance. In the market place (read: the front end of business) they fight fiercely among themselves for market share; at the back-end they are forming alliances and aggregating their orders for multitudes of items such as tyres and batteries (which are of standard specifications); they then approach the manufacturers of these items to renegotiate the bulk rate. Since the aggregated order quantity is higher, the negotiated bulk rate is lower. This boosts the bottom lines of the companies.

Telecom companies also follow this business model to bring down their costs. At the back-end they share transmission towers, but at the front-end they are involved in intense battles. If each of the telecom companies had to invest in building back-end towers their business would become unviable.

Pay As You Earn Business Model

During uncertain times, many businesses postpone capital and operating expenditure decisions. To overcome this barrier, vendors follow the 'pay as you earn business model', where payment is linked to future earnings. They install their products at the customers' site and receive payment only after the products start generating revenue. For customers, this business model offers an opportunity to align the payment to revenue generation. There are two primary types of payment options available to customers:

- Make an upfront 'token' payment, followed by fixed payments at predefined frequency.
- Make payments linked to the percentage of revenue. For example, if payment is fixed at 5 per cent of monthly revenue, the customer has to pay 5 per cent of the revenue to the vendor every month. If the revenue is low, the payment is proportionately lower and vice versa.

This business model is also called the 'deferred payment business model'. It has the advantage of guaranteeing that the vendor has some skin in the game. This will ensure that they do not overpromise while pitching the product. After all, their payment is linked to the product delivering results.

Outsource Business Model

Let us talk about schools now. Many schools provide pick-and-drop bus services. Do they have expertise in it? Of course not. Therefore, they follow the 'outsource business model' to provide this service. They outsource this service to a bus fleet owner. The service providers charge a rent that is paid at regular intervals (read: monthly). Every aspect required for providing the service is handled by the service provider. This frees up time for schools to focus on their core functions.

Many companies, including Apple outsource their manufacturing activity partly or completely, to third-party manufacturers. In addition, businesses actively outsource many other activities so that they can free up their resources and focus their energy on strengthening their core business.

Popular outsourcing functions include:

- Housekeeping
- Security
- IT infrastructure maintenance
- Pay roll
- Food and beverages

Product As Service Business Model

On my business trips to Singapore, on the return journey to Mumbai, I have to spend time at Changi Airport's business lounge. There I find a Nescafé coffee vending machine offering multiple options of coffee. Why have they kept a vending machine and not coffee powder? The answer is obvious: coffee connoisseurs desire coffee, not coffee powder. This is popularly referred to as the 'product as service business model'. Based on this insight, Nescafé, instead of offering a product (coffee powder) offers the desired benefit (coffee as a service) via its vending machine.

This business model also finds widespread application in the B2B space.

Let us go back to bus fleet owners. They buy, maintain and replace tyres to keep the buses running. Would they prefer to sign up with a tyre company which offers tyres free plus takes responsibility for their maintenance and replacement? Sounds too good to be true. How will the tyre company make money? By charging per rotation of the tyre which can be measured by placing sensors in the tyre. Sensors accurately count the number of rotations and feed this data to a central location from where the billing is done. The tyre company is not selling a tyre as a product but providing it as a service. The advantage of this model is that the fleet owners pay only when they are generating revenue.

Outcome-Based Business Model

Companies will be more amenable to giving their business to vendors who link payment to the delivery of promised business outcomes.

Take the example of aircraft engine manufacturers. Innovative companies, in this space, are experimenting with a new business model. Instead of merely selling the aircraft engines, they are promising to deliver 'outcomes' desired by its customers: less downtime of aircraft, more miles flown with lower fuel consumption and a lower carbon footprint. When they come good on the promise, they gain substantially; if they do not deliver the promised outcomes, they self-penalize. This model seems to be gathering traction because the 'vendor's skin is in the game.' Therefore, they do not tend to overpromise. Customers are happy with this model because they get what they are promised and compensation in case of failure to come good on the promise.

Let us shift the focus to advertising. Earlier, digital advertising took center stage, marketers, like me, paid media owners to telecast advertisements on TV. The media owners did not give me an ironclad guarantee that advertisements would be viewed by my target audience. The only assurance I got was that my advertisements would be telecast as per the agreed schedule. This left me, and possibly other advertisers, feeling frustrated. But since we had no option, we continued to advertise on TV.

Google understood this pain point and linked payment to outcome. Advertisers were expected to pay only when the link was viewed, giving rise to pay per view/impression. This made advertisers shift the advertising budget to digital marketing (refer table). In 2018, Google's adverting revenue was nudging $116.3 billion.[6]

Media & Entertainment (INR in Bilions)									
Segment	2016		2017		2018		2020 (Est)		CAGR
	INR Billion	%	INR Billion	%	INR Billion	%	INR Billion	%	%
TV	594	45	660	45	734	44	862	42	9.8
Print	296	23	303	21	331	20	369	18	5.7
Digital Media	92	7	119	8	151	9	224	11	24.9
Others	327	25	391	26	444	27	577	29	
Total	1309	100	1473	100	1660	100	2032	100	11.6

Advertising spends move to digital media[7]

---

6 Trefis Team, 'Did Google's Cloud Focus Mitigate Advertising Revenue Headwinds in Q2?' *Forbes*, 25 June 2019, https://www.forbes.com/sites/greatspeculations/2019/07/25/did-googles-cloud-focus-mitigate-advertising-revenue-headwinds-in-q2/#449f3fa6c618

7 FICCI & EY, Re-imagining India's M&E sector, March 2o18, http://ficci.in/spdocument/22949/FICCI-study1-frames-2018.pdf

Many sellers are offering performance guarantees and expect to be paid only when they deliver the promised outcome. This includes the emerging profession of stand-up comedy. Their payment is also being linked to delivery of outcomes. Aghast? How can the performance of comics be measured? Agents are experimenting with technology to help them with this issue. Systems that can measure the duration and intensity of claps, laughter and catcalls during a performance are being designed. An algorithm does an analysis and gives ratings to comedians based on which payments are released.

Co-Ownership/Time-Sharing Business Model

Let us shift our conversation to vacations. Ordinarily, people take a vacation for a short period in a year. Therefore, acquiring a vacation home that will only be used for a short duration in a year would be a bad investment.

The 'co-ownership/time-sharing business model' has evolved based on this insight. It sells time instead of property. For example, if fifty-two people buy one week of a vacation time in a year, then each member pays only 1/52 of the total price.

A world of caution: time-shares make for poor investment. It is a sunk cost for the buyer, with poor resale value. It starts depreciating from the moment it is acquired.

Time-sharing has its advantages too: for a fraction of the cost people can gain access to luxury vacation resorts or even private jets. Among the rich, those who desire to fly by private jet but cannot afford to own one, opt for the next best thing: fractional ownership. High-net-worth people can buy the 'time' of a jet. For the duration of time bought by them, the jet will be at their disposal.

Businesses are warming up to this idea. If a startup cannot afford to buy a product due to its high price, then a few of them get together to acquire it and use it for the period of time paid by them. For a fraction of a cost, a start-up can 'own' the product and, together with other co-owners, sweat the purchased asset to its limit.

Bottom line: if you desire to buy a product that is expensive, you can bring down the cost by co-owning it.

Negative Working Capital Business Model

It is said that business should be done with other people's money. Such companies collect money in advance from customers and vendors and hold out on paying others. In accounting terms, it is referred to as the 'negative working capital business model'.

E-commerce follows this business model. They get products from its vendors on credit. But when it sells to us, it collects payment immediately. Result: They collect money from customers immediately but pay the vendor—whose product was sold—later! In short, it does business with the vendors' money.

Bricks-and-Clicks Business Model

In this model a company integrates both offline (bricks) stores and online stores (clicks) so that customers have a seamless experience while engaging with the company (this model is discussed in detail later).

Online to Offline (O2O) Business Model

Domino's Pizza accepts orders online and delivers the pizzas offline in thirty minutes—to our homes. Zomato and Swiggy deliver orders placed online to people's doorsteps (this model, too, is discussed in detail later).

Linear Business Model

Steel and oil companies, including automobile and FMCG are patrons of this traditional business model. These companies source raw material and components and convert them into finished goods which they sell either directly or through channel partners to customers.

Low Touch Business Model

I was visiting an IKEA store in Singapore to buy a photo frame as a gift for my mother. The store is spread over a large area and I was feeling frustrated because I was unable to spot the photo frames section. Neither could I see a salesperson to guide me. As if on a cue, I heard an announcement on the PA system: customers may find a small number of staff members on the shop floor. It was because the store had few staff members so it could pass on the benefits to the customers through lower prices.

Upon hearing this announcement my feeling of frustration evaporated. I took a deep breath and, with renewed vigour, embarked on my hunt for the photo frames section. I did discover it, bought an elegant photo frame, and presented it to my mother. My father's photograph, even today, resides in that photo frame.

The business model followed by IKEA is popularly called the 'low touch business model': customers walk into a store, select what they desire, pay at checkout counters and depart.

Walmart is ranked no. 1 among the Fortune 500 companies (revenue: $500 billion FY 2018)[8]. It has reached this pinnacle by following a low touch model. It promises its customers that they can 'save money, live better' by offering products at attractive prices. Therefore, the store is designed to be largely based on self-service: the saving is passed on the buyers in terms of value pricing.

The value propositions offered by the low touch business model are attractive pricing and a wide assortment of merchandise. To offer these benefits they compromise on service, ambience and a few other amenities.

On the other end of spectrum is the high touch model: it is usually opted for by luxury brands where a salesperson is omnipresent to assist the customer. Here, service, not price, is the differentiator.

Direct Sale Business Model

This refers to selling products to end-users in a non-retail environment—be it home or office or other such locations. The intermediaries—distributor, wholesaler and retailer—are eliminated from the distribution chain.

Tupperware and Amway have perfected this business model. E-commerce companies too have followed suit: Amazon sells directly to customers, skipping intermediaries or middlemen. The middlemen margin that is saved is many

---

[8]   Fortune 500, Fortune, https://fortune.com/fortune500/2018/

a times deployed for providing attractive prices to buyers or making better products. Even technology companies, such as Tesla, follow this model.

Franchise Business Model

McDonalds[9] runs a very successful 'franchise business model'. It allows McDonalds to grow rapidly without having to spend substantially from its own coffers but still have control over the operations. This business model de-risks its business: if an operation is not successful the loss is largely borne by the franchise.

You may be wondering: why is the franchise bearing so much of risk? Because this business model offers an invaluable opportunity to a franchise: to access a recognizable trade name, a proven business model, upon payment of fees.

Dominos, Dunkin' Donuts and Pizza Hut are just a few successful businesses which have scaled up by leaning on the franchise model.

Licensing Business Model

Many of us use Microsoft Office. The software is licensed to us. We can only use it. The intellectual property (IP) rights reside with Microsoft.

In the 'licensing business model', a monetary compensation is paid to the licensor by the licensee for the right to use the intellectual property. The payment is called a royalty fee.

---

[9] Our Business Model, https://corporate.mcdonalds.com/corpmcd/about-us/our-business-model.html

The licensee can plug the licensed product and can quickly enter the market. For example, Uber has licensed Google Maps instead of developing it.[10]

Should You Select Only One Business Model?

In today's day and age, it is not enough to rely on just one business model. Look at Amazon for instance. It uses multiple business models: the razor blade model to sell the Kindle, the subscription model for Amazon Prime, the negative working capital model for its e-commerce business, O2O to provide a seamless experience to its customers, and so on. You too can embed as many business models as required to fully unlock the value of your business.

Multiple business model will ensure that a company has multiple revenue streams. If one revenue stream is unsteady or drying up, there are others that can pitch in. This will de-risk the business.

What Should You Do?

Take taxis for instance. They have been in the business of transporting people. But today their business is under threat from ride hailing companies. If you examine closely, the business of 'transportation' is not under threat. Ride hailing companies continue to transport us. They have introduced a new business model—pay as you use—and in the process made the business model of taxis seem dated.

---

[10] Jordan Novet, 'Uber paid Google $58 million over three years for map services', CNBC, 11 April 2019, https://www.cnbc.com/2019/04/11/uber-paid-google-58-million-over-three-years-for-map-services.html

What is the lesson for you? Business never dies, but business models do. Therefore, critically evaluate if your current business model is relevant. If not, identify an alternate business model/s in its place. Or, if you are planning to disrupt your industry, you can do it by introducing a new business model.

Here is a quick review of the business models to help you decide which ones to deploy so you can continue to rule the roost or start the journey towards it:

- **Advertising-based revenue business model:** When you do not wish to charge your customer, but charge advertisers who wish to 'speak' (read: advertise) to your customers
- **Razor-blade business model:** When the objective is to generate steady revenue
- **Pay-per-use business model:** To inspire confidence among customers that they will be charged only for the services they utilize
- **Freemium business model:** For generating trials
- **Subscription business model:** When the objective is to receive recurring payments at regular intervals
- **Frenemy business model:** Desire to improve margins
- **Payment-as-you-earn business model:** To align your payments to future earnings
- **Outsource business model:** So that you can focus on your core business
- **Product-as-service business model:** Where customers do not 'buy' a product but the benefits it provides
- **Outcome-based business model:** To generate confidence among your customers that they need to

pay only when the promised business 'outcome' is delivered

- **Co-ownership/time-sharing/fractional ownership business model:** If you cannot afford to buy a product and/or cannot use its capacity completely
- **Negative working capital business model:** To ensure smooth cash flow and obviate bad debts
- **Bricks and clicks or O2O:** If you wish to provide both online and offline conveniences to the customers
- **Linear business model:** If you desire to follow the traditional way of doing business
- **Low-touch business model:** When you sell your products with the least number of salespeople so that the cost-saving can be passed on to customers in the form of lower prices
- **High-touch business model:** When you wish to pamper your customer with high quality services
- **Direct sale business model:** If you wish to sell directly to end-customers
- **Franchise business model:** If you wish to be associated with an ongoing business and get it on a platter by paying a fee
- **Licensing business model:** When you desire to enter the market quickly by paying a fee.

Choosing the right Business Model is a critical business decision. Choose it wisely.

RULE 16

Disrupt Your Own Business at Regular Intervals

He who is not busy being born, is busy dying.

—Bob Dylan

One nightmarish question that occupies business leaders constantly is: will I be the next Nokia?[1]

Let me share with you a partial list of industries which have been disrupted, leaving the business leaders presiding over them wondering if the Nokia fate awaits them:

- **Retail business:** Flipkart and Amazon have put the shop in our hands and therefore pose a stiff challenge to traditional and modern retailers.
- **Taxis:** This century-old industry is facing serious competition from ride aggregators spearheaded by

---

[1]   Anton Troianovski and Sven Grundberg, 'Nokia's bad call on smart phones', *Wall Street Journal*, 18 July 2012, https://www.wsj.com/articles/SB10001424052702304388004577531002591315494

Uber and Ola. They have given us our personal driver 24 X 7.[2]

- **Banking services:** Paytm, Airtel Money, Jio Money, PayPal, Apple Pay, and so on, are making it simple for us to pay online to people or businesses. In the process they are attempting to disrupt the banking system by attempting to replace physical wallets with digital (mobile) wallets.

- **Entertainment:** Online content streaming companies like Netflix, Amazon Prime, Hotstar and are posing a serious threat to TV and multiplexes by putting entertainment in our palms.

Can you identify a common element which is responsible for these disruptions?

It is technology! When it collides with an industry it is likely to disrupt it. New age businesses are powered by technology. Therefore, every business is susceptible to disruption. Including yours.

No wonder the longevity of companies in the S&P 500 index—single gauge of large-cap US equities—of leading US companies has reduced by more than fifty years in the last century, from sixty-seven years in the 1920s to merely fifteen years, says Professor Richard Foster from Yale University.[3] Therefore, leaders need to be on their toes, because 'the rate of change is at a faster pace than ever before', he says.

---

[2] Uber Website: https://help.uber.com/riders/article/when–and–where–is–uber–available–in–my–city?nodeId=558929fa–b991–4810–b6db–8c823862d7d4

[3] Kim Gittleson, 'Can a company live forever?' BBC, 19 January 2012, https://www.bbc.com/news/business-16611040

Topple Rate, a measure of the rate at which companies lose their leadership position, has increased; some estimate it to be 39 per cent.[4]

Why Do Companies Get Disrupted?

There are myriad reasons why disruptions can happen. Here is a partial list:

- **The belief that past success is a guarantee of future success:** In this century the speed of change is swift and if businesses do not keep pace with it they will cease to be relevant. Therefore, relying on past success is similar to driving a car looking into a rear-view mirror. An accident is guaranteed.

- **Sunk costs:** Successful companies would have invested heavily in building factories, setting up infrastructure and training employees to establish dominance in the marketplace. Even if they wish to disrupt themselves, they find it difficult to overlook these 'sunk costs'. Therefore, to protect their past investments they ruin their future.

  A prime example is the American company, Kodak, founded by George Eastman and Henry Strong. During most of the twentieth century it held a dominant position in the photographic film market.

---

4   Rita McGrath and M Muneer, 'Disruption isn't just a buzzword. If you don't disrupt your own business, someone will', *Economic Times* (Blog), 15 September 2017, https://economictimes.indiatimes.com/blogs/et-commentary/disruption-isnt-just-a-buzzword-if-you-dont-disrupt-your-own-business-someone-else-will/

'Kodak moment', its tag line, entered common parlance to describe a personal moment that demanded to be recorded for posterity.

Although Kodak developed a digital camera in 1975, the first of its kind, it was dropped for fear that it would 'cannibalize' its existing photographic film business. Eventually, Japanese companies introduced digital cameras and delivered a crushing blow to Kodak from which it failed to recover. Kodak filed for Chapter 11 and subsequently sought bankruptcy protection.

Bottom line: a company should know when to cut its losses and not become victim to the sunk cost fallacy.

- **Cannibalization:** Dominant players fear that executing disruptive strategies will lead to cannibalization of their own brand. Therefore, they shun this strategy. In due course, an agile competitor comes along who eats into their business and eventually disrupts it. An apt example is Nokia. 'More than seven years before Apple rolled out the iPhone, the Nokia team showed a phone with a colour touch screen set above a single button. The device was shown locating a restaurant, playing a racing game and ordering lipstick. In 1990s, Nokia secretly developed another alluring product: a tablet computer with a wireless connection and touch screen-all features today of the hot-selling Apple iPad.' writes Anton Trioanovski and Sven Grundberg.[5] Fearing cannibalization, these

---

[5] Anton Troianovski, 'Nokia's Bad Call on Smartphones', *Wall Street Journal*, 18 July 2012, https://www.wsj.com/articles/SB100014240527 02304388004577531002591315494

innovative products were not launched in the market. Result: Nokia was dethroned by Apple's iPhone.

No wonder Steve Jobs said that if we do not cannibalize our products, somebody else will.[6]

- **Judging competitor's products using own norms:** Companies often measure competitors' products by the rules they hold dear. They sneer at their competitors if the latter's products fail to adhere to the norms. For instance, Nokia's engineers turned up their noses at the Apple iPhone because it failed the 'five-foot drop test'— where a device survives and remains in working condition after being dropped from chest height onto concrete from a variety of angles.[7] They did not realize that iPhone was a smartphone and was not designed to survive the five feet drop test!

- **Ignoring new disrupters:** Companies which get disrupted choose to ignore potential disruptors when they enter the market, believing they are too small and insignificant to disrupt them. Unchallenged, these disruptors scale up quickly till they become too big to be slain. Then the disrupted company panics and gets into reactive mode. But most often it is too late.

- **Failure to adapt to newer ways of doing business:** Take taxi drivers for instance. Many of them are still not familiar with some routes. They can overcome this problem by using the GPS. But they continue to

---

[6]   Walter Isaacson, 'Steve Jobs' (Little, Brown Book Group, 2015)

[7]   Troianovski, 'Nokia's Bad Call on Smartphones'.

be a slave to their habits. The same is the case with companies. They are so bound by the traditional ways of doing business that they turn a blind eye to newer and more efficient ways of working. This makes them vulnerable to getting disrupted.

Do 'Disruptors' Have Anything in Common?

- Most of them are small companies and possess limited resources. Despite these limitations they go on an offensive and win.
- Most of them are manned by a motley collection of young people (read: disruptors) sitting in the proverbial garage in a corner of the world.
- The majority of these disruptors were founded during this century.

A Disruptor's Mindset

You must be wondering what kind of mindsets these disruptors possess that make them such formidable foes.

- They believe in taking leaps, not incremental steps.
- They have an 'I can change the world' mentality.
- They are customer (user) focused. They believe in identifying the user's pain point and then working towards reducing or eliminating it altogether.
- They adapt with lightning speed to new realities.
- They are not afraid to kill their own darlings. If an idea has outlived its utility, no matter how

precious it is to them, they will not hesitate to kill it themselves.

- They do not fear failure. Their motto is 'Fail early, fail fast'. In fact, they take pride in failures and wear them like a badge.
- They do not wallow in self-pity; when they fail, they pivot in a quest to find new opportunities.
- They believe that ideas come with a shelf life. Therefore, they freely pitch ideas without being scared that they will be pinched.
- They are sharply focused on the issue they are trying to resolve and do not get distracted by other business opportunities.
- Their business is powered by intellect, not capital. They use it to write software which runs the computers whose computing power continues to follow Moore's Law and is relatively cheap to harness.
- They believe that the margins and inefficiencies of legacy companies offer them opportunities.
- They devise new and disruptive business models.
- They make things simpler.

The Nurturing Technology Ecosystem

These new age robber barons, armed with the mindset described above, have been assisted by a nurturing technological ecosystem that has given them wings to disrupt industries.

- **Rise in smartphone penetration:** India had 468 million smartphone users in 2017.[8] World-wide, it is estimated that more than 5 billion people have mobile devices, and over half of these connections are smartphones.[9] Adults in India are spending almost three hours per day glued to the screen.[10] In fact, many check their smartphones as many as fifty-two times a day.[11] It would not be out of place to say that the world is getting addicted to smartphones. Disruptors are taking full advantage of this to entice users on to their platform.
- **Internet access:** A huge number of people have access to the internet: 481 million people in India[12]

[8] 'Smartphones users expected to rise 84% to 859m by 2022: Assocham-PwC study', ET Bureau, 10 May 2019, https://economictimes.indiatimes.com/tech/hardware/smartphone-users-expected-to-rise-84-to-859m-by-2022-assocham-pwc-study/articleshow/69260487.cms?from=mdr

[9] Kyle Taylor and Laura Silver, 'Smartphone Ownership Is Growing Rapidly Around the World, but Not Always Equally', 5 February 2019, https://www.pewresearch.org/global/2019/02/05/smartphone-ownership-is-growing-rapidly-around-the-world-but-not-always-equally/

[10] G Seetharaman, 'Indians spend roughly 3 hours a day on smartphones, but are they paying big bucks for apps?' *ET Panache*, 11 February 2018, https://economictimes.indiatimes.com/magazines/panache/indians-spend-roughly-3-hours-a-day-on-smartphones-but-are-they-paying-big-bucks-for-apps/articleshow/62866875.cms

[11] Todd Spangler, 'Smartphones? U.S. Consumers Check Their Phones 52 Times Daily, Study Finds', Variety Intelligence Platform, 14 November 2018, https://variety.com/2018/digital/news/smartphone-addiction-study-check-phones-52-times-daily-1203028454/

[12] Surabhi Agarwal, 'Internet users in India expected to reach 500 million by June: IAMAI', 20 February 2018, *Economic Times*, https://economictimes.indiatimes.com/tech/internet/internet-users-in-india-expected-to-reach-500-million-by-june-iamai/articleshow/63000198.cms

(35 per cent of the country's population) and over 4 billion people around the world.[13] This enables the disruptors to reach their users in a very cost-effective manner across the globe to communicate and engage with them.

- **Data usage:** Data usage is growing rapidly on the back of low prices. This enables disruptors to share content with the users and engage them in a two-way dialogue.

- **Death of distance:** The internet has killed distance. Disruptors utilize this feature to get users from all across the world on to their platform.

- **Death of intermediaries:** Intermediaries have been made redundant. Disruptors are able to connect directly with their users. This enables them to collect the users' personal data and offer them personalized solutions. This in turn deepens the relationship between the disruptor and the users.

Since the business of disruptors is powered by technology, it enables them to scale up rapidly with paltry requirements of capital. To illustrate the point, let us pull the hospitality industry into our discussion. If Ginger, a budget hotel chain, wishes to add five rooms to its existing property, it will require adequate capital and time before these can be built and added to the inventory. But if OYO Rooms wants to add five additional rooms to its inventory, it has to merely list them on its platform and they can start generating revenue instantly.

---

[13] Nathan Mcdonald, 'Digital in 2018: World's Internet Users Pass the 4 Billion Mark', 30 January 2018, https://wearesocial.com/us/blog/2018/01/global-digital-report-2018

This advantage helps technology companies scale-up faster and makes them formidable competitors.

Change the Rules of the Industry

Take the shave market for instance. New entrants are changing the rules of the industry. Instead of selling through traditional retail channels, they are opting for online channels. Take Harry's for instance. It is an online seller of shaving products. Each time its product is sold, it knows when, where and to whom it is sold. It collects this data, analyzes it and presents customized offers to its users. No wonder it has been growing 35 per cent year-on-year, between 2014 and 2016, which is three times faster than the average industry rate. Take Gillette for instance. Its shaving products are sold through traditional retail outlets. The company cannot come to know when, where and to whom its product is being sold.[14] Not surprisingly Gillette sales are struggling as customers shift their business to Harry's or other popular online brand like Dollar Shave Club.[15]

Take the telecom industry in India for instance. Reliance Industries, a cross-industry competitor, has changed the

[14] Howard Yu, 'What Big Consumer Brands Can do to Compete in a Digital Economy', *Harvard Business Review*, 4 December 2018, https://hbr.org/2018/12/what-big-consumer-brands-can-do-to-compete-in-a-digital-economy

[15] Amelia Lucas, 'Protector & Gamble shares jump on earnings beat, optimist 2020 outlook despite Gillette write-down', CNBC, 30 July 2019, https://www.cnbc.com/2019/07/30/procter-and-gamble-q4-2019-earnings.html

rules of the industry and landed a punishing blow to well-entrenched players.

On 5 September 2016, it launched Jio, offering free voice calls and messages, no roaming charges within India. All of it at the lowest LTE data rates in the world![16] In two years, it acquired 315 million users (April 2019)[17].

Metaphorically speaking, Jio has become the cat among the pigeons. Long-time rivals Vodafone India and Idea Cellular have merged to put up a joint fight. Many more alignments are in the offing to take on the new 800-pound gorilla in town.

How Can You to Protect Yourself from Disruptors?

It does seem that getting disrupted is the new normal. What should you do to bullet-proof your enterprise from such a catastrophic situation?

The answer may surprise, even alarm, you: you have to become your own fiercest competitor and disrupt or destroy your own business before the competition does it. Then you must reinvent yourself in a more formidable avatar. Because if you do not embrace this counter-intuitive strategy, you may

---

[16] 'Reliance Jio to be launched on Sep 5, says Mukesh Ambani', *Business Today* Online Journal, 1 September 2016, https://www.businesstoday.in/sectors/telecom/reliance-jio-to-be-launched-on-sept-5-says-mukesh-ambani/story/236770.html

[17] 'At 8mn, Jio adds the most subscribers in April; Airtel loses the most at 3.3 mn', Livemint, 24 June 2019, https://www.livemint.com/industry/telecom/at-8-mn-jio-adds-the-most-subscribers-in-april-airtel-loses-the-most-at-3-3-mn-1561380855275.html

become the next Nokia. You will first be rendered irrelevant and eventually decimated.

Has any successful enterprise disrupted its own business and reinvented itself?

iPhone believes in being its own fiercest competitor. At regular intervals, it destroys its existing models by launching newer ones which are more advanced, rendering the older models obsolete. Since its birth in 2007, it has destroyed itself almost every year by launching a more advanced model. By following this seemingly counter-intuitive strategy, iPhone has managed to remain ahead of the competition.

Let us pull Amazon into our discussion. In early 2000, Apple was reviving under the innovative leadership of Steve Jobs. Jeff Bezos, the Amazon boss, feared Apple might come up with a device that would disrupt its successful online book retailing business. In 2004, Bezos 'started a secretive Silicon Valley skunkworks with the mysterious name Lab126. The hardware hackers at Lab126 were given a difficult job: they were to disrupt Amazon's own successful bookselling business with an e-book device. In 2007, Amazon unveiled the result of this effort. Kindle.'[18]

Kindle is the child of Amazon's efforts to disrupt its own business. Today, it is an important artillery in Amazon's product range to ward off competition.

Let us move to Netflix. Before its current avatar, Netflix's business model involved sending DVDs by mail to its

---

[18] Brad Stone, 'The Everything Store and Age of Amazon' (Little, Brown and Company, 2013).

customers. Customers could get the next DVD only after they returned the previous one.

Netflix witnessed unprecedented success, but it did not rest on its laurels. It had the foresight to realize that physical delivery of DVDs would soon become obsolete. So, instead of waiting for a potential competitor to take the lead on delivering content over the internet, it proactively destroyed its own mail order business and adopted the streaming-over-Internet business model. But Reed Hastings, Netflix's flamboyant founder, was determined to pursue this strategy. The results of this strategic shift started showing later in 2010 and Hastings was nominated Business Person of the Year by *Fortune* magazine.

Is this strategy the fiefdom of new age companies? Of course not. Traditional companies have been following this strategy to protect their dominant position, since 1940s.

Take P&G's Tide.[19] It was the first synthetic detergent to be launched in 1946. It made 'white clothes look whiter'. Prior to it, all soaps were 'natural'—manufactured by heating vegetable or animal fats in water with an alkaline base. P&G management feared that it would cannibalize into its 'natural' soap business. Except William Cooper Procter, Chairman of P&G. He explained, 'this (synthetic detergent) business may ruin the soap business. But if anybody is going to ruin the soap business, it had better be Procter & Gamble.'

Gillette, owned by P&G, every few years launches a razor that makes the earlier versions redundant. In effect, it

---

[19] Howard Yu, 'What Big Consumers Brands Can Do to Compete in a Digital Economy, Harvard Business Review, 4 December, 2018, https://hbr.org/2018/12/what-big-consumer-brands-can-do-to-compete-in-a-digital-economy

actively disrupts its own razor. It started with a single-blade safety razor, then launched a double-blade razor, followed it up with a three-blade razor, and now its Fusion Razor has five blades.

Have Indian Companies Adopted this Strategy?

There is long list of Indian companies which have adopted this strategy and benefited from it.

'Hamara' Bajaj was the numero uno scooter brand in India and had acquired a cult status. Marriages were held up because the Bajaj scooter, which was customarily demanded in dowry, could not be delivered since it had a waiting period stretching over years. Despite this, Bajaj exited the scooter business because there was pressure on its profitability. It decided to self-destroy the scooter business and shifted focus to the motorcycle segment. 'If we are to be a motorcycle specialist, we cannot make scooters,' said Bajaj Auto managing director Rajiv Bajaj.[20]

Today Bajaj is recognized as a leading profitable motorcycle company.

Priya Cinema was a single-screen theatre in Delhi showing Hollywood films. Business was steadily dwindling, so it decided to proactively disrupt and reinvent itself.

It entered into a joint venture with Australian company Village Roadshow, christened PVR (Priya Village Roadshow).

---

[20] 'Focus on bikes market, no scooter: Rajiv Bajaj', Live Mint, 13 February 2011, https://www.livemint.com/Companies/iQ3dCzq4qS60 GRRlt0WTHN/Focus-on-bikes-market-no-scooters-Rajiv-Bajaj.html.

This was the birth of India's first multiplex.[21] It was a roaring success. In its wake, a tsunami of multiplexes followed which swept away (read: disrupted) a majority of single screens—most of them later resurrecting as multiplexes themselves.

Take the banking industry for instance. It is getting disrupted by fintech companies. Aditya Puri, Managing Director of HDFC Bank, visited California to get first-hand understanding of the fintech companies who are disrupting the industry by sanctioning loan in seconds, offering digital wallets and providing wealth advisory services using Alorthem.

Upon his return, he posed a series of deliberative questions to his senior team members, 'Why can't we give a loan in ten seconds? Why can't we invent something to transfer money in just a click? Why can't we reduce friction in the banking system? Finally he posed a defining question to all: Why don't we disrupt ourselves instead of waiting to be disrupted by fintech companies?[22] The bank has embraced digital strategy and in the process transformed into a hunter instead of being the hunted.

Finally, let's get religion, I mean cricket, into our discussion. Cricket, too, is in throes of disruption. For almost a century, cricket was synonymous with Test cricket. It was played in white apparels, spread over five days, with each team batting twice. Advent of colour TV and live broadcasting of matches created a fertile ground for disruption which happened with launch of One Day Cricket. It changed the established rules

---

[21] Business Standard, https://www.business-standard.com/company/pvr-14622/information/company-history

[22] Tamal Bandyopadhyay, 'How HDFC disrupted itself', 16 July 2019, *Telegraph* (online edition), https://www.telegraphindia.com/business/how-hdfc-bank-took-on-the-digital-colossus/cid/1694586

of cricket. In this format each team bat only once, that too for limited number of overs and players wore colour clothing emblazoned with advertising messages. Spectators thronged to the stadium to witness these matches, while millions more watched it over TV. Even before it could stabilize, it was disrupted by T20 format. It is a shorter version of 'One Day' and has mixed cricket with entertainment.

Have these disruptions in cricket paid dividends? The proof of the pudding is in eating it. Today, One Day and T20 draws the more crowd and sponsership money than Test cricket!

Non-Violent Ways of Disrupting Your Business

If the disruptive strategy sounds too violent, you can adopt a more benign path: just buy out the competition.

That is what Facebook did to an emerging competitor, WhatsApp. Facebook bought it for a whopping $19 billion.[23] Walmart did it in India by acquiring Flipkart for $16 billion for roughly 77 per cent stake.[24]

Needless to say, such a strategic move will leave a hole in your pocket. If the cost of acquiring an ongoing business seems steep, invest in promising start-ups and nurture them into great businesses. The benefits of these investments

---

[23] Reed Albergotti, Douglas MacMillan, and Evelyn M. Rusli, 'Facebook to Pay $19 Billion for WhatsApp, *Wall Street Journal*, 19 February 2014, https://www.wsj.com/articles/facebook-to-buy-whatsapp-for-16-billion-1392847766

[24] Nandita Bose, Sankalp Phartiyal, 'Walmart to pay $16 billion for control of India's Flipkart, shares slide', Reuters, 9 May 2018, https://www.reuters.com/article/us-flipkart-m-a-walmart/walmart-to-pay-16-billion-for-control-of-indias-flipkart-shares-slide-idUSKBN1IA14H

will fructify in the future. Alphabet, the parent company of Google, is pursuing this strategy and is betting on multiple areas like retailing, personalized medicine, transportation, robotics, education and clean energy. It is thus diversifying its portfolio and de-risking its own business.

Countries Can Also Disrupt Themselves

It is not just companies, brands and people that are embarking on the mission to disrupt themselves. Countries, too, are enthusiastically embracing this strategy.

Despite holding 9 per cent of the world's proven oil reserves, Abu Dhabi has set up Masdar City, which is designed to be a hub for clean tech companies. They are charged with the responsibility of discovering new sources of renewable energy through which the state can continue to dominate the energy market even after its oil fields run dry.[25]

To many, it may seem that Abu Dhabi is investing its resources in developing an alternative source of energy that could potentially destroy its oil business. But by proactively challenging its oil business, Abu Dhabi is protecting its own future. When the oil fields dry up—which they will one day—Abu Dhabi could dominate the energy market with its expertise in solar and other clean, renewable forms of energy.

How to Handle the Threat of Disruption?

Take Apple for instance. Not only has it disrupted industries but also protected itself from getting disrupted—till now.

[25] 'Vision, Mission and Values', Masdar, https://masdar.ae/en/about-us/management/vision-mission-and-values.

The credit for this goes to Steve Jobs. He organized Apple to be the biggest start-up on the planet. To achieve this, he made sure there were no committees in the company. Instead people were put in charge—one person each for iPhone iOS software, Mac hardware, worldwide marketing, operations, and so on. 'There is tremendous teamwork at the top of the company—which filters down throughout the company. Team work is dependent upon trust. Trusting the other folk to come through with their part without watching them all the time. That's what we do really well—all work on the same thing, touch base frequently and bring it all together into a great product.' He said, in an interview.

So what did Jobs actually do? 'I meet with teams of people and work on ideas and solve problems to make new products, new marketing programs.' He said.

What is the message for rest of us? Your job is to build a company which has a start-up culture, where the best ideas win. Your company should be run by ideas not hierarchy. [26]

Does any other successful business leader subscribe to Steve Jobs' philosophy? Jeff Bezos does. He wants Amazon to stay Day One—to be always in start-up mode. 'Even though it's a large company, I want the heart and spirit of a small one,' he said.[27]

Expounding on it, he say, 'Staying Day One requires you to experiment, plant seeds, protect saplings and double down when you see customer delight.'

---

[26] Jonathan Nasution, Apple as a Startup, YouTube, 11 May 2011, https://www.youtube.com/watch?v=gce55_Mb4eY

[27] Laura Stevens, 'Leadership and Life Lessons from Amazon's Jeff Bezos', *Wall Street Journal*, September 14, 2018, https://www.wsj.com/articles/leadership-and-life-lessons-from-jeff-bezos-1536938179

In contrast what does Day Two look like? 'It is stasis. Followed by irrelevance. Followed by excruciating, painful decline. Followed by death. And that is why it is always Day One,' triumphantly concludes Bezos.[28]

Lesson for you: Work towards making your company Day One. It should never slip into Day Two. If that happens then certain death awaits you.

For successfully implementing strategies proposed by Jobs & Bezos, adopt Founder's Mentality, propounded by Bain & Company.

Most large, successful companies began as insurgents-fast, agile and adaptable. They focused on customers. They hated complexity. But too many companies accept a troubling trade-off. They achieve scale, but lose their Founder's Mentality—the very core strength and values that helped them succeed and grow.[29]

Research done by Bain indicates that one in nine companies that achieve a decade or more of sustained, profitable growth, the majority are those that have preserved- or resorted-their Founder's Mentality.

Let us now shift our discussion to you. How should you respond to or deal with the threat of disruption?

Let me share the 'revolving door' strategy that you can follow to deal with an impending disruption.

---

[28] Anita Balakrishnan, 'Bezos shareholder letter: Don't let the world push you into becoming a Day 2' company, CNBC, 12 April 2017, https://www.cnbc.com/2017/04/12/amazon-jeff-bezos-2017-shareholder-letter.html

[29] 'Founder's Mentality', Bain & Company, https://www.bain.com/founders-mentality/

In 1985, Andy Grove, then Intel's president, and Gordon Moore (of Moore Law's fame), its CEO, faced a dilemma. Intel's memory chip business had come under assault from Japanese memory chips, whose quality level was beyond what Intel thought they could achieve.[30] The memory chip business continued to bleed copiously, which led to an all-pervasive gloom inside Intel. Finally, the day dawned when the Japanese stole the bulk of the memory chip business from right under Intel's nose.

Around this time, a small team working inside Intel had developed a microprocessor which, as luck would have it, was picked by IBM to be the brain of a new personal computer. Andy Grove, fearing the worst, turned to Gordon Moore and asked: 'If we got kicked out and the board brought in a new CEO, what do you think he would do?'

'He would get us out of memories,' replied Moore.

'Why shouldn't you and I walk out of the door, come back in, and do it ourselves?' asked Grove.

Grove and Moore decided to fire themselves—metaphorically, of course—and walked out of the room. Once outside, they 'hired' themselves and entered the room as new custodians of the business. They analyzed the business without the burden of legacy—as if looking at it for the first time. With this fresh perspective, they decided to take the radical decision of pulling the plug on the memory business. This decision made Intel even more competitive and turned it into a technology powerhouse. If they had not acted decisively

---

[30] Chip Heath and Dan Heath, 'The Revolving Door Test: How Intel overcame fear by gaining an outsider's perspective', The Water Cooler, http://watercoolernewsletter.com/the-revolving-door-test-how-intel-overcame-fear-by-gaining-an-outsiders-perspective/

and taken steps to disturb their existing business, Intel too could have suffered the same fate as Nokia.

What Should You Do to Be the Hunter Instead of Being the Hunted?

- Adopt a disruptor's mindset.
- Disrupt your business and resurrect in a stronger avatar.
- Do not judge competitor's product from your yardstick. Chances are they might have changed the norms.
- Leverage technology to disrupt the industry you are operating in.
- Do not be afraid of cannibalizing your own business. It is better you do it, instead of a competitor.
- Never ignore a new entrant and dismiss it off as being too small to merit your attention. A few of them will metamorphosize into a formidable foe over time.
- Do not allow success to seduce you into believing that your company is invincible. Acquire Day One mindset.
- Do not fall victim to sun cost fallacy. It has the power to sink you.
- Institute a start-up mentality and run your company on the strength of good ideas not hierarchy.
- Institutionalize a Day One (start-up) way of working. Never allow Day Two to sneak in.
- Keep the Founder's Mentality alive.
- Be open to disrupting yourself by following revolving door policy.

It would be wise to remember that disruptors and disruptions cannot be wished away. It would be prudent to follow the advice of Twitter founder, Jack Dorsey: 'Expect the unexpected. And whenever possible, be the unexpected.'

Postscript: Secure Your Future

Some of my friends and I were fascinated with climbing and mountaineering. As a first step, we decided to acquaint ourselves with the basics of mountain climbing. We hired an instructor.

He started the session by posing a question: What is the first thing you would do to climb Mount Everest?

'Develop stamina, undergo endurance training, get insured, buy safety equipment . . .' we answered, one by one.

He waited for us to exhaust our answers and said, 'Mount Everest is first climbed in the mind. So, you need to prepare your mind first.'

The same is true for you. You have to first prepare your mind for these 'new rules' and approach them with an open mindset.

The next step is to discard dysfunctional rules. I can already sense a question stirring in your mind: How will I determine which rules to discard and which ones to adopt?

Here's the answer: through experimentation!

Select the 'new rules' which resonate with you. Modify them suitably to serve your unique requirements. Share them with people whose judgement you trust, actively seek their feedback and make modifications based on it.

What happens if the rule (read: decision) turns out to be incorrect?

Let me paraphrase Jeff Bezos[1] to allay your fear: Most decisions are changeable or reversible; they are two-way doors. If they prove to be suboptimal decisions, you don't have to live with the consequences. You can re-open the door and re-enter. But not taking decisions fearing failure will result in slowness, unmindful risk-aversion, insufficient experimentation and consequently, reduced innovation.

The rules that govern the future need to be entirely different than those that delivered results till recently. To remain relevant, you will have to proactively arm yourself with the new rules.

By embracing the new rules of business, you will take a decisive step towards securing your and your company's future.

---

[1] 'A rare insight into Amazon's experimental culture', Conversation Rate Experts, https://conversion-rate-experts.com/amazon/